*Donated by
Dr. Reene Shue Alley
to the Department of Educational Administration, Research,
and Foundations at Youngstown State University for use in the
Doctoral Library*

SCHOOL-BASED MANAGEMENT:
CURRENT THINKING AND PRACTICE

ABOUT THE AUTHORS

This book is written by two authors whose combined experiences include teaching at the elementary, junior high, senior high, and junior college levels; serving as building principals, as central office curriculum specialists at both the elementary and secondary levels, as an assistant superintendent for instruction, as staff developers, as consultants to school districts and other organizations, as a superintendent of schools for twenty years, as a state department of education researcher, as university professors of educational leadership, and as a university administrator. In view of this kinship of author perspective, it is clear that this book serves as a valuable resource for practicing administrators.

SCHOOL-BASED MANAGEMENT: CURRENT THINKING AND PRACTICE

By

JERRY J. HERMAN, PH.D.
*Professor and Area Head
Area of Administration and Educational Leadership
College of Education
The University of Alabama at Tuscaloosa*

and

JANICE L. HERMAN, PH.D.
*Associate Professor
Department of Educational Leadership
School of Education
The University of Alabama at Birmingham*

CHARLES C THOMAS • PUBLISHER
Springfield • Illinois • U.S.A.

Published and Distributed Throughout the World by

CHARLES C THOMAS • PUBLISHER
2600 South First Street
Springfield, Illinois 62794-9265

This book is protected by copyright. No part of
it may be reproduced in any manner without
written permission from the publisher.

© *1993 by* CHARLES C THOMAS • PUBLISHER

ISBN 0-398-05817-2

Library of Congress Catalog Card Number: 92-22922

With THOMAS BOOKS *careful attention is given to all details of manufacturing and design. It is the Publisher's desire to present books that are satisfactory as to their physical qualities and artistic possibilities and appropriate for their particular use.* THOMAS BOOKS *will be true to those laws of quality that assure a good name and good will.*

Printed in the United States of America
SC-R-3

Library of Congress Cataloging-in-Publication Data

Herman, Jerry John, 1930-
    School-based management : current thinking and practice / Jerry J. Herman and Janice L. Herman.
       p.   cm.
    Includes bibliographical references and index.
    ISBN 0-398-05817-2
    1. School management and organization—United States.   2. Teacher participation in administration—United States.   3. Educational change—United States.   I. Herman, Janice L.   II. Title.
LB2805.H42   1992
371.2′00973—dc20
                                                                     92-22922
                                                                          CIP

We dedicate this book to our very valued stakeholders; our grandchildren: John, Keith, Jessica, Kelsey, Eric, Erin, and Hannah, and to all those grandchildren yet to come, in the belief that their twenty-first century schools will provide the superb learning environments which we have always envisioned and striven to create.

PREFACE

For Whom This Book is Written

This book is written for those practitioners who are considering implementing school-based management or who are mandated by state law or local board of education directive to implement it. It also will serve as a reference for professors of educational administration.

Structure of This Book

The chapters in this book are designed to consider the participants' change processes and roles in school-based management; attention is focused on the teacher, professional organization, principal, central office staff member, superintendent, school board, community, and state department of education. They also provide an overview of local, state, and national patterns of practice. Related references are summarized in these chapters. The text concludes with future trends and implications for school-based management and shared decision making.

Benefit to the Reader

As a means of school improvement, as an employee empowerment process, and as a characteristic of current educational leadership practice, school-based management is becoming a powerful restructuring innovation. Practitioners considering this innovation, whether from a voluntary entry-level position, from an in-place implementation position, or from a state or district mandated implementation position, will be provided insights, techniques, and process details by this book. School-based management, its structural and process elements, holds potential for meaningful restructuring of the school operations and cultures. The book will prove to be a guide and perspective about implementation of this restructuring innovation.

PROLOGUE

DECISION MAKING: A WHODUNIT AND A WHY?

It was the Year 1820 when settlers first decided to settle a piece of land in the sparsely settled mining territory of the Upper Peninsula of Michigan. The area, which was later to be incorporated as a town, was small in population; having merely two hundred and eighty-six inhabitants. This number included the miners, their wives, their children, and the mine owner and his family.

Mostly, the inhabitants were uneducated (in the sense that, today, we view schooling). But, they were very wise in the ways of life; which, at best, were difficult. The miners came to the Upper Peninsula as immigrants from Wales, Finland, Italy, Norway, Sweden, and France. They worked with pick and shovel during their sixteen hour days and for six days each week in their underground place of employment. The only time each day that they escaped from their mole-like existence in their damp and dirty underground cave was when they came to the surface for one hour, during which time they were met by their wives who served them a pasty (a crusted meat, potato, carrot, and turnip self-contained pie) for lunch.

The mine owner and the bosses he selected comprised the management king and princes hierarchy. The owner made all the decisions and the bosses enforced them, making certain that the slave (economically deprived) workers produced the maximum tonnage of ore without ever daring to question the orders given them.

The women in this place, which eventually acquired the Indian name of Chicannon, possessed their own long and tedious work hours. Their major tasks included: giving birth and raising numerous children, growing and caring for a garden, milking the cow and tending to the rabbits and chickens, chopping wood for the cooking and heating stoves, keeping house, washing clothes, and taking in borders to assist in eking out an extremely spartan existence.

Eventually the town constructed a school for the children. Some children stayed in school until they were twelve years of age, at which time the boys trudged down into the mines to assist in raising income to support the family; and by the age twelve, most of the girls were kept home to help their mothers raise the younger children and assist with a multitude of chores. For the boys and their parents, the ever present threat on mine cave ins, blacklung, and miscellaneous serious injuries did not weigh sufficiently heavy in the equation to overcome the survival needs of the family.

As we move ahead to 1921, we discover the owner (who at this time was the original owner's grandson) served as the king. This king decided to sell his mine to a mining company for a huge amount of money. However, the mining company decided to employ the former owner as its king who was to manage this mining operation. Nothing much really changed from 1820 to 1921; the king was still king, the bosses were still princes, the miners were still economic slaves, and the children were still very much undereducated.

The population of Chicannon, by 1921, had swollen to over twelve thousand people, and the original school had expanded into a school district with two primary schools, a grammar school and a very small high school. The schools' management structure mimicked that of the mine's management structure. The superintendent, who was selected by the king of the mine, was made educational king; the teacher-principals were the princely bosses; and the teachers, who each had two years of normal school training, were the working slaves.

Very few children ever graduated from high school, and the male students practically all left to go to work in the mines after eighth grade or even before they entered eighth grade. Some little progress, however, was noted in 1921, as the high school graduation class numbered eleven graduates—ten females, and the king of the mine's son who was to attend the University of Michigan in the fall.

In 1938, a very interesting event occurred. Another mining company purchased a huge section of the iron ore rich land about twenty miles from Chicannon. They proceeded to build a model town, construct a beautiful set of school buildings, and recruited miners from all over the United States to join the company in achieving the vision of an economically successful and socially desirable venture. The company decided to give the model town an Indian name, which translated into the word heaven.

Heaven prospered. The miners' work was cut to a five-day week and to an eight hour day, and technology was incorporated into the mining operation which made the work safer and easier and which made the mining of the iron ore more efficient and profitable. In addition, the owners were concerned about the welfare of the miners and their families; and the supervisors were told that they were to serve as monitors of production and as helpers to the miners—not play the roles of "bosses" or "princes."

The two most dramatic changes, however, were: (1) the miners were asked to work with the supervisors to suggest and implement improvements in the efficiency of the mining operations and to help in improving the working conditions under which they toiled, and (2) the owners shared the expanding profits with the workers and with the townspeople.

In the schools that were created in Heaven, the same type of management structure was implemented. The superintendent and the principals were cast in the roles of facilitators, coplanners, and helpers of the teachers. All children were encouraged to finish high school by the mine owners, the parents, and the community at large. Indeed, the interest was so high that the employees' union and the mining company's management jointly established a scholarship fund to assist high school graduates, who wished to continue their education, to attend college.

By 1940, Chicannon's mine was closed, as it could not profitably compete with mines like those operated in Heaven. Chicannon's schools, with many less students than previously attended, still had the autocratic management style of operation; and it was a rarity to find a student who graduated from Chicannon High School.

From 1940 to this day, Heaven prospers. Both the mine and the schools have empowered people, have become economically and educationally productive, have utilized technology well and continuously; and they have achieved their visions, missions, and desired outcomes; and both the mines and the schools provide wholesome, satisfying and healthy environments in which to study, work and live. The result is a town, its citizens, and a company combining their talents and acquiring broad-based ownership of the educational system as well as agreeing on high level aspirations for the youth of the community.

Studying the histories of Chicannon and Heaven provides important lessons that illustrate guideposts which can well serve those who read this book and who are contemplating involvement in, or are currently operating within, the educational restructuring movement called *school-based management*. These guideposts include the following:

- Those persons who are most closely involved with the activity should be given an important voice in the decisions related to that activity.
- All stakeholders should combine their efforts for the purpose of attaining the desired outcomes and process results.
- Technology is many times useful in accomplishing goals and results.
- Ownership of the system by stakeholders brings support for the activities offered by the system.
- Environment, the force-field within which one works and lives, should be a caring, healthful, and productive one which stresses high aspirations and receives high level quality results.
- People; regardless of their title, rank, wealth, or educational level; want respect, opportunities, care giving, and input. In turn, they will join together to make their heaven-like scenario come true.

ACKNOWLDGMENTS

A debt of gratitude is owed to our two graduate students, Dr. Vicki Oliver and Dr. Christine Tomberlin, for their scholarly and technical assistance in the preparation of this book. Thanks also go to Sandra Miller and to Evelyn Kelly at The University of Alabama at Birmingham for support of the research part of this work. Finally, particular appreciation is due to Kentucky Superintendent Dr. David Gover, and to the members of the Kentucky case study's Local School Councils, whose cooperation made much of this text possible.

CONTENTS

	Page
Preface	vii
Prologue	ix
Chapter One—SCHOOL-BASED MANAGEMENT:	
A HISTORICAL AND DEVELOPMENTAL OVERVIEW	3
BEGINNINGS	3
ORIGINS IN ORGANIZATIONAL THEORY	4
RATIONALES FOR SCHOOL-BASED MANAGEMENT	6
DEFINITIONS OF SCHOOL-BASED MANAGEMENT	9
KEY COMPONENTS OF SCHOOL-BASED MANAGEMENT	12
EXPERIMENTATION AND IMPLEMENTATION IN SCHOOL SYSTEMS: FIRST STRATEGIES AND DESIGNS	13
COMMON EXPERIENCES AND PATTERNS OF DEPLOYMENT	19
SUMMARY	20
EXERCISES	21
REFERENCES	22
Chapter Two—SCHOOL-BASED MANAGEMENT:	
IMPACT ON SCHOOL CULTURE	25
MAJOR CHANGES TAKING PLACE IN THE UNITED STATES AND IN THE WORLD WHICH IMPACT THE SCHOOLS	27
TECHNIQUES WHICH CAN BE USED TO CAUSE CULTURAL CHANGE	30
School Climate Assessment	30
Empowering Activities	32
Marketing Strategies and Tactics	33
Employees and SBM Committee Members Training	34
STRATEGIC PLANNING AND OPERATIONAL PLANNING RELATED TO SCHOOL BASED MANAGEMENT	35
Scoping	36

Data Collecting	38
Planning	38
Implementation and Evaluation	40
CONCLUSION	40
SUMMARY	41
EXERCISES	42
REFERENCES	42
Chapter Three—SCHOOL-BASED MANAGEMENT: VEHICLE FOR TEACHER EMPOWERMENT	**44**
DEFINITIONS AND RATIONALES FOR EMPOWERMENT	44
BACKGROUND OF TEACHER EMPOWERMENT AND SBM	48
REQUIRED SUPPORT AND FACILITATION: COMMON PRACTICE	49
OBSTACLES TO TEACHER EMPOWERMENT AND LEADERSHIP	53
STATE AND NATIONAL TRENDS OF TEACHER EMPOWERMENT IN REFORM AND RESTRUCTURING	55
SUMMARY	57
EXERCISES	58
REFERENCES	59
Chapter Four—SCHOOL-BASED MANAGEMENT AND TEACHER ORGANIZATIONS: NEGOTIATIONS AND PARTNERSHIPS	**61**
EARLY EXPERIENCES AND COLLABORATIVE DESIGNS	61
QUALITY OF WORK LIFE BASICS	64
Board of Education Policy	64
West Bloomfield School District's Employees Communication and Development Council Bylaws	65
WIN/WIN NEGOTIATIONS	68
INHERENT PROBLEMS AND LOGICAL CONNECTIONS	70
Connections and Problems of Implementing SBM in School Districts with a History of Collaborative Decision Making	71
Connections and Problems of Implementing SBM in School Districts with a History of Adversarial Union/Management Relations	72

IMPLEMENTATION OF SBM AS PEER COACHING AND AS A PROFESSIONAL DEVELOPMENT VEHICLE	73
Peer Coaching	73
UNION CHANGE, DECENTRALIZATION, AND SHARED DECISION-MAKING IMPLICATIONS	74
NEW ACCOUNTABILITY STRUCTURES	75
SUMMARY	77
EXERCISES	79
REFERENCES	79
Chapter Five—SCHOOL-BASED MANAGEMENT AND THE PRINCIPAL: AUTHORITY, ACCOUNTABILITY, AND AUTONOMY	**81**
FOCUS ON THE PRINCIPAL'S ROLE	82
PRINCIPAL RELATIONSHIPS IN SCHOOL-BASED MANAGEMENT	84
PRINCIPAL SBM STRATEGIES FOR SHARING LEADERSHIP	87
IMPLICATIONS FOR TRAINING	91
SUMMARY	92
EXERCISES	93
REFERENCES	94
Chapter Six—SCHOOL-BASED MANAGEMENT AND THE CENTRAL OFFICE: FLATTENING THE PYRAMID	**96**
NEW ROLES AND ORGANIZATIONAL PATTERNS OF CENTRAL OFFICE PERSONNEL	97
INHERENT PROBLEMS AND SOLUTIONS TO THE DISPERSAL OF CENTRAL POWER	99
TRANSITIONS DEMANDED BY SBM: LARGE DISTRICTS ALTER CENTRAL OFFICE STRUCTURE AND FUNCTION	101
IMPLICATIONS AND RECOMMENDATIONS: FOCUS ON THREE KEY AREAS	105
School-Based Budgeting	106
School-Based Personnel Management	108
School-Based Management and Curricular and Instructional Management	109
CONCLUSION	111
SUMMARY	111

EXERCISES	112
REFERENCES	113
Chapter Seven—SCHOOL-BASED MANAGEMENT AND THE SUPERINTENDENT: CHANGE CATALYST AND ACTIVE PARTICIPANT	115
TRANSITIONS AND NEW ROLE PERCEPTIONS RELATED TO THE SUPERINTENDENT IN DISTRICTS WHICH INITIATE SCHOOL-BASED MANAGEMENT	116
DESIRABLE PRAGMATIC SUPERINTENDENT'S SKILLS AND BELIEFS CHECKLIST	128
THE SUPERINTENDENT'S SYMBOLIC LEADERSHIP FUNCTIONS AND SUPPORT DEMANDS IN A DISTRICT CONSIDERING IMPLEMENTATION OF SCHOOL-BASED MANAGEMENT	130
SCHOOL-BASED MANAGEMENT INTERROGATORY CHECKLIST	131
IMPLICATIONS FOR REALIGNMENT OF INTERACTIONS WITH THE SCHOOL BOARD AND CENTRAL OFFICE PERSONNEL	133
NEW RELATIONSHIPS WITH BUILDING PRINCIPALS AND TEACHERS	134
COMMON NATIONAL AND STATE PATTERNS OF IMPLEMENTATION	135
IMPLICATIONS FOR TRAINING AND ROLE CHANGE	136
SUMMARY	138
EXERCISES	139
REFERENCES	139
Chapter Eight—SCHOOL-BASED MANAGEMENT AND THE SCHOOL BOARD: ALTERING TRADITIONAL GOVERNANCE AND POLICY	142
TRANSITIONS AND NEW ROLE FUNCTIONS DEMANDED BY SBM	142
Kentucky Law	143
KRS Chapter 160, Sections 12, 14, and 15	143
NEED FOR BOARD LEADERSHIP AND SUPPORT	145
SCHOOL-BASED DECISION-MAKING POLICIES FOR THE HOPKINS COUNTY SCHOOL SYSTEM	146

INSTRUCTIONAL IMPACT: PROCESS MONITORING AND ACCOUNTABILITY	147
SCHOOL COUNCIL: MECHANICS AND STRUCTURE	149
IMPLICATIONS FOR PROVIDING RESOURCES AND FOR RESTRUCTURING RELATIONSHIPS WITH THE SUPERINTENDENT, PROFESSIONAL STAFF, AND WITH INDIVIDUAL SCHOOLS	158
AREAS OF SCHOOL-BASED DECISION MAKING POSSIBILITIES	159
COMMON IMPLEMENTATIONS AND RECOMMENDATIONS	159
SUMMARY	161
EXERCISES	161
REFERENCES	162
Chapter Nine—SCHOOL-BASED MANAGEMENT AND THE COMMUNITY: NEW STRUCTURES FOR COLLABORATION	**164**
TRANSITIONS AND NEW ROLE FUNCTIONS DEMANDED BY SBM	164
Preplanning Phase	166
Phase One	
Overview Planning	166
Phase Two	
Awareness	168
Phase Three	
Change Model Development	168
Phase Four	
Detailed Five-Year Plan Development	169
Phase Five	
Initial Implementation	169
Phase Six	
Evaluation	169
Phase Seven	
District Implementation or Recycling	169
WEST BLOOMFIELD SCHOOL DISTRICT'S SITE-BASED COMMUNICATIONS-GOVERNANCE COMMITTEES	170
Why Develop a Communications-Governance Structure that Empowers Stakeholders at the School Building Level?	171

What are the Potential Advantages and Disadvantages of Creating This Empowerment Structure?	172
What Format Shall Be the Best One to Utilize?	174
How Will the Degree of Success of the Empowerment Structure be Measured?	176
A Final Comment	176
PARENT AND NONPARENT STAKEHOLDER PARTICIPATION ON SBM SCHOOL COUNCILS AND IN DECISION MAKING	177
CORPORATE PARTNERSHIP OPPORTUNITIES	178
COMMON NATIONAL PATTERNS AND RECOMMENDATIONS FOR IMPLEMENTATION	179
RECOMMENDATIONS AND IMPLICATIONS FOR TRAINING OF COMMUNITY MEMBERS INVOLVED IN SBM ACTIVITIES	180
SUMMARY	181
EXERCISES	182
REFERENCES	183
Chapter Ten—SCHOOL-BASED MANAGEMENT AND STATE DEPARTMENTS OF EDUCATION AND LEGISLATURES: LIBERATING THE INDIVIDUAL SCHOOL THROUGH MANDATE	185
SCHOOL-BASED MANAGEMENT: STATE RESTRUCTURING STRATEGY	186
TEXAS AND KENTUCKY: STATEWIDE SBM LABORATORIES	187
Restructuring for Diversity: The Texas Model	187
Kentucky Perestroika	190
EARLY IMPLEMENTATION OF SCHOOL-BASED DECISION MAKING: CASE STUDY OF A KENTUCKY SCHOOL DISTRICT	194
Description of Case Study Schools	195
School-Based Management Interview Responses	195
Common Interview Response Patterns	207
School-Based Management Questionnaire	208
Common SBDM Council Questionnaire Responses	213
Combined Conclusions from Interviews and Questionnaires	213
CONCLUSION	214
SUMMARY	216

EXERCISES	217
REFERENCES	217
Chapter Eleven—SCHOOL-BASED MANAGEMENT AND SCHOOL REFORM: RESTRUCTURING FOR COLLABORATION	219
THE DECADE OF REFORM: SPRINGBOARD FOR SCHOOL-BASED MANAGEMENT	219
SCHOOL-BASED MANAGEMENT AS A STRUCTURAL AND MANAGERIAL TOOL OF REFORM	221
Summary of Common Reform Report Points	223
SBM ROLE IN THE RESTRUCTURING OF EDUCATION	223
CONNECTIONS WITH EFFECTIVE SCHOOLS RESEARCH AND SCHOOL IMPROVEMENT	228
FEDERAL INITIATIVES AND SCHOOL-BASED MANAGEMENT	230
SUMMARY	233
EXERCISES	234
REFERENCES	234
Chapter Twelve—SCHOOL-BASED MANAGEMENT AND THE FUTURE	237
SUMMARY OF CHAPTERS ONE THROUGH ELEVEN	237
COMBINED TRENDS WITHIN THE CONTEXT OF THE EDUCATION REFORM AND RESTRUCTURING MOVEMENT	243
EDUCATIONAL LEADERSHIP TRENDS AND SBM	245
IMPLICATIONS FOR PROFESSIONAL PREPARATION AND TRAINING	246
SUMMARY OF STATE AND NATIONAL SBM IMPLEMENTATION PATTERNS AND FUTURE IMPLICATIONS	247
CONCLUSION	248
SUMMARY	249
EXERCISES	251
REFERENCES	252
APPENDIX: State-by-State Implementation of School-Based Management	253
GLOSSARY	263
Index	267

SCHOOL-BASED MANAGEMENT:
CURRENT THINKING AND PRACTICE

Chapter 1

SCHOOL-BASED MANAGEMENT: A HISTORICAL AND DEVELOPMENTAL OVERVIEW

The controversy which has characterized American education over the last decade has had, at best, a diverse and diffused focus. From the Effective Schools studies to the succession of state-of-education national reports and commission studies which have impacted the field since 1983, there has been a range of topics, discussion points, and recommendations. School-based management can be traced, by direct reference or by inference, in almost all of these (see Chapter 11). As a structural or organizational innovation, however, SBM has a much earlier record; the essential operations of decentralization and shared decision making have long been a tradition in some districts. Clune and White (1988) mention the 34-year-old tradition of school autonomy which exists in Chesterfield, Missouri. SBM as a differentiated concept, however, is relatively new to the practitioner field, in terminology if not in practice.

BEGINNINGS

This tradition of local control of schools dates back to the last century, with separate, individual boards of education for each school building, and was overtaken during this century by centralization, by increasing district size, and by consolidation factors, virtually disappearing through the 1960s (Oliver, 1992).

After the Second World War until the late 1960s, school site decision making was done informally in the school's hallways, or through quick meetings between principal and staff. However, authority in the schools gradually became more centralized, and the union conflicts of the decade impaired collegiality. In 1965 the IGE (Individually Guided Education) school improvement program created research and instruction units in schools, which gradually evolved to include the principal and to require district support for coordination of effort. During the 1970s, some early SBM forms began to appear in an attempt to respond to the changing characteristics of desegregated and increasingly multicultural neighborhood and community schools (Taylor and Levine, 1991).

Early indicators of SBM appeared in New York in the 1971 Fleischman Commission school-based management development, and in Florida in 1973 in a report to the Governor's Citizens Committee on Education, which promoted "a school-centered organization of instruction" based on the following principles: allocation of funds to schools based upon the needs of the children in the schools, development of educational objectives by those associated with the school, determination of curriculum at the school level, and participation of parents in decision making (Oliver, 1992). Some efforts were encouraged by state legislation. In 1979, a Florida law granted funds to establish advisory committees at each of a district's schools. California's Early Childhood Education Act and School Improvement Program included councils and parent involvement. Other factors, such as desegregation and collective negotiations, impacted the initiation of SBM, in such locations as Cleveland in 1976 and in Dade County, Florida. Also documented are the investigations of the Boston School District, which considered the Florida model for implementation, and the consideration of the Edmonton (Alberta, Canada) model by the San Diego School District and the Cleveland Public Schools. Grant-sponsored initiatives provided SBM pilots funding in Minnesota, Oregon, Washington, and New Jersey (Clune and White, 1988). During the 1960s and 1970s, decentralization and some local-level budgeting innovations were present in scattered districts; these were adopted to give political power to local communities, to balance state authority, or to achieve an administrative efficiency gain (Wissler and Ortiz, 1986, David, 1988). All of these initiatives preceded the substantial school-based management thrust which occurred during the educational reforms of the 1980s, and which is described in greater detail in Chapter Eleven.

ORIGINS IN ORGANIZATIONAL THEORY

The beginnings of school-based management as a distinct concept lie in organizational theory and in private sector managerial innovation. Much of organizational theory has been developed over the last three decades, and public sector-related research is even more recent. The idea of loosely coupled systems, and the resulting and inevitable cultural uniqueness of each individual school, supports the push for decentralization and the view of each school as a center for change (Bailey, 1991). The more recent patterns found in productive businesses have included employee involvement, high levels of participation, a team approach, decentralization of decision making, and, most significantly, a downsizing of structure—scope, management, and governance (Bailey, 1991; Christopher, 1980). SBM has borrowed from this recent corporate practice, a logical strategy, since schools are, indeed, workplaces.

Examination of contemporary organizational theory and current corporate innovation reveals patterns of participation, involvement, smallness, work teams, and decision making at the lowest level—various forms of self-determination which have decentralized the workplace (Bailey, 1991). The common thread which runs through the substantial body of contemporary corporate and managerial study is the key function of *decentralization*, in critical linkage with the increase of productivity. The absences of centralization and entrenched bureaucracies in exemplary organizations is well documented (Peters and Waterman, 1982; Bennis and Nanus, 1985).

In Peters and Waterman 1982 study of the nations "best-run companies", they identified a shared sense of ownership as a key ingredient of successful organizations. *Business Week* reported in 1989 that an increasing number of major corporations had adopted employee ownership, trading traditional line assembly for self-managing teams which assumed responsibility for a larger scope of the production process or product (Toch, 1991).

Downsizing as a pervasive application in scope, management, and governance/regulation has been a hallmark of the corporate field (Lewis, 1988). Theories of how people work together effectively in organizations have characterized managerial research and practice for the past two decades. Companies are looking for ways to place responsibility closer to the activity; deciding which functions can be decentralized, and giving autonomy to units while also incorporating them into the overall operations (Lewis, 1988). There has been substantial restructuring at 78-year-old IBM, which has resulted in the ground-breaking spinoff of virtually all divisions into decentralized and autonomous units. These new subsidiaries are free to develop distinctive marketing strategies, to set salary levels, and to report fiscally to stockholders. The purpose of this divestiture (of one of the most undeniably classic bureaucratic organizations) is to eliminatea stifling bureaucracy and to enable the newly-emancipated units to compete more skillfully in a global market.

Such decentralization and shared decision-making patterns among companies vary greatly, but the essential issues of retooling the American workplace, Lewis (1988) notes, are the challenges of rethinking mission, doing more with less, and doing things better. These challenges are common to both business and education, and can evoke similar responses of downsizing (reassigning central-level responsibility to the site-level manager) and blurring "the traditional lines of demarcation between labor and management" (Siegal and Smoley as quoted in Lewis, 1988, p. 107), in order to assign that responsibility closer to the delivery point. Collaborative management, as demonstrated in shared decision making, and rewarding performance, as demonstrated in teamwork incentives for productivity and quality, are two powerful business concepts (Siegal and Smoley, as cited in Lewis, 1988) which underlie the concept of school-based management, and which are hallmarks of SBM practice in many early implementations.

RATIONALES FOR SCHOOL-BASED MANAGEMENT

A new balance of centralization and decentralization, as recommended by the body of corporate theory, is evident in education; many of the conditions and catalysts which began the change in business two decades ago are now present in the field. Historically, there has always been a struggle between autonomy and control; the undeniably strong, though frequently corrupt, local control tradition of nineteenth century schools. The historical and reactive twentieth century depoliticization of schools occurred with the inception of the role of the superintendent and the substantial increase in the size of many school districts. This was combined with the application of the 1920s industrial model of management, and control shifted strongly to a top-down model. Common deficiencies of such centralization include the loss of creativity and innovation, and strong arguments began occurring in the late 1950s in educational circles against centralized educational management (Lindelow and Heynederickx, 1989).

There are many reasons and rationales why school-based management is currently being touted as a means of improving school districts. Ever since *A Nation at Risk* was published, warning all readers of the deplorable condition of our schools and urging the necessity to quickly attend to the restructuring and innovations required to improve them, a wide variety of reports, evidences, and legislative actions have suggested ways to improve our schools. Some of the major reasons for the current emphasis on school-based planning as a method of restructuring are:

- Current effective schools research on schools and teaching indicate that the best way to ensure improvement in schools is to focus on the individual school building.
- Current research on the principalship indicates that the "key" instructional leader in a school district is the building principal.
- Business and industry want schools to improve in order that the schools' products (students) are more productive workers; which, in turn, should make business and industry more competitive with foreign nations.
- The number of adult illiterates and the huge student drop out rates that exist, especially in large cities and in minority populations, alarm practically everyone; as this leads to an undereducated populace and an expensive drain on the finances of the national, state and local levels to take care of the dependency that this undereducation creates.
- Organizations like the Commission of the States, governors' organizations, and federal and state legislatures are being made aware of the political necessity to support school improvement efforts by the lobbyists for business, industrial and educational groups; and they are reacting politically to this pressure by mandating or pressuring in other ways for restructuring of our schools (J.J. Herman, 1990, p. 2).

Additionally, the American Association of School Administrators', the National Association of Elementary School Principals', and the National Association of Secondary School Principals' joint task force on school-based management identified nine advantages to SBM, in that it:

- Formally recognizes the expertise and competence of those who work in individual schools to make decisions to improve learning.
- Gives teachers, other staff members, and the community increased input into decisions.
- Improves morale of teachers, because staff members see they can have an immediate impact on their environment.
- Shifts the emphasis in staff development. Teachers are more directly involved in determining what they need.
- Focuses accountability for decisions. One individual—typically the superintendent or a building principal—has ultimate responsibility for any decision.
- Brings both financial and instructional resources in line with the instructional goals developed in each school.
- Helps to provide better services and programs to students.
- Nurtures and stimulates new leaders at all levels. As one task force member said, "Super stars emerge from the process. There is a rebirth."

- Increases both the quantity and the quality of communication, which is more likely to be informal—in face-to-face meetings, for example (AASA, 1988).

Pierce in 1980 noted that proponents of SBM view educational organizations as loosely structured, with little control existing between the levels. The autonomy of each level is evident in that each chooses whether or not to comply with central-level rules and regulations. In light of this loose coupling, SBM may be the only way to administer schools. Without the voluntary compliance of such participants, no real change will occur. In 1986, Guthrie insisted that the school is the logical unit for decision making, asserting that the faculty and principal make a natural team, and that, in reality, parents and students usually "give their allegiance" to a particular *school*, not to a school system or state educational system. Guthrie also felt that SBM could potentially reduce the conflict between state policymakers and local school personnel.

In 1988, Sirotnik and Clark emphasized the importance of the school as the center for change, suggesting that site educators should not just be given programs to implement, but should focus on the problem and become involved in active solutions, employing the knowledge and talent available in the schools. Through inquiry and discussion, understanding can be translated into action. In asserting that decisions should be made where the action is, they note, "the ultimate power to change is in the heads, hands, and hearts of the educators who work in the schools" (p. 664). Echoing Pierce Sirotnik, and Clark have also recognized that schools and districts systems are not closed systems; they interact continuously with surrounding environments, and, in the process, develop their own distinct cultures—cultures which must be considered when change and improvement are contemplated. Similarly, David (1989) describes the rationale for school-based management as emerging from two well-established propositions:

1. The school is the primary decision-making unit; and, its corollary, decisions should be made at the lowest possible level (with reference to Smith and Purkey's 1985 work on the policy implications of Effective Schools literature), and,

2. Change requires ownership that comes from the opportunity to participate in defining change and the flexibility to adapt it to individual circumstances; the corollary is that change does not result from externally imposed procedures (with reference to Fullan's 1982 work on educational change). (David, p. 2)

These rationales represent a range of views and convictions: the successful business restructuring followership model; the common findings on leadership from Effective Schools and principal research; the current demographic and social dysfunction impetus; the recommendations from collective national task force reports (which address teacher morale, staff development, instructional improvement, communication, and leadership stimulation); and the organizational dynamics of loose coupling, logical unit of decision making, and logical locus of viable action. The press for widespread implementation of SBM seems, therefore, to be supported by a national leadership consensus, (derived, in part, from exemplary corporate and organizational practice), the national concern for sociocultural realities, and a broadly-based anticipated impact on the effectiveness of the individual school. Considering this sheer weight of common rationale, the focus on SBM as an essential tool of restructuring is understandable.

As SBM backdrop and catalyst, the history of Effective Schools, school improvement, and school reform are substantially intermingled with school-based management concepts and terminology, whether directly indicated or logically implied. In Chapter 11, a separate and more focused consideration is given to these issues; the reader will find there further rationales for school-based management, underpinned by the reform/restructuring consensus for its implementation.

DEFINITIONS OF SCHOOL-BASED MANAGEMENT

Definitions for school-based management abound in the literature, but, as a relatively new concept in educational practice, there is no existing clear-cut definition. The SBM process has a variety of names in the field: site-based management, building-based management, school-centered management, decentralized management, school-site autonomy, the autonomous school concept, responsible autonomy, school-based budgeting, school-site lump-sum budgeting, school-improvement process, school-based curriculum development, teacher empowerment, shared governance, administrative decentralization, and shared decision making (Oliver, 1992). The differences in terminology are less important than the shifts in authority implicit in the process (Kolderie as cited in Lewis, 1989).

Various descriptions have appeared in journals and texts. In 1980, Pierce described SBM as a means of accountability. The AASA/NAESP/NASSP School-Based Management Task Force, which has summarized SBM recommendations in *School-Based Management: A Strategy for Better Learning,* provides a definition of a "process that involves the individuals responsible for implementing decisions in actually making those decisions. In general, under school-based management, decisions are made at the level lowest to the issue being addressed" (AASA, 1988). Rennie (1985) defines SBM as a system of educational management which provides the "appropriate balance of authority and accountability." Carl L. Marburger (1985), the former New Jersey Commissioner of Education, defines it as a process in which a number of policy and budgeting decisions are made at the school building level rather than by the school board or central administration of the school district. In general, Clune and White noted in 1988, SBM refers to increased authority at the school site. Burns and Howes (1988) report a definition used by the National Committee for Citizens in Education: "A form of district organization and management in which the school-community is the key unit for educational change and improvement." Lindelow and Heynederickx (1989), in their leadership text, describe SBM as "a system of administration in which the school is the primary unit of educational decision-making" (p. 109).

David's 1989 synthesis of research on SBM notes that "Under school-based management, professional responsibility replaces bureaucratic regulation; districts increase school autonomy in exchange for the staff's assuming responsibility for results. . . . it represents a change in how the district operates—how authority and responsibility are shared between the district and its schools" (p. 2). In a similar research overview, White in 1989 noted that SBM "refers to a program or philosophy adopted by schools or school districts to improve education by increasing the autonomy of the school staff to make school site decisions" (p. 1). NASSP's *Practitioner* (1989) publication, reviewing SBM issues and practice, simplified it as embodying "the concept that decisions should be made at the lowest possible level in organizations" (p. 1).

In an SBM-teacher empowerment text (1989), James Lewis, Jr. insists that school-based management goes beyond many more limited definitions, indicating that it is "the practice of giving teachers the authority, responsibility, information, freedom, autonomy, support, and resources they need to perform those duties usually reserved for administrators. It is not a process, but, rather, a democratic management style" (p. 20). In a reform movement summary text, Boyd (1990) comments that "school-based management is founded on the belief that many key decisions inescapably must be made at the school level.... (and) thus involves the creation of a school council.... which is responsible for a variety of programmatic and operational decisions as well as the allocation of a small budget.... School-based management is consistent with trends in modern business management that emphasize the advantages of maximum delegation of decision making to the operational level within a centrally-coordinated framework" (p. 90). In a text on restructuring, Raywid (1990) describes "site management" as a "proposal to decentralize and, at least to this extent, debureaucratize school control.... it is also a proposal for shared decision making within the school" (p. 156).

Canadian educator Daniel Brown (1990) notes that SBM, "As a manifestation of decentralization, means simply that schools within a district are allotted money to purchase supplies, equipment, personnel, utilities, maintenance, and perhaps other services according to their own assessment of what is appropriate" (p. 4). In Bailey's 1991 landmark text on school-site management, he indicates that "school-based or site-based management is usually defined in terms of a process that involves the individuals responsible for implementing decisions to be involved in making those decisions" (p. 56). Candoli's 1991 text on planning for SBM describes it as meaning "achieving a balance between accountability and freedom in all parts of the educational system.... The primary idea is that the greatest possible improvements in the school system will be attained when local schools are given the freedom to solve their own problems" (p. 34).

Brown's 1991 work on decentralization uses the term school-based management "to mean the decentralization of a school district or school's authority to make key decisions affecting it" (p. 11). Guthrie's 1991 policy text describes SBM as a further "effort to infuse schools with greater citizen participation.... intended to gain a greater measure of lay control and to provide more 'accountability' by using the school, rather than the district, as the basic decision-making unit for personnel and curriculum" (p. 37–38). In Hanson's 1991 administrative and organizational text, SBM "involves a transfer of decision-making power, or at a minimum the manner in which decisions are made" (p. 383). Eastlund (1991) further carries this transfer notion in describing SBM as a system where "principals confer authority on others within the system and promote the autonomy of teachers" (p. 25). SBM has been described by Ambroisie and Haley, (1991) as an organizational model in which individuals are empowered to determine and manage the programs at the building level.

Three common elements can be discerned in this range of definitions:

- The shift/exchange, and balance of decision making authority with regard to autonomy and accountability.
- The consensus that those closest to, most impacted by, or primarily responsible, for any decision implementation, should be the decision makers.
- The empowerment and involvement of principals, teachers and other staff, and community, in school decision making.

KEY COMPONENTS OF SCHOOL-BASED MANAGEMENT

These three elements are quite clearly related to the common points of the current rationales for SBM. A similarity can also be found in the common key components of SBM, though the variety of implementation of SBM is substantial and logical, given that "Variation in the implementation of SBM programs is implicit in the definition of SBM" (Clark, 1992). The success of any SBM program will depend upon the amount of latitude individual schools have to adapt new policies or develop innovative solutions to problems (Cohen, 1983). In 1991, Taylor and Levine contended that the development of uniform guidelines for decision making is an impossibility; such guidelines will vary enormously depending upon the particular organizational culture and individuals involved. Mojkowski and Fleming in 1988 noted that the mass of literature on SBM is accumulating at a faster rate than is actual knowledge about the practice. Considering the wide range of components that constitute SBM, it is difficult to identify salient characteristics of the practice, but there are some commonalities of implementation. Clune and White in 1988 found decentralization of authority and the creation of a decision-making SBM council to be key elements. David (1989) reported Cawelti's listing of the key elements of SBM: various degrees of budgeting affording alternate use of resources; a team operation to expand the basis of decision making; site advisory committees; increased authority for personnel selection; curriculum modification options; regulatory waiver options; and the expectation of an annual report on progress and school improvement. Common key components identified in the literature on SBM include: strategic planning (J.J. Herman, 1989); a decision-making model incorporating decision areas, the types of representational groups, and the nature of that representation (Solokoff,

1990); role and responsibility (Harvey & Crandall, 1988), annual plans and performance reports (Guthrie, 1986) and exemption from statutory regulation through waivers (Cawelti, 1989).

In 1990, J.J. Herman addressed the key component and definition question of SBM: "Most schools or school districts that have implemented school-based management processes have included one or more of the following: (1) some or a great deal of decision making, which traditionally has been done at the central office level, is now done in collaboration with building level functionaries, or decisions which were traditionally central office-made are delegated to the building level; (2) the building level has greater control of instructional, staffing and/or budgetary decisions; (3) the building level can get exemptions for cause from district policies and rules and regulations; (4) the building level initiates its own policies and rules and regulations; and (5) the building level decisions are made by a variety of stakeholders which can include any combination of teachers, classified personnel, parents, students, community members, business or industrial representatives and building level administrators" (p. 2–3). Herman's definition of school-based management combines the essence of the common elements of current definitions of SBM: "A structure and process which allows greater decision-making power related to the areas of instruction, budget, policies, rules and regulations, staffing, and all matters of governance; and a process which involves a variety of stakeholders in the decisions related to the local individual school building" (p. 3).

EXPERIMENTATION AND IMPLEMENTATION IN SCHOOL SYSTEMS: FIRST STRATEGIES AND DESIGNS

These key components were present to some extent in the initial SBM implementation efforts and pilot programs which were scattered across the country during the 1970s and 1980s. Some were individual district efforts, such as those in Boston, Massachusetts; Charleston County, South Carolina; Duval County, Florida; San Diego, California; Sarasota, Florida; St. Louis, Missouri; and Tulsa, Oklahoma. Some were state department of education-initiated (see Chapter 10); some were court-ordered in combination with desegregation directives (Cleveland, Ohio is an example) or came as a result of collective bargaining contracts, as in Dade County, Florida. Some were initiated by a grant-sponsoring agency; this was the case in Saint Paul, Minnesota and in New Jersey (Clune & White, 1988). A description of some specific SBM implementations follows:

East Baton Rouge Parish School System in Louisiana in 1988 implemented SBM in combination with open enrollment, as a federally-approved experiment. Twelve pilot schools have school advisory councils, appropriate staff development, curricular flexibility aimed at magnet school-type specialization, and some financial discretion. If successful, the program was to be implemented at each of the district's 100 schools within four years.

Memphis School System in 1988 selected 8 schools to comprise a deregulated school district reporting directly to the superintendent; they were exempted from guidelines in exchange for establishing school-based decision making, assuming increased responsibility for instructional leadership, and developing local programs and services. Implementation of school-based decision making via local councils was planned for 1990–91; with the intent to limit the initial council term to one year. Waivers of district rules and regulations were available.

Tulsa, Oklahoma had a 1988 superintendent-instigated program of shared decision making; Toward Educational and Management Success (TEAMS). The school system involves parents and citizens in decision making, and includes teachers on the management team. SBM has helped the district to deal with the problem of downsizing due to enrollment decrease, and the need to desegregate via magnet schools.

Hammond, Indiana, responding innovatively to depressed local economic conditions and in conjunction with the teachers' union, created a school-site plan through the collective bargaining process. Design teams charged with school improvement and staffed by teachers, administrators, and parents, have received training in group dynamics. This locally-funded and grant-supported effort has resulted in dramatic changes in structure, curricular design, and use of school time.

Jefferson County, Kentucky in 1986 used a strong base of an academy (grant-supported); this professional development institute created school teams that developed shared vision and decision making, and used flexibility in policies and procedures. Developmental design support also came from the University of Louisville and from the district's central office staff. Superintendent Don Ingwerson indicated that the restructuring is encompassing participatory management at all levels, causing site-based activities, and is creating a change in the levels of decision making. One hundred and fifty principals report directly to him.

Rochester, New York traded substantial salary increases for union concessions that facilitated a career ladder with mentoring lead teachers, school-based planning and decision making. Like Dade County's structure, the 1987 program was designed around the Carnegie Forum's *A Nation Prepared*. Guidelines for school-based teams were presented in 1989; with an effort to make sure that all stakeholder groups were represented on the teams.

In 1988 **San Diego** implemented a strategic planning process which resulted in the publishing of school board beliefs that schools: need greater autonomy and shared decisionmaking; can be responsible for student outcomes; need time (at least 3 years) before site change can be felt; and can restructure schools within existing district resource allocations.

Toledo, Ohio instituted a lighthouse restructuring design in 1981. The Toledo Plan has facilitated union-board collaboration on many issues, including the creation of individual building committees for each school. (Lewis, 1988; Hanson, 1990a).

Monroe County, Florida phased in a school-based management system between 1971 and 1976, as a result of state reform legislation; the superintendent, together with central office staff and principals, implemented an SBM program, supported by four state universities and some grant funding. Extensive training in team management and decision making and was provided for the principals; each school determines goals and allocated funds expenditure; in-house personnel school teams were created, and each school has an advisory committee composed of parents, teachers, students, and citizens.

Martin County, Florida began an SBM system in 1976, spurred by teacher and parental desire for more participation. Training was provided during the first five years for school advisory groups. The level of individual school autonomy is substantial; with input from various groups, principals have decision-making purview in areas of budget, curriculum, and personnel. The next step planned was to increase the involvement of parents in the decision-making process.

Fairfield-Suisun Unified School District, California began to decentralize in 1973, aiming at the implementation of SBM and at the provision of community and staff input in a discretionary funds-based budget process. School site councils and principals can plan their own programs, and purchase materials and equipment.

Irvine Unified School District, California was created by a 1972 election; the problems of significant district enrollment growth which followed were greatly facilitated by the district's agreed-upon school site management format. Principals were given responsibility for a wide range of management areas, including planning and personnel decisions, with the caveat that staff be fully involved. While recent fiscal developments have reduced discretionary latitude, the district has managed to employ SBM instructional flexibility while adhering to a highly centralized state reform-mandated curriculum.

Lunenburg, Massachusetts in 1982 began alterations of its school-site management structure, supported by the superintendent's vision of the principal as responsible for curriculum, teacher and student evaluation, discipline, purchasing, and monitoring of achievement and morale. The small size of the district, which has been impacted by severe reductions in funding, requires the variety of input and opinions of people in making decisions.

Cherry Creek, Colorado has changed its school-based management system over a long period of time; in 1980 one principal reported having 95 percent or more autonomy in such areas as personnel and curriculum. The central office staff has remained small, and many traditional central functions are performed by the principals. Decision-making latitude extends to a personnel selection consensus process and to the inclusion of parents in the development of school policy.

Portland, Oregon's 92 schools have a partial form of SBM; with budget and personnel decentralized, and with curriculum being a shared area between schools and the central office. Community and school-site input into decision making is important; schools receive "consolidated building budgets" and principals have virtual expenditure control. Each school selects its own personnel and can design the instructional delivery systems which impart district-common curricular content. Local advisory committees, consisting of teachers, parents, and community members, work with the principal in decision making; there is also a separate budget review committee at each school. (Lindelow and Heynderickx, 1989).

Richardson, Texas uses school site budgeting as part of its school effectiveness managerial design. Principals receive equitable nonpayroll funds and personnel units, and many apply for special programmatic allotments. School effectiveness teams provide an advisory function to the principal; they are responsible for developing school improvement plans and performance reports.

Prince William County, Virginia began SBM in five pilot schools in 1987, with a goal of complete implementation by 1990. Principals were given budget and hiring authority, maintenance and utility payment options, and the allocation of instructional funds. Waivers were allowed for district regulations, but adherence to state standards was a maintenance requirement.

Savannah-Chatham County, Georgia in 1989 phased in a three-year site-based budgeting process; principals assumed control of inservice training, instructional supplies, and staff travel. The importance of interacting with other staff on such expenditures was emphasized.

Sarasota, Florida's plan allows for collaborative school site development of budget requests. A school advisory board of parents and a teacher representative work with the principal in determining school priorities, budget, and staff allocations. A school management team assists the principal in dealing with instructional matters, including school improvement, and in managing day-to-day issues and problems.

Granville County, North Carolina in 1991 had six pilot sites set up for the LEAD teacher program. Lead teachers assume liaison authority with other site constituencies; the school may waive most state regulations in order to facilitate classroom authority. The schools create their own goals and budgets.

Key Largo, Florida by 1980 had a decentralized management structure which emphasized teacher decision making in budgetary and curricular areas.

Fairfax County, Virginia in 1988 had elected school faculty/staff advisory councils charged with providing a link between staff and program managers.

Knox and Giles Counties, Tennessee have school site councils made up of the principal and several faculty representatives, who address such areas as curriculum, discipline, inservice, and facilities.

Charleston, South Carolina began implementation of SBM in 1982 through an application and selection process; the ten pilot schools were required to execute short- and long-range planning keyed to Effective Schools models. Local school management teams composed of the principal, teachers, parents, and citizens were given intensive management practice training.

Spring Branch, Texas has been identified by the National Clearinghouse on SBM as among the top ten SBM districts in the United States; its implementation of SBM had been followed by increases in such quality indicators as student achievement, SAT score gains, increased parental involvement, improvement in teacher morale, and a reduction in dropout rates.

Temple, Texas in 1989 required individual schools to conduct site planning as part of the overall district strategic planning process; each school's team was composed of school personnel, parents, and community leaders. In adopting a district participative management policy, individual schools were given control over budget, curriculum, staff assignment and development, scheduling, program design and selection, and implementation of strategies.

Pinellas County, Florida had a school in 1986 which, as one of the NEA's Mastery in Learning project schools, included a site-based decision making process. Across-the-board participation of stakeholders produced a school profile, vision, and perceived needs. Flexibility in the district's collective bargaining agreement took school-based decision making a step further by alloting supplemental salary funds to its twelve schools. Later contract provisions facilitated: the provision of funds to schools desiring SBDM participation, options for contractual waivers, and grant support for district-wide SBDM (Oliver, 1992).

Two large district implementations have been more widely publicized, due to the dramatic nature of the urban system restructuring in Chicago, and to the sustained time period, breadth of collaboration, and phased-in process which characterized Dade County's implementation.

In 1988, the **Chicago** School Reform Act established local councils for each of the system's 590 schools; these councils can hire and evaluate the principal, set improvement priorities, and make budgetary expenditure (within city-wide guidelines); the principals hire staff without regard to seniority, and Teacher Advisory Councils, (charged with curricular change and improvement) were created at every school. The local school councils are represented on the District Council, which selects the district superintendent. The central district budget was to be cut by $40 million and the funds passed on to the schools (see also Chapter 6).

Dade County, Florida, drawing on the strong positive relationship between the district and the teacher's union, created a joint union-management team which selected 33 schools from 55 applicants to participate in SBM. This implementation was designed with the specific recommendations of the Carnegie Forum Task Force report on the teaching profession in mind. By 1989, 100 of the district's schools were participating in school-based management, and were being provided lump-sum flexible funding (90% budgetary control), waivers on district and state regulations, flexible governance structures (which must involve teacher decision making), and extra funds for staff development. The Dade County model uses leadership circles (modeled after Japanese and American Quality Circles) of teachers that address issues involving budgetary, academic, and staffing decisions (Hanson, 1990a).

COMMON EXPERIENCES AND PATTERNS OF DEPLOYMENT

The earlier SBM implementations—those occurring in the 1970s and early 1980s—had some common characteristics:

- began with schools that volunteer
- supported with waivers from local or state constraints
- involved staff in developing goals and actions
- made cooperative agreements with unions
- gave schools staffing and materials budgets
- provided incentives for principals to include teachers in site decisions
- developed and tried out new SBM models during the summer
- used multiple measures of accountability, including those defined by the schools
- provided professional growth for principals and teachers in management, clinical supervision, and instruction
- provided time for staff to work with colleagues to make decisions
- sought supplementary (usually grant) sources of funding (Lewis, 1988)

Common implementation conclusions from 1988s *School-Based Management: Institutional Variation, Implementation, and Issues for Further Research* by Clune and White were:

- Decisions on budget, curriculum, and hiring represent the three crucial areas for school-based management.
- Budget decisions tended to be given first, then hiring, and finally, curriculum.
- The most aggressive plans decentralized all three areas at once.
- Smaller districts found the process easier; larger districts confronted more obstacles.

- The central person in school-based management programs is the principal, whose roles changes as instructional leader, as mediator of shared governance, and as a more authoritative figure in the district chain of command.
- Communication with students and parents improves in these schools, especially through the school governance councils.
- School-based management represents a unique blend of accountability and autonomy.

The later SBM innovations and implementations, demonstrated by those district efforts extending from the 1980s into the 1990s, seem to extend and refine those early characteristics:

- There is a definite emphasis on the creation and further empowerment of school councils, especially in the efforts to assure wide-ranging stakeholder and representational membership.
- The early participant training has been enhanced and amplified to include broad managerial training, especially consensus and group process skills. The terminology is subtly changing to emphasize shared decision making (SDM) as a companion, but distinct concept.
- SBM curricular innovation has become more definitive, substantially impacting the technical core. Collaborated change has been wrought in such powerful instructional components as grade and content area organization, time allotments, and instructional program/textbook adoption alterations.
- School-based management has become more definitely linked with and structurally intertwined with school improvement efforts.
- School-based management has also become a vehicle and tool for school district strategic planning efforts.

SUMMARY

In this chapter the origins of SBM were traced from its historical practice to its linkage with and adaptation to contemporary corporate managerial theory. Productive business patterns of decentralization and employee empowerment underlie much of the collective rationale for SBM. The history of educational administration has been one of evolution from strong local school control to one of district consolidation and strong central regulation. The rationales for SBM, as a field-based reaction to this situation were outlined, drawn from current literature. They reflect common themes: leadership research and recommendations, social impact needs, and productive organizational dynamics.

A range of definitions for SBM was reported, derived from two decades of research literature and practitioner thought. Three common definitional elements were discernible: the shift/exchange, and balance of decision-making authority with regard to autonomy and accountability; the consensus that those closest to, most impacted by, or primarily responsible, for any decision implementation, should be the decision makers; and the empowerment and involvement of principals, teachers and other staff, and community, in school decision making. These key components of SBM, clearly related to the rationales which appear in some of the literature, include: strategic planning, a decision-making model incorporating decision areas, the types of representational groups, and the nature of that representation, role and responsibility, annual plans and performance reports, and exemption from statutory regulation through waivers.

The chapter briefly described a substantial number of both early and more recent school district SBM implementations, drawn from a variety of states, which began at a number of points in time over the last two decades. The common experiences and patterns of SBM deployment demonstrated by these pioneer districts include: a pilot, waiver-supported status; involvement of principal, staff, and employee organizations; transfer of budgetary authority and personnel decision-making latitude; frequent employment of external funds and innovative scheduling to support training activities and meeting time; and the use of multiple measures of accountability. Further common SBM themes included: implementation in the areas of budget, hiring, and curriculum; a variety of amounts of decision-making latitude; a focus on the principal as key player; an enhancement of public relations; and a theme of blended accountability and authority. Later SBM trends, derived from the implementations of the late 1980s, extend and refine the earlier hallmarks by their emphasis on local council formation and empowerment, the broadening of training content, and the increase in the emergence of curricular change as an arena of SBM impact.

EXERCISES

1. Given the historical and local control model of nineteenth century education, what similarities and linkages do you see in the evolution of

other local and state governmental structures? Are there definable local examples of gradual bureaucratization which can be identified?

2. Conversely, what are some examples of decentralization within the private and public sectors?

3. If you were presenting the idea of SBM to your school board, what would be the thrust of your arguments with regard to rationales and key components?

4. With regard to the SBM patterns of implementation and the list of district program detail, which structures would work best in your district, and why?

REFERENCES

A cooperative model for a successful secondary school (1986). The National Association of Secondary School Principals/National Education Association. Reston, VA: NASSP, NEA.

A nation prepared: Teachers for the 21st century. (1986). New York. Carnegie Forum on Education and the Economy, pp. 56–61.

AASA. (1988). *School-based management* (AASA Stock Number 0221-00209), Washington, D.C.: American Association of School Administrators, National Association of Elementary School Principals, and National Association of Secondary School Principals.

Bailey, W.J. (1991). *School-site management applied.* Lancaster, PA: Technomic Publishing Company, pp. 24–26, 37.

Bennis, W. & Nanus, B. (1985). *Leaders: The strategies for taking charge.* New York: Harper & Row, pp. 16–18.

Boyd, W.L. (1990). Balancing control and autonomy in school reform: The politics of perestroika. In J. Murphy (Ed.), *The educational reform movement of the 1980's* (pp. 89–93). Berkeley, CA: McCutchan Publishing Corporation.

Brown, D.J. (1991). *Decentralization: The administrator's guidebook to school district change.* Newbury Park, CA: Corwin Press, Inc., p. 11.

Burns, L.T. & Howes, J. (1988). Handing control to local schools: site-based management sweeps the country. *The School Administrator, 45* (7), 8–10.

Candoli, I.C. (1991). *School system administration: A strategic plan for site-based management.* Lancaster, PA: Technomic Publishing Company, p. 34.

Cawelti, G. (1989). Key elements of site-based management. *Educational Leadership, 46* (8), 46.

Christopher, W. (1980). *Management for the 1980s.* Englewood Cliffs, NJ: Prentice-Hall.

Clark, C.R. (1990). Site-based management. *Site-based management information folio.* Arlington, VA: Educational Research Service, pp. 1–9.

Clune, W.H. & White, P.A. (1988). *School-based management—institutional variation, implementation, and issues for further research.* Center for Policy Research in Education, p. 12.

Cohen, M. (1983). Instructional, management, and social conditions in effective schools. In A. Odden & L.D. Webb (Eds.), *School finance and school improvement: linkages for the 1980s.* Cambridge, MA: Ballinger.

David, J.L. (1989). Synthesis of research on school-based management. *Educational Leadership, 46* (8), 45–53.

Eastlund, J.O. (1991) Site-based management as a tool for reform. *Music Education Journal, 34* (4), 25–29.

Guthrie, H. (1986). School-based management: The next needed education reform. *Phi Delta Kappan, 68* (4), 305–309.

Hansen, E.M. (1990a). *Educational administration and organizational behavior.* Boston, MA: Allyn and Bacon, pp. 382–385.

Hansen, E.M. (1990b). School based management and educational reform in the United States and Spain. *Comparative Education Review, 34* (4), 523–537.

Harvey, G. & Crandall, D.P. (1988). *What restructuring is: In search of a definition.* Andover, MA: Regional Laboratory for Educational Improvement of the Northeast Islands.

Herman, J.J. (1990). School-based management. *Instructional Leader, III* (4), Texas Elementary Principals and Supervisors Association, 1–4.

Lewis, A. (1989). *Restructuring America's schools.* Washington, D.C.: American Association of School Administrators, pp. 20–25, 143–150, 152–169.

Lewis, J., Jr. (1989). *Implementing school-based management... by empowering teachers.* Westbury, NY: J.L. Wilkerson Publishing Company, p. 20.

Lindelow, J. & J. Heynederickx. (1989). School-based management. In S.C. Smith & P.K. Piele (Eds.), *School leadership: handbook for excellence* (2nd ed.) (pp. 109–110). Eugene, OR: ERIC Clearinghouse on Educational Management.

NASSP. (1989). School site management. National Association of Secondary School Principals' *The Practitioner, 16* (2), 1–6.

Oliver, V. (1992). *A study of school-based management in selected southern states: extent of implementation and comparison of attitudes, perceptions, and concerns of principals and teachers.* Unpublished doctoral dissertation, The University of Alabama at Birmingham.

Peters, T.J. & Waterman, R.H. (1982). *In search of excellence: Lessons from America's best-run companies.* New York: Warner Books, pp. 112, 121–213, 312.

Pierce, L.C. (1980). School based management. *OSSC Bulletin, 23* (10), 6–21.

Raywid, M.A. (1990). Rethinking school governance. In R.F. Elmore and Associates, *Restructuring schools — the next generation of educational reform* (p. 156), San Francisco: Jossey-Bass Publishers.

Rennie, R.J. (1985). School-centered management: A matter of style. *School Business Affairs, 51* (4), 64–66.

Sirotnik, K.A. & Clark, R.W. (1988). School-centered decision making and renewal. *Phi Delta Kappan, 69* (9), 660–664.

Sokoloff, H. (1990). Ideas for making shared governance work. *The School Administrator, 47* (3), 43.

Taylor, B.O. & Levine, D.U. (1991). Effective schools projects and school-based management. *Phi Delta Kappan, 72* (5), 394–397.

Toch, T. (1991). Public schools of choice. *American School Board Journal, 178* (7), 18–21.

White, P.A. (1989). An overview of school-based management: What does the research say? *NASSP Bulletin, 73* (518), 1–8.

Wissler, D.F. & Ortiz, F.I. (1986). The centralization process of school systems: A review of the literature. *Urban Education, 21* (3), 280–294.

Chapter 2

SCHOOL-BASED MANAGEMENT: IMPACT ON SCHOOL CULTURE

Recently, we were attending a three day meeting in Washington, D.C., and we were staying at a very upscale hotel which had just opened that week. After two days we were so impressed with the treatment we received from everyone associated with the hotel; busboys, doorman, limousine driver, room service, concierge, desk operators, and all other employees with whom we came in contact, that we started talking to the employees to try to determine why this particular hotel had treated us so much better than any other hotel in which we had stayed. We probably spent about three hours asking a wide variety of employees a series of questions related to the way they treated their customers.

The employees shared the following with us:

- We are hired after multiple interviews and we are convinced that our employer is very selective in the people who are hired for any type of job category.
- We were trained, with full pay, for a full month before the hotel opened its doors for the first time.
- We are taught that people who stay with us are not to be thought of as customers; rather, they are to be treated as our house guests.
- We are told that if any house guest indicates that he or she has a problem, it immediately becomes our problem; and we are to stay with it, no matter how long it takes, until it is solved.
- We are instructed that if any house guest asks directions to any place in the hotel, we do not merely tell them how to get to the desired spot; but we are to take whatever time it takes to physically accompany the house guest to that destination.
- We are rewarded for excellent service, and we are recognized for good work.
- Training updates continue as long as we work for the hotel.

Recently, we stopped for breakfast at an area restaurant and as we waited in line to be seated we noticed a plaque on the wall the stated the corporate mission. The mission stated: "We offer good quality food at a reasonable price." The food was quite standard and the price was reasonable. What we remember most, however, was that the service was terrible. If this mission statement was intended to guide all employees in ownership of the corporate culture, then the slogan used to state the corporate culture of the restaurant chain missed the most important ingredient—that of excellent customer service.

Because of our interest in organizational culture, we have purposely read annual statements, talked to employees as we go about our daily living, and looked for slogans or other evidences which would indicate the culture that the organization has developed and maintained. In most cases, the organizations do not appear to have an identified culture; and many of them, like the restaurant with the mission statement, have not inculcated their desired culture into their daily operation (Sergiovanni, 1990). Thus, the culture desired by leadership remains a wish that remains unfulfilled because the employees have not bought into the ownership of it, nor have the organizational leaders developed action programs to make certain that the desired culture permeates every act of the organization and every act of each of the organization's employees (Herman & Herman, 1988).

Culture is defined by Webster (1984) as: "the customary beliefs, social forms, and material traits of a racial, religious, or social group" (p. 314). For the purposes of this chapter, we shall define *school district culture* as the beliefs and values held, the standard processes and activities utilized, and the traditions maintained by the students and employees of the school district and by the community members who live within the geographical bounds of the school district.

If it is true that society, to some extent, affects what happens in the schools of this nation; it is a time of significant and important changes which will impact our schools. School districts will have to consciously recognize these changes and make modifications to adapt to these changes (Prince, 1989). As these adaptations are made, modifications in the culture of the school district will result.

The key question to be answered is: Will the school district personnel plan these cultural changes or will they result from trial and error over time? It is our belief that some aspects of the culture can be changed by taking purposeful actions over an extended period of time (Deal & Kennedy, 1982).

This chapter will be devoted to a discussion on the topic of a school district's organizational culture. The major areas to be discussed within this chapter include: (1) some of the major changes taking place in the United States and in the world which have and will continue to impact the schools of this country, (2) some of the techniques which can be used to cause cultural changes, and (3) the restructuring process and structure called school-based management and whether this restructuring method will conflict with or complement school culture.

MAJOR CHANGES TAKING PLACE IN THE UNITED STATES AND IN THE WORLD WHICH IMPACT THE SCHOOLS

The only thing certain about change is that it will continue and it will accelerate. If school districts cannot develop a tolerance for change and if they cannot make the modifications in culture that are required to make the school districts productive, effective, exciting, and rewarding places to learn and work, it is quite possible that other profit and nonprofit organizations will take over many of the roles now played by the school districts of this country. This type of radical restructuring will not take place in the United States because of a punitive motive; but, rather, it will take place from a clear-cut survival need as a corporate, political, and economic world power.

Obviously, this is more and more becoming a world wide network of forces that influence the individual countries. Also, within the political boundaries of the United States vast changes are taking place which can be plotted as trends. Both the world forces and the internal forces causing change many times impact the roles, tasks, missions and visions of the school districts of this country (Kaufman & J.J. Herman, 1991b). Some of the major changes which are or soon will impact our school districts include:

- A trend in employment opportunities from agriculture and manufacturing to service and knowledge-related jobs. In the near future, it is predictable that service employment opportunities will decrease with additional automation and that knowledge-related jobs will continue to employ an increasingly greater number of the work force.
- The graying of America will continue, and an increasing number of adults will not have children in the K–12 school ages. For school

districts that depend on local property taxes or other local income sources, the maintenance of an adequate level of local financial support will be an increasingly difficult challenge.

• The United States has a huge deficit balance of trade which affects the federal government's ability to assist in the adequate financing of the nation's schools.

• There is a great deal of pressure being placed upon the schools by corporate America, because the corporate leadership feels that the school districts of this country aren't producing the high quality of graduates that will be required to more successfully compete with Japan, Germany, and other countries that are high tech, manufacturing, business, commercial, and financial giants of the world with whom the United States must compete. State legislatures are reacting to the urging of corporate America by passing legislation which mandates restructuring and choice programs for schools.

• Teacher unions are promoting empowerment legislation which provides the teachers employed by the school district boards of education a greater voice in the decision making of the schools.

• As more women advance in the leadership and administrative positions within education, the "good old boy" network is undergoing changes which may very well have an impact on the culture of the school districts.

• With the influx of Asian, Mexicans and other immigrants, the school populations and the communities in which they live are truly becoming multi-cultural. States like Texas, Florida, and California have a much different nationality mix than they had just a relatively few years ago, and this will definitely impact the culture within the individual school districts.

• With the increasing number of children coming to school from single parent homes, the traditional nuclear family, in many cases, no longer exists to inculcate the young with traditional values.

• With an increasing number of single parent homes where the parent works and with an increasing number of two parent home where both parents work outside the home, the school may have to assist in a broader societal need by providing latchkey programs before and after normal academic school hours (Cetron, Soriano, & Gayle, 1985).

An article in *Business Week* included a section entitled: "Supply: Our

New Labor Force", which presented other significant trends that have an impact on our schools and the society within which the schools exist:

- 82 percent of the new entrants during the next 12 years will be women and minorities.
- Urban school dropout rates are 50 percent plus.
- One of eight seventeen year olds is functionally illiterate.
- One of five children lives in poverty.
- One million teenage girls become pregnant each year.
- 50 percent of all teenage mothers end up on welfare.

In 1991 a similar publication written by Harold L. Hodgkinson and published jointly by the American Association of School Administrators and the National School Boards Association in part stated:

- Each year, about 350,000 children are born to mothers who were addicted to cocaine during pregnancy. Many of the surviving children have strikingly short attention spans, poor coordination, and other physical problems, including drug addiction.
- About 40,000 children annually are born with alcohol-related birth defects, which can cause a range of impairments, including mental retardation, hypersensitivity, and language problems.
- About 6.7 percent, or 260,000 children, are born each year with lower than normal birth weights. Those babies are one-and-a-half to twice as likely to need special education services.
- One-fourth of pregnant mothers get no physical care of any sort during the crucial first trimester of pregnancy. About 20 percent of handicapped children would not be handicapped if the mother had received just one physical examination in the first trimester.
- Since 1987, one-fourth of all preschool children in the United States have lived in poverty.
- In 1987, 2.2 million reports of child abuse or neglect were made to child protective service agencies. This was triple the number in 1976.
- Today, 15 million children are being reared by single mothers, whose average family income is about $11,000. This is within $1,000 of the poverty line, which in 1988 was set at an annual income of $10,000 for a family of 3. (The average family income for a couple with children was slightly more than $34,000 per year in 1988).
- At least 2 million children of school age have no adult supervision after school.
- On any given night, from 50,000 to 200,000 children have no home. In 1988, 40 percent of shelter users were families with children."

The listing could be continued *ad infinitum,* but suffice it to say that the world within which our schools operate is undergoing many and very significant changes; and as the students change, the communities change, the United States experiences change, and the world undergoes change; the schools are impacted. As the impacts caused by these changes create different ways for educators dealing with students, with one another, with their communities and with other stakeholders; the culture of the individual schools and the school districts will change (Hall & Hord, 1987). The challenge is to adjust to the external and internal impacting variables in a manner that will make the changes positive ones, and in a way that will positively improve the culture within which students learn and educators teach.

In order to change the culture in positive directions, there are some techniques that can assist in causing positive cultural changes. We shall now briefly illustrate some of the techniques that may be utilized to cause positive changes in the schools' culture.

TECHNIQUES WHICH CAN BE USED TO CAUSE CULTURAL CHANGE

Although there are numerous techniques which can be utilized to attempt to cause cultural change, there are four basic techniques that we recommend to anyone who is courageous enough to attempt to change the culture of their school district or of their individual school. The four techniques are: (1) assessing school climate periodically to develop trend lines, and using these trends to intervene with action programs that improve the school climate, (2) implementing empowering activities which change the manner in which decisions are made which affect the schools' structure and processes, (3) marketing strategies which tend to build support for the schools from the external and internal stakeholders (a stakeholder is an individual student, parent, employee, or community member who has a reason for an interest in schools, or who is impacted by the activity of the schools), and (4) training of employees in the areas of knowledge, skills, or attitudes (Kaufman & J.J. Herman, 1991a). A brief discussion will serve to elaborate upon these three techniques.

School Climate Assessment

Changing the culture of any organization, especially one of a very traditional and conservative school district, is a long-term and difficult task (Deal & Kennedy, 1982). One means of intervening to cause a change in culture is to systematically assess the current state of culture and to continue to assess systematically at least once a year. These data can then be given as feedback to the individuals working and learning within the school district, and action plans can be developed to improve the areas of school culture that the employees and students feel a need (a need is a gap or discrepancy between "what is" and "what should be" or "what could be") to improve (Kaufman & J.J. Herman, 1991b). In fact, it could be wise to involve the parents and, perhaps other members of the community, in providing their perceptions related to the various important items of school culture.

If multiple groups assess the culture, the district's decision makers will have data that will not only identify cultural areas of concern among all respondent groups, but they will also have data which will allow them to assess major discrepancies in the responses between and among respondent groups (Margolis, 1991). In both cases, the decision makers have important information from which to plan action programs intended to overcome any serious discrepancies of either the total respondents or of the sub groups of respondents.

Some of the major items of school culture that a school district should assess are:

- Are the buildings safe and do they meet good health standards?
- Is there an emphasis on high achievement by students and employees?
- Are achievement levels constantly monitored, and is action taken if achievement does not match up to desired standards?
- Is it a place that allows for input from individuals?
- Is it a place where individuals feel cared for and cared about?
- Is it a place where individuals are trusted?
- It is a place where the work done by students and employees is interesting?
- Is it a place where individuals are recognized for their contributions?
- Is it a place that has a clear vision of what it is and what it wants to be?
- Do the employees treat others as they would like to be treated?
- Is it a place where one can easily get help?
- Are there other climate items, in addition to the above, which apply to the individual school building?

Let's assume two example results, using a ten-point rating scale where a ten is the best and a one is the worst situation. Example One finds that all respondent groups, overall, rate allowing for input from individuals as a two. Obviously, this is an area that could be addressed by the development of action programs to correct this deficiency.

Example Two finds that the teachers feel that they can easily obtain help, and they rate this area a nine; but parents see this as a major area of concern and they rate this area a one. This issue may stem from a perception that help is not given or that there is not sufficient communication with parents describing the method of obtaining assistance for the various types of concerns they might have. Action plans targeted specifically to the parents can be developed to correct this deficiency (J.J. Herman, 1990a).

Over time such data feedback on school climate, coupled with successfully implementing corrective action plans in areas of need, will have a positive effect on the organizational culture of the school district. Let's now turn to another means of changing culture over time: that of developing and implementing empowerment activities for the various stakeholders of the school district.

Empowering Activities

Empowering implies giving additional and nontraditional decision-making power to individuals or groups who previously were not given the authority to make those decisions. When an individual or group is newly empowered, two very important concepts must be reinforced: (1) with the delegation of decision-making power comes delegation of the responsibility for the decisions made, and (2) there must be a quality assurance standard attached to the decisions made in order to assure that the results are positive (J.J. Herman & J.L. Herman, 1991).

Empowering activities can include very limited newly delegated decision-making power, such as teachers in each school building being given the power to choose a textbook different from that used in other school buildings in the district; or it can be a comprehensive delegation of decision making power, such as situations where parents and teachers are given the power to select employees, determine schedules, select curricula, select the materials and equipment, and have budgetary input. (More on this topic is provided in Chapter 3). Regardless of the degree of delegation, or regardless to which individual(s) or group(s) the decisions are delegated; the two criteria of *responsibility* and *quality assurance* should follow the delegation of decision-making power.

Now that we have briefly dealt with the empowerment concept, let's turn to a discussion of marketing strategies. For not only do the school district's decision makers rely on those empowered to implement school based management, they must also develop active strategies and tactics to gain approval of the community at large.

Marketing Strategies and Tactics

If a school district's decision makers decide to implement school-based management throughout the school district in an effort to change the way that business is done and decisions are made in the school district, which eventually should change the culture of the school district and that culture which existed prior to the implementation of SBM in the individual school building, those decision makers should develop marketing strategies and tactics as a part of the overall strategic plan. There are a variety of marketing tactics available to the school district's decision makers, which relate to the three major SBM strategies of: (1) getting maximum involvement, (2) obtaining positive media coverage, and (3) spreading the ownership in SBM among the maximum number of individuals and groups (Prasch, 1990). The major tactics that fall under these three strategies include the following.

- Probably the single most effective way to market school-based management is to have a large number and a great variety of stakeholders successfully involved in the process. If these stakeholders gain ownership and if the results are positive, they will pass the good word to their neighbors, their business acquaintances, and their social acquaintances (J.J. Herman, 1989a).
- Another successful strategy is to publicize attitudinal survey results of the increased satisfaction about what is happening in the schools. These surveys should include students, parents, employees, and the community at large (Kaufman & J.J. Herman, 1991a).
- Another significant method of marketing the advantages of the school district's and individual school buildings' approaches to school-based management is to create media opportunities by having newspapers and TV stations visit and interview people involved. Radio and TV spots can also be of great assistance. Also, don't forget the old standard press release, which deals with the Who?, Why?, What?, When?, Where? and How? questions (J.J. Herman, 1988)

- A final suggestion is to obtain business, industrial, and civic partnerships for the individual schools. As these firms and organizations become active participants in the planning processes and in the action activities, they will acquire ownership; and if they like what they do and see, they will become cheerleaders for school-based management (King & Swanson, 1991).

Now that the strategies and implementation tactics have been decided upon, the school district's decision makers must not forget the requirement for training. Those persons and groups who are delegated new decision-making power and who are not used to making decisions within the areas delegated will probably be frustrated and make poor decisions if they are not given training opportunities to assist them with their newly delegated responsibilities.

Employees and SBM Committee Members Training

The depth of training required will vary from individual to individual and from group to group. A training needs assessment should be conducted which includes responses from each individual involved and each group involved. From this needs assessment, specific training activities should be designed to meet the identified needs. The school district's decision makers must remember that these training needs assessments and training activities are ongoing, as the employees leave the district and as members of the SBM committees change over time (Harrison, Killion, & Mitchell, 1989).

Although the training should be differentiated, the general areas of training should definitely include the following:

- Communication skills which include: (1) active listening (listening to the emotions of the speaker, not just the words spoken), (2) paraphrasing (to make certain that the message is clear), (3) negotiating for meaning (conducting discussion until everyone agrees on the meaning of the agreement reached), (4) listening (not just hearing), and, (5) wait time (providing silent time to clarify thoughts before uttering them).
- Planning skills which include: (1) defining a vision of "what should be," (2) developing a clear mission statement, (3) arriving at goals and objectives, (4) devising action plans to carry out the agreed upon goals and objectives, (5) collecting monitoring data with which to evaluate

the level of achievement of the identified goals and objectives, and (6) conducting evaluations.
- Team building schools which include: (1) group decision making, (2) group caring, (3) group involvement strategies and tactics, and (4) group celebration techniques (McKenzie, 1991).

Once we have assessed our climate, empowered people, marketed SBM, and initiated training activities, we can address the complex issue of strategic planning and its value to the SBM processes. A model for strategic planning is presented here, and a brief elaboration on each step of the model is provided.

STRATEGIC PLANNING AND OPERATIONAL PLANNING RELATED TO SCHOOL-BASED MANAGEMENT

Once we have empowered people to make decisions and carried on training activities for employees and other members of the school-based management teams each school-based management committee should proceed to develop a strategic plan, an operational plan, and the tactics and activities to implement those plans. Strategic planning can be defined as long-term planning to achieve a future vision of "what should be" or "what could be." Operational planning, on the other hand, is short-term planning (usually no more than one year in length) geared to actions which are designed to achieve specific short-term objectives (Kaufman & J.J. Herman, 1991b). Of course, the operational planning should be synchronized with the strategic plans of the school building and the school district.

The school-based management committee should spell out a vision of "what should be" for their specific school. Once this is done, they can do a comprehensive assessment to delineate the "what is" current state of the school.

The differences, or discrepancies between the future "what should be" or "what could be" state when compared to the "what is" current state will define the needs (gaps between the states) of the school. These needs can then be translated into strategic goals and specific objectives. Once the goals and objectives are clarified, the school-based management building level committee can develop action programs (the how-to-do-it's) to achieve the objectives. Those action programs that are short term involve operational planning, and those objectives and action programs designed to achieve the long-term future vision involve the process and results of strategic planning (J.J. Herman, 1989b).

A more comprehensive planning model is presented in Figure 2.1, and the elements of this model are reviewed below. It is crucial for any group that wishes to achieve its vision of "what should be" or "what could be" to make certain that vision is clear and known to all stakeholders. It is also crucial for any group to know how to develop the detailed plans and to evaluate the results of those plans if the group's vision is to be achieved.

The strategic planning model illustrated in Figure 2.1 involves four specific clusters which are: (1) scoping, (2) data collecting, (3) planning, and, (4) implementing and evaluating. Each of these planning clusters involves concepts and activities, which are outlined below.

Scoping

Scoping involves choosing among the three foci levels of planning: (1) Mega Level Planning, (2) Macro Level Planning, and (3) Micro Level Planning (Kaufman & J.J. Herman, 1989a). Although starting at the mega level is preferred, any level can be used as the primary focus. However, multiple levels must be closely articulated in order to assure a good fit.

- **Mega Level Planning** is society-oriented, and it usually employs a time frame several years into the future. The unit of improvement is society as well as the total school district and all of its parts. However, the primary client and beneficiary should be society, now, and in the future.

- **Macro Level Planning** is addresses the total school district's organization, and it addresses the efficiency and effectiveness of the total school district. Its primary client is the organization itself; and when it is concerned with external clients (outcomes), it seeks to determine the extent to which the client is satisfied with the organization.

- **Micro Level Planning** is a subset of Macro Level Planning. It takes individuals or groups within the total organization as the primary clients. Its operational time frame is usually short-term. Some might call this level of planning, "tactical" planning.

FIGURE 2.1
STRATEGIC PLANNING MODEL

SCOPING

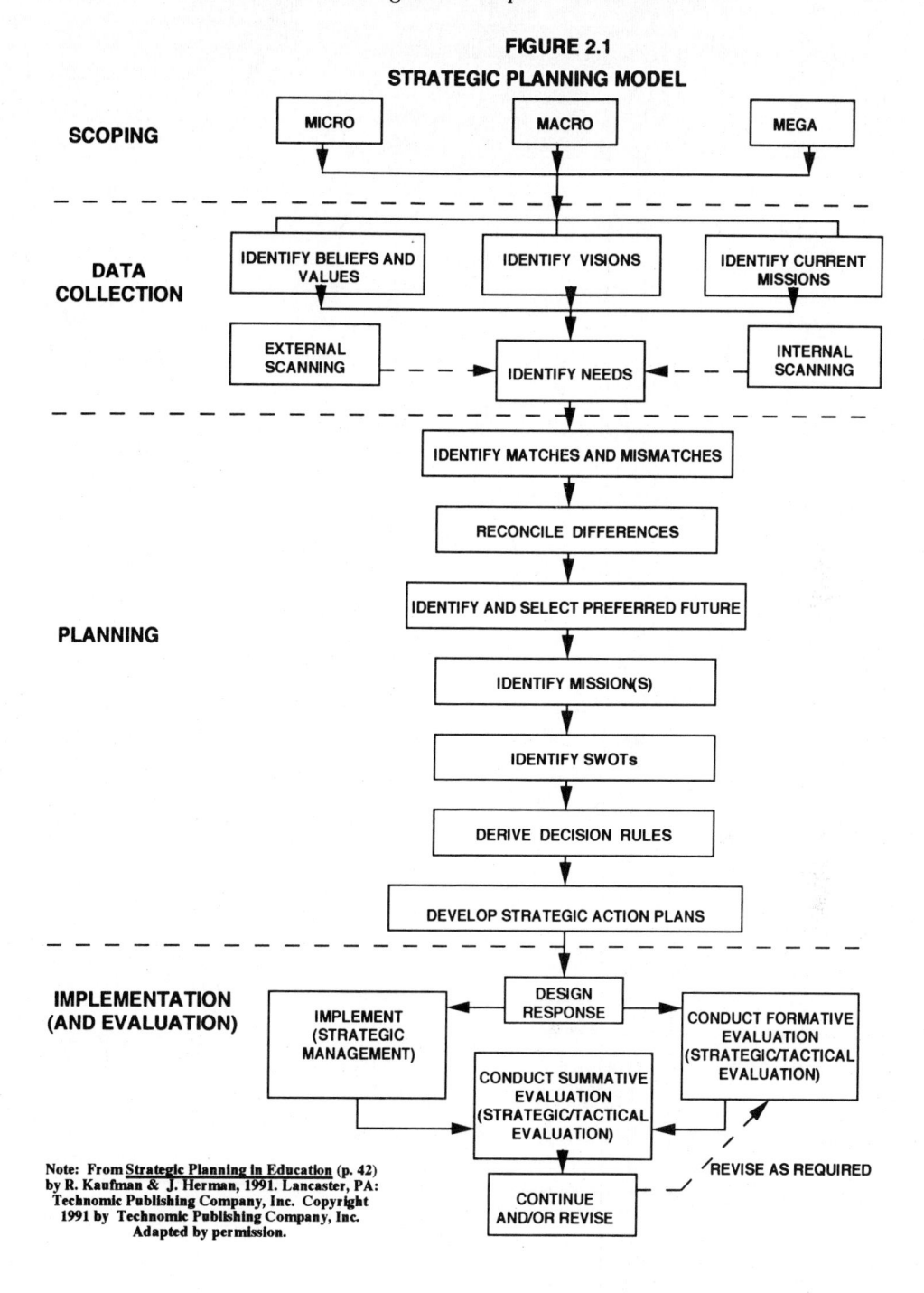

- MICRO
- MACRO
- MEGA

DATA COLLECTION

- IDENTIFY BELIEFS AND VALUES
- IDENTIFY VISIONS
- IDENTIFY CURRENT MISSIONS
- EXTERNAL SCANNING → IDENTIFY NEEDS ← INTERNAL SCANNING

PLANNING

- IDENTIFY MATCHES AND MISMATCHES
- RECONCILE DIFFERENCES
- IDENTIFY AND SELECT PREFERRED FUTURE
- IDENTIFY MISSION(S)
- IDENTIFY SWOTs
- DERIVE DECISION RULES
- DEVELOP STRATEGIC ACTION PLANS

IMPLEMENTATION (AND EVALUATION)

- DESIGN RESPONSE
- IMPLEMENT (STRATEGIC MANAGEMENT)
- CONDUCT FORMATIVE EVALUATION (STRATEGIC/TACTICAL EVALUATION)
- CONDUCT SUMMATIVE EVALUATION (STRATEGIC/TACTICAL EVALUATION)
- CONTINUE AND/OR REVISE
- REVISE AS REQUIRED

Note: From *Strategic Planning in Education* (p. 42) by R. Kaufman & J. Herman, 1991. Lancaster, PA: Technomic Publishing Company, Inc. Copyright 1991 by Technomic Publishing Company, Inc. Adapted by permission.

Data Collecting

This is the second cluster in the model. It involves the identification and consensus among the school-based committees about their: (1) beliefs and values (the stuff of culture), (2) visions, (3) currently identified and held missions, and (4) needs (J.J. Herman, 1988, 1989c).

• **Beliefs and values** are those basic items which guide the behaviors and attitudes of the employees and other members of the school-based management team. Consensus must be reached on those values and beliefs which will guide the district as the future "what should be" or "what could be" visions are developed. Without achieving consensus on the guiding values, the planning operation will fail (J.J. Herman, 1990b)

• The **visions** of "what should be" and "what could be" for the school district, compared to the "what is state" identifies the *needs* (discrepancies between the states) that provide the working matter for the development of action programs to achieve the results identified by the needs. By scanning important external and internal data over a period of five to ten years, one can arrive at trendlines which will assist the planners in the development of their future visions and their *preferred future vision*.

• As part of determining **current mission(s)**, formal consideration of existing laws, rules, regulations, and policies should be included. In addition, a determination should be made of the operational missions for each part of the system. Doing a conflict (match/mismatch) analysis of missions—relating the different parts of the organization and each one's contribution to the overall purposes—should also be completed at this step.

• The **needs** (gaps between "what is" and "what should be" or "what could be") of the individual school buildings and of the school district as a whole can be determined from the collection of hard data and soft data. Both external and internal scanning for trendlines should be conducted. Hard factual data on the degree of results achieved, the impact of external financial and regulatory trends, and numerous other pieces of hard data will be helpful. Also, collecting attitudinal soft data from students, employees, parents, and community members and community groups will assist in identifying important needs to be met.

Planning

This third cluster includes: (1) identifying the agreements among visions, beliefs, and the current mission; (2) reconciling differences,

(3) selecting the preferred future; (4) identifying missions; (5) identifying strengths, weaknesses, opportunities, and threats; (6) deriving decision rules; and (7) developing strategic action plans (J.J. Herman, 1989d, 1989e).

- It is crucial that agreement be reached by those involved in SBM about the visions, beliefs, and current mission(s) held by various individuals and groups. If agreements are not reached, further planning activities will hit a bumpy road as plans will be railroaded to a side track simply because of strongly held but widely varying visions, beliefs, and current mission(s) by the planners.
- Finding a common ground based on reality is the major product of this step. Using previous data and information in negotiating what is right, (not just what is acceptable), requires patience, and often the collection of more data. This step must be handled with concern and care for people's deep-seated values and biases. Planners must remember that this is not a *quick fix* exercise; but, rather, it is a long-term process.
- The trendline data and the hard and soft data collect may lead the planning group to identify alternative vision scenarios. This may be a necessary prerequisite to agreeing upon a preferred future vision which will guide all future planning activities for the individual school building's planners, or for all planners in the entire school district.
- From the foregoing steps and their products, this function delivers a written mission statement based upon visions, beliefs, and needs. This often requires some changes to the existing mission statement. The skills of preparing measurable performance indicators, and writing mission statements, in terms of results, at the appropriate (and selected) level are the keys to success at this step.
- A SWOT's (strengths, weaknesses, opportunities and threats) analysis is a technique that permits the external scanning data to be utilized to identify the external opportunities (which should be capitalized upon during planning) and threats (which should be eliminated or their impact reduced). Also, the internal scanning for trendlines permits a factual analysis of the strengths of the school building or school district (which can be capitalized upon during planning) and an analysis of the weaknesses (which can be overcome or neutralized).
- The step of deriving decision rules is a very important one. Decision rules, or policies, are necessary in order that all planning partners have the same "marching orders," visions, and intentions. These decision rules provide strategic goals and objectives with measurable criteria

(performance requirements). Part of this step includes prioritizing needs (on the basis of the question: what do you give and what do you get?)

• Developing strategic action plans is the last step in the Planning Cluster. The needs, visions, beliefs, and missions are integrated at this step. Based upon the SWOT's and the decision rules, the product of this step is arrived at by answering the key questions:

What?

How?

Who?

When?

Why?

Where?

At this step is also the identification of desired outcomes (results), and in-process milestones for implementation are established, along with consideration of alternative approaches to achieve the desired results.

Implementation and Evaluation

This is the fourth and final planning cluster. In a purist sense, this is not planning; rather, it actually involves putting the plan into action and getting the required results. It involves *management* of the strategic plan that has been developed. Once the plan is enacted, it involves formative (in-process) data collection and evaluation which are geared to making any corrective adjustments in the action plans. At the end of a stipulated time frame, it also implies the collection of data and the conduct of a summative (end of activity) evaluation which is designed to measure the degree to which the desired objectives (results) have been achieved (Herman, 1989b, Herman, 1989f).

CONCLUSION

It was noted at the chapter's beginning that modifications in the culture of the school district will occur when the organization is impacted by change. A traditional school district's culture—the beliefs and values held, the standard processes and activities utilized, and the traditions maintained by the students and employees of the school district and by the community members who live within the geographical bounds of the school district—will alter dramatically as a result of SBM implementation. Unless the SBM cultural change desired by leadership is proactively and purposefully addressed, it will occur haphazardly, and, perhaps, nonproductively. Organizational leaders should develop action programs to make certain that the desired SBM culture permeates every act of the organization and every act of each of the organization's employees.

Strategic planning could be considered as an SBM prerequisite or companion process in school district restructuring. There is a natural affinity between the two, considering the strong planning components involved in school-based management. Scoping and data collection are appropriate structures for districts and schools as they create the common reference framework—the informal goal-setting process—which allows the relatively autonomous schools to operate in accord with mutual goals and expectations. The implementation and evaluation part of the strategic planning process must be carried out in order to effectively operationalize and assist the SBM implementation process at the school level.

SBM is not an event or stand-alone innovation, as indicated in Chapter 1. For traditional schools, it represents profound and dynamic cultural change, and therefore requires careful structuring and strategic management of the institutional change process.

SUMMARY

In this chapter, school district culture was defined as the customary beliefs, social forms, and material traits of a racial, religious, or social group. Schools must make modification in their culture to adapt to environmental change. One major area which was discussed were the significant changes taking place on a national level, such as age, gender, racial, and demographic shifts, imbalance of trade, increasing pressure on schools, the push for empowerment, and the changing nature of education's clientele. The internal and external forces impacting the roles, tasks, missions, and visions of the nation's school districts also include employment change trends and international competition. The culturally-related problems of America's youth were outlined. Four basic techniques which can be utilized to cause cultural change were given: assessment of school climate; discerning trends to order to intervene in that climate, implementing empowering activities to change decision-making processes, and marketing strategies to build support for schools. All of these techniques build a climate in which SBM can flourish.

Strategic and operational planning are a next logical step. Strategic planning was defined as long-term planning to achieve a future vision of "what should be" or "what could be." Operational planning was defined as short-term planning (usually no more than one year in length) geared to actions which are designed to achieve specific short-term objectives. A comprehensive strategic planning model was presented including the four specific clusters of scoping, data collecting, planning, and implementing and evaluating. Each planning cluster was expanded upon with concepts and activities. The two types of planning—strategic and operational—can be synchronized through the process of school-based management, as vehicles and facilitating strategies for the cultural change SBM demands.

EXERCISES

1. Of all the significant trends and changes described as impacting the schools, which do you think are most significant to your school district? Why are these factors the most impacting in your situation?

2. Use the major items of school culture as checkpoints to informally assess the climate of your district. Are there areas of need?

3. Which of the three major SBM marketing strategies would work best in your district, and why?

4. Select one of the strategic planning model clusters, and simulate its implementation in your district. Which groups and individuals would complete the process, and what would be the outcome?

REFERENCES

Cetron, M., Soriano, B., & Gayle, M.E. (1985). *Schools of the future: How American business and education can cooperate to save our schools.* New York, NY: McGraw-Hill, pp. 37–43. 66–77.

Deal, T.E. & Kennedy, A.A. (1982). *Corporate cultures: The rites and rituals of corporate life.* Reading, MA: Addison-Wesley Publishing Company, pp. 157–158, 164–169.

Hall, G.E. & Hord, S.M. *Change in schools: Facilitating the process.* Albany, NY: State University of New York Press, pp. 8–10.

Harrison, C.R., Killion, J.P., & Mitchell, J.E. (1989). Site-based management: The realities of implementation. *Educational Leadership, 46* (8), 55–58.

Herman, J.J. (1988). Map the trip to your district's future. *The School Administrator, 45* (9), 16, 18, 23.

Herman, J.J. (1989a). A decision making model: Site-based communications governance committees, *NASSP Bulletin, 73* (521), 61–66.

Herman, J.J. (1989b). A vision for the future: Site-based strategic planning. *NASSP Bulletin, 73,* (518), 23–27.

Herman, J.J. (1989c). Site-based management: Creating a vision and mission statement. *NASSP Bulletin, 73,* (519), 79–83.

Herman, J.J. (1989d). External and internal scanning: Identifying variables that affect your school. *NASSP Bulletin, 73,* (520), 48–52.

Herman, J.J. (1989e). School business officials' roles in the strategic planning process (part II). *School Business Affairs, 55* (3), 20, 22–24.

Herman, J.J. (1989f). School district strategic planning (part I). *School Business Affairs, 55* (2), 10–14.

Herman, J.J. (1989g). Strategic planning: One of the changing leadership roles of the principal. *The Clearing House, 63* (2), 56–58.

Herman, J.J. (1990a). Action plans to make your vision a reality. *NASSP Bulletin, 74* (523), 14–17.

Herman, J.J. (1990b). Strategic planning: Reasons for failed attempts. *Educational Planning, 8* (3), 36–40.

Herman, J.J. & J.L. (1991). *The positive development of human resources and school district organizations.* Lancaster, PA: Technomic Publishing Company, pp. 39–45, 151–153.

Hodgkinson, H.L. (1991). *Beyond the schools: How schools and communities must collaborate to solve the problems facing America's youth.* Alexandria, VA: American Association of School Administrators and National School Boards Association, 1991.

Kaufman, R. & Herman, J.J. (1989). Planning that fits every district: Three choices help define your plan's scope. *The School Administrator, 46* (8), 17–19.

Kaufman, R. & Herman, J.J. (1991a). Strategic planning for a better society. *Educational Leadership, 48* (7), 4–8.

Kaufman, R. & Herman, J.J. (1991b). *Strategic planning in education.* Lancaster, PA: Technomic Publishing Company, pp. 3–7, 45, 56, 92–95, 99.

King, R.A. & Swanson, A.D. (1990). Resources or restructured schools: Partnerships, foundations, and volunteerism. *Planning & Changing, 21* (2), 94–107.

Margolis, H. (1991). Understanding, facing resistance to change. *NASSP Bulletin, 75* (537), 1–8.

McKenzie, J.A. (1991). *Site-based management: A practical guide for practitioners.* Flemington, NJ: Correct Change Publishers, pp. 35–52.

Merriam-Webster, Inc. (1984). *Webster's ninth new collegiate dictionary.* Springfield, MA: Merriam-Webster, Inc., p. 314.

Prasch, J. (1990). *How to organize for school-based management.* Alexandria, VA: Association for Supervision and Curriculum Development, pp. 17–26, 50.

Prince, J.D. (1989). *Invisible forces: School reform versus school culture.* Bloomington, Indiana: Phi Delta Kappa, p. 11.

Sergiovanni, T.J. (1990). *Value-added leadership.* Orlando, FL: Harcourt Brace Jovanovich, p. 54.

Supply: Our new labor force. (May, 1992). *Business Week,* p. 2.

Chapter 3

SCHOOL-BASED MANAGEMENT: VEHICLE FOR TEACHER EMPOWERMENT

The trend towards teacher empowerment is a direct and logical outgrowth of the organizational patterns found in productive businesses, in the guise of employee involvement, high levels of participation, and a team approach, as described in Chapter 1. The common thread which runs through contemporary corporate and managerial theory is the key function of *decentralization,* which Raywid (1990) elaborated upon in considering restructuring strategies aimed at accomplishing changes in governance patterns. The strategy of SBM returns authority to the school and democratizes its exercise—effectively empowering the site level participants. As one of the basic tenets of the restructuring movement, the *Instructor* (1990) notes that SBM is being reviewed by think tanks, touted by union leaders, and supported by government policy analysts as a prerequisite for enhanced teacher effectiveness. There are many pushes for restructuring, one of the strongest of these is teacher involvement, since change is best facilitated when those responsible for its implementation are involved in the process from the outset (Lewis, 1988).

In this chapter the definitions and rationales for teacher empowerment as part of that restructuring are described, followed by a perspective on the related background of this movement. Common practice in support and facilitation of teacher empowerment through the implementation of school-based management is reported, and an overview given of the current obstacles to empowerment. The broader viewpoint of state and national trends and views of enabling and empowering teachers ends the chapter.

DEFINITIONS AND RATIONALES FOR EMPOWERMENT

Empowerment (Bailey, 1988) creates professionals out of educators, who, ideally, are then accountable, possess a professional expertise, and progress intellectually. School-based management as a restructuring can best accommodate these demands by placing quality control at the lowest possible level.

In 1988 Barth found the concept of shared leadership within a school to be both fashionable and controversial; touting teachers as leaders in contemporary times is uncomfortable. Speaking of teachers as harborers of "extraordinary leadership capabilities" and of that leadership as "a major untapped source for improving U.S. schools" (p. 640), he recommends the removal of the present impediments to exercise those talents and the provision of conditions to enhance them. He holds the beliefs that all teachers have leadership tendencies; that schools badly need this leadership (which has not been forthcoming), and that the fate of such leadership in creating a community of leaders lies in the relationships between principals and their faculties.

Glickman (1990) speaks of *empowerment* as the banner word of the restructuring movement, and defines professional empowerment as the theory that, "when given collective responsibility to make educational decisions in an information-rich environment, educators will work harder and smarter on behalf of their clients: students and their parents" (p. 69). Empowerment has emerged from the current reform movement in response to the regulatory and compliance-ridden nature of the first wave of reform; the issue has shifted from that viewpoint to one of the issue of the treatment of educators in their own settings, particularly in the provision of greater latitude over curricular and instructional decisions, accompanied by caveats concerning accountability.

Maeroff, in 1988, supported the empowerment of teachers: "But the input of teachers must give shape to the forming of education; it cannot be left to others to make all of the important decisions.... In part, taking greater regard for teachers and what they have to say means enhancing their role.... this is the reason why teachers should be empowered" (p. xiii). He likewise speaks of the empowerment issue as somewhat synonymous with professionalization.

Bailey (1991) makes the distinction between the type of empowerment historically practiced by teachers through classroom isolation (termed "slippage" and "loose coupling," or "autonomy by default"), and the more formal and school-focused empowerment which occurs with school-based management. The SBM structural changes actually needed are groups of teachers who work collaboratively to establish the best possible schoolwide instructional program.

Moses and Whitaker (1990) list ten educational restructuring components, including the enhancement of the teaching profession through, foremost, empowerment. With it, a teacher's role "requires a redefinition from the custodial job of dispensing information to the more sophisticated one of facilitating growth" (p. 33).

The Carnegie Forum's *A Nation Prepared* (1986) expands upon the recommendation for a professional environment for teaching, noting how one element of such an effort is dependent upon another, as policymakers withhold autonomy until they are assured of teacher accountability, and teachers resist accountability unless they have substantial control over service delivery. It describes the bureaucratic management of schools as stemming from the view that teachers lack the talent or motivation to think for themselves. *A Nation Prepared* recommends that, within the context of a clear but limited set of student goals, teachers must be free to collaborate to exercise collective professional judgment on how to attain those goals, including the ability to make decisions about instructional materials and methods, staffing structures, student assignment and school day organization, and allocation of resources. Their particular suggestion is to accomplish this through the use of Lead Teachers, who will create collegial communities, and through school-site budgeting and state deregulation. A conversation by Brandt (1989) pointed out that this empowerment of teachers does not mean that principals will be banished; it is, rather, the enabling of teachers to participate in group decision making and to make key choices.

AASA's 1990 publication on empowerment in education indicates that schools are more effective places for learning because empowered individuals:

- "Use their insights and experience to make better decisions,
- Have the flexibility and support to try new approaches and custom-fit what they do to meet the needs of schools and students,
- Learn and grow on the job,
- Work together to solve challenging problems. Empowerment creates "team" spirit among administrators, teachers, students, and citizens.
- Believe that improved instruction is everyone's responsibility" (p. 1).

Lane (1991) describes SBM as providing a place where students, parents, teachers, and other community leaders come together to support the teaching-learning process to create a school community. In that

SBM situation where teachers are regarded as professionals, some of the responsibility for their supervision and formative evaluation is shifted from the principal to the teachers, who assess their own needs and requirements, and prepare staff development activities based on that assessment. Lane calls these "communities of reflective practitioners" (p. 121), with teachers exercising professional judgement in the facilitation of learning.

Sergiovanni (1990) speaks of enabling and empowerment as having less to do with rights than with responsibilities; with the placement of the emphasis on the school site, these are firmly linked. He describes the empowerment process as supporting a shared covenant built by successful schools, where teachers and principals are free to do things that make sense to them as professionals, with the provision that those decisions embody the shared values and requirements of the school covenant. He describes empowerment as being practiced when authority and obligation are shared in a way that authorizes and legitimizes action, correspondingly increasing responsibility and accountability. Teachers and principals must be put in charge of their practice, and schools must be allowed to create their own destiny. This is a perspective in strong contrast to the current perception of most teachers and principals; that they do not control their fate, and are on the receiving end of policies developed elsewhere. He warns that SBM plans must include the balance of empowerment and enablement, or principal dictatorships may form, as power is shifted downward from the central office. A recent Carnegie study has reported low teacher involvement in setting discipline standards, assigning students, designing inservice programs, setting of student performance standards, and deciding budgets; there is minimal teacher involvement in such personnel matters as the evaluation of teaching performance and selection of candidates.

The neglect of teachers as change agents was noted in an *America 2000* response document, *Voices from the Field* (1991). The president of the National Council for the Accreditation of Teacher Education spoke as one of the essayists: "An important lesson from the past is that we cannot improve the schools without improving the ability of the teachers in them.... It is the teachers on the front line who will make the difference." Summarily, the common definitional elements of teacher empowerment seem to be a culmination and fulfillment of professional status through the attainment of new levels of educational process efficiency and effectiveness. Empowerment creates collegial communities, and there is a tradeoff of accountability for professional discretion and decision-making latitude. Rationales include the efficacy of placing control at the lowest level of delivery, a sense of the field-based need for rank and file leadership, the removal of constraints on teacher talent, the push for collective responsibility for educational decisions and for the facilitation of learning in a collegial and collaborative environment.

BACKGROUND OF TEACHER EMPOWERMENT AND SBM

In 1987 Benson and Malone spoke of teachers' sensations of powerlessness, and of their sense of minor impact in influencing decisions which are actually implemented. The bureaucratization of the teaching workplace is well documented (Lieberman, 1988), and it increased as the decade of reform was launched. Relatively little initial attention was paid to the role of teachers in school reform and restructuring in the early 1980s, during the first wave of reform.

In 1988 Lewis considered the opinions of teachers with regard to that decade, citing a state-by-state report on teacher involvement in decision making, which reported some teacher participation in curricular decisions, but very little in more crucial areas such as evaluation, staff development, budget, and student policy development. She reported that Richard Elmore, a Michigan State University researcher, feels that twenty years of top-down reform efforts have eroded the responsibility of students and teachers, insisting that instructional effectiveness is best accomplished by "creating schools in which teachers and students are expected as a condition of their work to take responsibility for their learning and to act on their knowledge" (p. 69).

The existing educational structure, which is designed around teacher isolationism and individual allegiance to union or district, is possibly, Bailey (1988) suggests, the greatest weakness of the public school system. Snyder and Anderson (1986) likewise point out that the history, culture, and physical structure of schools encourage this isolationism (however, over the years, the pattern has been broken by such earlier successful innovations as team teaching, nongradedness, differentiated staffing, and individually guided education). More recent successful innovations have included subject area work teams, vertical curriculum teams, task forces, and faculty advisory groups; Snyder and Anderson categorize these and similar innovations as permanent teaching teams, temporary task groups, and leadership groups. Bailey (1988) describes participation in these as appropriate to transition to more broadly-based, school-based management governance structures. Development of a collegial professional climate is a philosophical shift which must precede shared decision making.

Lieberman (1988) pointed out that the first wave of reform standardized the curriculum, a direct ignoring of the enormous diversity of students, teachers, and principals; she likewise points out the inappropriateness of the notion that the principal is the only instructional leader, which is in direct contradiction to research on effective leaders. There is a cultural inhibition in the current labor-management climate which prevents many teachers from assuming empowering responsibilities; a continuation of the "we-they" divisiveness prevails. Teachers and principals who would prefer to collaborate must confront this ethic.

REQUIRED SUPPORT AND FACILITATION: COMMON PRACTICE

Bailey (1988) recognizes that little of teacher preservice training prepares them for the role of empowered professionals, nor is there typically any assistance offered by normal staff development opportunities. New teacher role and task dimensions emerging from empowerment will include personal and collaborative goal setting, peer interaction with principal and colleagues, spokesperson responsibilities, small and large group leadership demands, group decision making, curricular and instructional content area expertise, peer coaching, budgeting, mentoring, and involvement in hiring personnel. He likewise stresses the parallel need for role clarity in a school-based management setting, particularly concerning job descriptions and definitions of any delegated supervisory or leadership roles.

Conley, Schmidle, and Shedd (1988) indicted that teachers felt slighted by the early reform recommendations, and note that the second reform wave began to rectify this imbalance. The case for teacher participation and empowerment stems from the need to take advantage of employees' irreplaceable knowledge of work processes; teacher participation must be seen as something that school boards and administrators receive, rather than confer. They suggest a caveat, however, to employee participation; that unsupported involvement in decision making does not necessarily empower. A number of contextual and intervening factors, such as the circumscription of any decision making discretion by prescribed agendas, organizational norms, and resource limitations, will minimize or eradicate any benefits of participation. Questions concerning what instructional leadership is and who should exercise it are interwoven with the issues of teacher empowerment, says Rallis (1988). Since one side emphasizes strong principal leadership and the other encourages maximum teacher responsibility for professional growth and work, it becomes a turf debate, with the assumption of leadership as a limited commodity—a zero-sum game. While the framework of effective schools can encompass a variety of leadership roles, Rallis cautions that two conditions must exist simultaneously if teachers are to be empowered to act as instructional leaders:

- "Policy makers and administrators must establish the structures and send the signals that enable teachers to undertake such leadership, and,
- teachers must become responsible professionals, willing to devote the time and the energy that leadership requires, willing to be held accountable for the decisions they make, and willing to listen to one another and to accept leadership from within their own ranks" (p. 643).

Rallis further distinguishes between the instructional leadership function and role required by schools—which can be met by a range of empowered professionals acting in a variety of curricular content and instructional areas—and the somewhat managerial and "big picture"-driven role of the principal; there is no need, therefore, to consider empowerment as causing turf conflict.

The empowerment of teachers will require changes in the power relationships between teachers and principals (Hallinger and Richardson, 1988). Existing models of teacher decision making may serve as vehicles for larger, school-wide decision making councils; such structures as Instructional Leadership Teams, Principals' Advisory Councils, School Improvement Teams, and Lead Teacher Committees are prototypes for SBM empowerment models.

Maeroff in 1988 proposed that teacher empowerment be viewed as professionalization, rather than in terms of power and notions of who is in charge. Three guiding principles toward empowerment (status, knowledge, and access to decision making) separate needs and vantage points of teachers and autonomy. Lagan (1989) echoes the notion of empowerment as a more focused process for school improvement; educators must be trained to take risks, however, and to be exposed to challenging conditions, in order for empowerment to flourish. Lieberman (1988) points out that researchers say that collegiality is a prerequisite to an increased professional climate in schools, and it is especially effective when encouraged by principals. Collaborative schools which encourage and create opportunities for empowerment usually go through a stage of initial staff mistrust of those self-selected practitioners who opt to engage in leadership activities. It takes a period of time for them to be perceived as leaders who can organize new ways for teachers to gain competence and to simultaneously build colleagueship. Not only must the organizational structures be in place to allow for such teacher mobilization, but they must persist long enough for the mistrust effect to be replaced by new norms of openness and trust—the cultural change effect described in Chapter 2. Additionally, in order for the change to take place, teachers must be given sufficient contact time with each other to allow the trust-building and collegiality to develop; which may take away significant amount of classroom contact time, and, hence, require resources to support it. Frequently, individuals are designated as mentor teachers who work with other teachers. These leadership positions, in practice in some pioneering SBM districts, are supported by distinct job descriptions and higher pay. In a study of three schools practicing shared governance, Karant (1989) indicated that peer supervision and teacher empowerment are compatible concepts. The key elements of success are patience and an administrative philosophical commitment to the sharing of decision making.

A criticism similar to Bailey's (1988) was leveled by Kreptovics, Farber, and Armaline in 1991 concerning the failure of the top-down reforms, due to their removal of teachers, parents, and principals from the process. In designing their successful Toledo schools urban reform initiative (Project SHAPE), they envisioned a project which would empower teachers to develop curriculum materials and instructional strategies as they addressed student achievement. They facilitated the process by creating a common planning period for ease of collaboration, and established an extensive program of professional development to support the collegial process. Customized university coursework which complements the project is provided in order to help teachers revitalize their long-unused skills of curriculum development and instructional creativity; to "reclaim the intellectual heritage of teaching" (p. 298). Maeroff described a similar project (CHART) in New York, and stressed that making teachers more knowledgeable is an obvious step in enhancing their power; part of the reason teachers hesitate to exert authority is that they do not feel adequately informed to do so. Strengthening the intellectual foundation of the teaching staff is the beginning of true professionalization. The deliberate provision for collaborations and connectedness described in the Toledo project was present in CHART, also. Dillon (1990) reported on teachers themselves speaking out on empowerment, citing the need for solid knowledge to support authority and describing the empowering characteristics of self-direction, self-confidence, and high energy.

In 1991 Weinholtz focused on the restructuring efforts of an urban high school, and offered some specific lessons to be learned about empowerment in an SBM setting:

- "The principal and teachers should perceive themselves as generalists first and specialists second; staff should expect multiple obligations (teacher-counselor-manager) and a sense of commitment to the entire school.
- Ultimate administrative and budget targets should include, in addition to total students loads per teacher of 80 or fewer pupils, substantial time for collective planning by teachers...." (p. 36).

The outcome of these strategies is the arranging of circumstances for unleashing of the creative powers of the staff; the engineering of necessary conditions is an essential prerequisite for true teacher empowerment. Lieberman and Miller (1990) describe the role of teachers in restructuring as involving two behaviors; colleagueship and leadership, and point out that teachers are best able to develop these decidedly new behaviors in schools which have a shared culture, one collaboratively shaped by both teachers and administrators. A web of new organizational connectedness occurs; one that is such a departure from traditional structure and practice that it requires a great deal of relearning.

Sato and McLaughlin (1992) note, in an article comparing Japanese and American teachers, that the former have a similar strong involvement in their own professional growth activities, and work within a context of high collaboration and collegiality. A whole-staff meeting format provides a school-level integrating structure. Teachers work in cooperative groups to reaffirm purpose, set goals, and to participate in school management and administration, dealing with such areas as finance, textbook selection, and schoolwide curriculum management.

Conley and Bacharach in 1990 reported that a 1988 NEA publication maintained that school-based decision-making programs offered many opportunities for local associations. They caution that the same bureaucratic strategies employed previously to manage teachers may re-emerge if a professional work environment is not created. It is quite possible to have decentralized resources placed, as many districts traditionally do, in the hands of the principal, and still not achieve true collegial and collective management. A key issue and prerequisite in school-based management is not just the decisional decentralization about use of resources, but also the participation of the school's professional staff. SBM management teams of teachers and administrators have become the broad interpretation of what was more narrowly construed in the earlier implementations. They recommend participatory decision making as the appropriate vehicle for daily school governance, preceded by the critical necessity of principals viewing teachers as true professionals capable of dealing with managerial uncertainty and as the holders of key of information. Principals must perceive themselves as indeed dependent on teachers. Conley and Bacharach pose strategic questions which they feel are necessary in considering new forms of participation. The definition of the areas of decision making in which teachers will be involved can be derived from research on teachers' working conditions; they wish to influence both classroom operational and interface areas— those decisions which impact student and teacher assignment, for example. Likewise, the cross-impact and matrix effect of decision making in a school organization must be considered; how much influence does one group of stakeholders, such as central office personnel, have on various areas of decision making, such as curriculum? SBM mediation structures should be created to resolve inevitable decision making conflict.

OBSTACLES TO TEACHER EMPOWERMENT AND LEADERSHIP

Encouragement of leadership within the teacher ranks is uncommon in the current educational climate, notes Rallis (1988). There is some general administrator resistance and hostility, and some demonstrated teacher avoidance of leadership and aversion to power. The way to overcome this impasse is for structures to be established to enable teacher leadership, and for teachers to acknowledge and demonstrate professional responsibilities, even at the cost of extra time and effort. Administrative risk-taking is the tradeoff for teacher investment of effort. The catalyst to bring the two together, Ernest Boyer has said, is the provision of resources—time and money for training and implementation—as well as the creation of those enabling structures. In some schools, however, such empowerment programs are failing because of lack of principal commitment/administrative support, or teacher initiative. The two elements must both be present for successful teacher empowerment and for the effective blend of leadership.

Lieberman (1988b) speaks of the community of leaders (much as Lane later did in 1991) as a way of conceptualizing a school and its necessary leadership tasks, rather than focusing on any mutually exclusive leadership roles of teacher and principal—the "zero-sum game" power perspective. Fear of encroachment on principal role and the move to professionalize will "inevitably conflict with the bureaucratic orientation of schools and of schoolpeople who have held positions in the hierarchy" (p. 649). Traditional models of teacher involvement, such as superficial representation on committees, must give way to the sharing of larger responsibilities, provision of resources, and the support of teachers as they cope with new collegial interactions. One of the significant impoverishments of teachers' professional lives, because of the constant custodial nature of the job, is limited contact with peers and limited time for professional growth. Some good models exist to overcome this limitation; the creation of formal roles (and funds to support them) such as mentor, specialist, advisor, assistant, and lead teacher, are examples. However, new leadership positions for teachers are budgetary items at high risk in the present fiscal climate of many school systems.

Sirotnik and Clark (1988) pose the question of the concept of schools as *targets* for change, rather than *centers* for change, and make the point that *school-based* management seems to imply that all decisions are made at the school or are made somewhere else, disregarding the reality that decisions made at school sites are part of a broader environment. They do not imply an ignoring of the true dynamics and impact of a school's surrounding district, county, and state educational agencies, and accompanying parents and stakeholders. Rather, they focus on the school as a center for renewal, not simply an isolated base for management; this is a direct link to the strategic planning process described in Chapter 2. They recommend the kind of empowering effort that puts educators at the center of a process of generating and using knowledge; to assist teachers in the process of "reknowing" pedagogical knowledge in the context of their own value-based human activity. To accomplish this, they suggest the release of teachers and administrators for significant periods of time from instructional and routine duties in order to engage in this kind of critical inquiry. Techniques to facilitate this include organizing and integrating the curriculum, using human resources, time, and technology more efficiently, and 11-month appointments for all educators.

As a contrast, Prager (1991) reports on some critical teacher training, undertaken to support a Milwaukee school-based management implementation, which was eliminated because of budgetary constraints. She comments on the necessary SBM fiscal and technical support: "Perhaps fragile and variable district supports are a sign of tough economic times for almost all schools and districts. Will the engines of restructuring continue to rely on the fuel of exceptional dedication by teachers?" (p. 15).

STATE AND NATIONAL TRENDS OF TEACHER EMPOWERMENT IN REFORM AND RESTRUCTURING

Clune and White (1988) noted that one objective of SBM is to make schools more teacher-centered, and that the outcomes of early implementation were greater flexibility and the opportunity to make changes. Council membership increased teacher influence, and teachers were trained in group skills. Teacher reaction to SBM has varied, but a common finding is that teachers feel enthused and positive about themselves and their efforts.

Maeroff reported on the empowerment of teachers, indicating that, by 1988, restructuring had not really impacted the average teacher or principal: "School systems cannot be counted on to initiate programs aimed at empowering teachers"—because they work under so many constraints" (p. 70). National or local foundations have provided successful and publicized opportunities to work collegially. This is not a viable solution for national scale restructuring and empowerment; however, the body of research and accumulating practice and preparation, and the leadership of the unions (see Chapter 4) are combining to create an emerging trend for empowerment (Lewis, 1988). The professional desire for this emerging trend was evident in a 1988 AASA survey of Teachers of the Year; they strongly supported the reorganization of district structure and governance, an increase in teacher accountability, a reorganization of faculty practices, the establishing of restructuring experiments, and the vesting of greater authority in the school and in teachers (Lewis, 70–76).

The Center on Organization and Restructuring of Schools at the

University of Wisconsin at Madison has begun a five-year research program to develop new knowledge on how schools can be organized for improvement. One of their defined arenas of change includes the professional life of teachers; redefining their work in relationship to peers, administrators, and parents. They are searching for public schools to participate in the program's investigations; in Prager's *Issues for Restructuring Schools* (1991), they list school-based, management-type of qualifying criteria which include differentiated teacher function (to include peer coaching, mentoring, and supervising), teacher involvement in staff development, and teacher control over curriculum and policy.

Local, state, and national trends of this empowerment have been codified as recommendations in a series of reports:

> A publication of the Education Commission of the States, *The Next Wave*, (Green, 1987) is a synopsis of recent education reform reports, summarizing the outcomes achieved when almost every state raised standards and implemented other commission-recommended improvements. Reform reports which address the issue of school-based management include:
>
> • The 1985 California Commission Report, *Who Will Teach Our Children?*, recommends the involvement of teachers in decision making.
> • The 1986 *Tomorrow's Teachers: A Report of the Holmes Group*, which recommends changing the structure of schools by developing models for new divisions of authority among teachers and administrators.
> • The 1986 Carnegie Task Force on Teaching as a Profession *A Nation Prepared: Teachers for the 21st Century*, which recommends restructuring schools to provide a professional environment for teachers to decide how to meet goals; and suggests restructuring the teaching force to introduce "lead teachers" to help redesign the schools.
> • The 1986 Education Commission of the States *What Next? More Leverage for Teachers* suggests that current policies must decentralize responsibly, neither too specifically nor too piecemeal. Things such as giving teachers control over time and materials are more important than money. Berkeley's Dean of Education stated in that report, "If we are ever going to make a dent in the problems we face in public education we're going to have to find ways of permitting talented teachers to play a much larger role. We need to find ways of giving talented people, first rate professionals, extra leverage."
> • The 1986 National Governors' Association *Time for Results: The Governors' 1991 Report on Education* recommends allowing a real teacher voice in decisions, and the provision of incentives and technical assistance to districts to promote school-site management.
> • The National Association of Secondary School Principals/National Education Association's 1986 *A Cooperative Model for a Successful Secondary School*

called for a collegial model that strongly emphasized teacher participation within a framework of school-level decision making.

The National Governors Association couched policy making in terms of empowering leadership at the school level (Lewis, 1988). School-based management is built on two basic beliefs, according to a joint statement of the American Association of School Administrators, the National Association of Elementary School Principals, and the National Association of Secondary School Principals. These beliefs are:

- Those most closely affected by decisions ought to play a significant role in making those decisions; and
- Educational reform efforts will be most effective and long-lasting when carried out by people who feel a sense of ownership and responsibility for the process.

The 23rd Annual Gallup Poll of the Public's Attitudes Toward the Public Schools (Elam, Rose, & Gallup, 1991) is the most comprehensive survey to date of American attitudes on education, since the series began in 1969. The report inquired about control of schools; noting that the reform movement had highlighted the call for school-based management, and described it as one of restructuring's foundation stones. The general public shared that view, with 76 percent of the respondents in favor of allowing principals and teachers more say in how schools are run, especially through local councils of teachers, principals, and parents (as in Chicago), rather than leaving decision making to boards and central office administrators—79 percent were in favor of such councils. This was a finding which had appeared in the 1990 poll, indicating, also, support for more parental say in such policy areas as budget, hiring, and curricular and instructional matters. In a similar vein, *Leadership News* reported a 1990 poll conducted by the National Center for Education showed that 90 percent of teachers believe they ought to have more authority in running schools, and 60 percent think that involving parents in running school would improve the nation's education system.

SUMMARY

The connection between teacher empowerment and contemporary corporate managerial theory was established, and definitions and rationales for school-based management were presented. Common points of both included the professionalization effect; the enhancement of the learning process as empowered practitioners make collaborative decisions in a collegial environment, and the heightened effectiveness of empowering those at the product and process delivery point.

The background of teacher empowerment draws on the historical isolation of teachers in classrooms and from the traditional bureaucratization of the workplace. This existing educational structure has been somewhat changed by such SBM transitional innovations as teaching teams, temporary task groups, and leadership groups. For the most part, however, the labor-management divisiveness between the teacher and principal persists.

Support and facilitation for empowerment raises questions of the division of responsibility and authority; the role of instructional leadership must be seen as one diffused across teachers and administrators, while the more managerial responsibilities may remain in the principal domain. The exercise of empowerment will typically require developmental and cultural change facilitation, as well as the more practical and critical elements of released collaboration time and training resources. The actual breadth of teacher involvement in decision making must be defined and resolved in the face of new distributions and district patterns of autonomy; some initial mediation of conflicts over decisional areas may be required. There are inherent obstacles to teacher empowerment; principal reluctance to relinquish authority, and teacher avoidance and aversion to power. Formal structures for shared leadership and change, and the provision of resources—time, training, and money—are needed to eliminate inbred reluctance and fear of encroachment.

There are discernible state and national trends of teacher empowerment; there is an accumulating body of research, practice, and teacher preparation which reflects shifts in district structure, the redefinition of professionalism, and new differentiations of teacher function. A series of reports which address the teacher empowerment issues of school based management included publications from the Education Commission of the States, the Holmes Group, the Carnegie Task Force on Teaching as a Profession, the National Governors' Association, the NASSP, the NEA, and the Annual Gallup Poll of Public Attitudes Towards Schools.

EXERCISES

1. What definitional elements of teacher empowerment do you feel are the most critical, and why do they seem to be key points?

2. What is the nature of the relationship between teachers and principals in your district, and how would it be affected by the implementation of school-based management?

3. What SBM cultural change preparation and training for teachers and administrators would be needed in your district?

4. What would be the facilitations or impediments to shared decision making as it might be practiced in your district?

REFERENCES

AASA (1990). *A new look at empowerment.* (AASA Stock Number 021-00278). Washington, DC: American Association of School Administrators.

A cooperative model for a successful secondary school (1986). The National Association of Secondary School Principals/National Education Association. Reston, VA: NASSP, NEA.

Bailey, W.J. (1991). *School-site management applied.* Lancaster, PA: Technomic Publishing Company, pp. 45–46, 116–128.

Barth, R. (1988). Principals, teachers, and school leadership. *Phi Delta Kappan, 69* (9), 639–642.

Benson, N. & Malone, P. (1987). Teachers beliefs about shared decision making and work alienation. *Education,* Spring, 1987, 244–251.

Brandt, R. (1989). On teacher empowerment: A conversation with Ann Lieberman. *Educational Leadership, 46* (8), 23–26.

Carnegie Forum on Education and the Economy (1986). *A nation prepared: Teachers for the 21st century.* New York. Carnegie Forum on Education and the Economy, pp. 56–61.

Clune, W.H. & White, P.A. (1988). *School-based management—institutional variation, implementation, and issues for further research.* Center for Policy Research in Education, pp. 21–22.

Conley, S.C. & Bacharach, S.B. (1990). From school-site management to participatory school-site management. *Phi Delta Kappan, 71* (7), 539–545.

Conley, S.C., Schmidle, T., & Shedd, J.B. (1988). Teacher participation in the management of school systems. *Teachers College Record, 90,* (2), 259–280.

Dillon, D. (1990). Pinning down empowerment. *Instructor, 99* (5), 26–36.

Elam, S.M., Rose, L.C., & Gallup, A.M. (1991). The 23rd annual Gallup Poll of the public's attitudes toward the public schools. *Phi Delta Kappan, 73* (1), 41–56.

Glickman, C. (1990). Pushing school reform to a new edge: The seven ironies of school empowerment. *Phi Delta Kappan, 72* (1), 68–75.

Green, J. (1987). *The next wave: a synopsis of recent education reform reports.* Denver, CO: Education Commission of the States, pp. 1–10.

Hallinger, P., & Richardson, D. (1988). Models of shared leadership: Evolving structures and relationships. *Urban Review, 20* (4), 229–245.

Karant, V. (1989). Supervision in the age of teacher empowerment. *Educational Leadership, 46* (8), 27–29.

Kreptovics, J., Farber, K., & Armaline, W. (1991). Reform from the bottom up: Empowering teachers to transform schools. *Phi Delta Kappan, 73,* (4), 295–299.

Lagana, J. (1989). Managing change and school improvement effectively. *NASSP Bulletin, 73* (518), 52–55.

Lane, J. (1991). Instructional leadership and community: A perspective on school based management. *Theory Into Practice, 30,* (2), 119–123.

Leadership News. 1990. Teachers polled want more authority, parent control. American Association of School Administrators' *Leadership News,* September 30, 1990, p. 6.

Lewis, A. (1989). *Restructuring America's schools.* Washington, D.C.: American Association of School Administrators, pp. 34–35, 69–76.

Lieberman, A. (1988). Expanding the leadership team. *Educational Leadership, 44* (5), 4–8.

Lieberman, A. (1988). Teachers and principals: Turf, tension, and new tasks. *Phi Delta Kappan, 69* (9), 648–653.

Lieberman, A. & Miller, L. (1990). Restructuring schools: What matters and what works. *Phi Delta Kappan, 71* (10), 759–764.

Maeroff, G. (1988). Teacher empowerment: A step towards professionalization. *NASSP Bulletin, 72* (511), 52–54, 56–60.

Maeroff, G. (1988). *The empowerment of teachers.* New York: Teachers College Press, p. xiii.

McDonnell, L. & Pascal, A. (1988). *Teacher unions and educational reform.* Rutgers, NJ: RAND Corporation, with the Center for Policy Research in Education.

Moses, M.C. & Whitaker, K.S. (1990). Ten components for restructuring schools. *School Administrator, 8* (47), 32–34.

Pinning down empowerment. (1990). *Instructor, 99* (5), 26–36.

Prager, K. (1991). Issues in restructuring schools. Madison, WI: *National Center on Organization and Restructuring of Schools,* pp. 2, 7, 15.

Rallis, S. (1988). Room at the top: conditions for effective school leadership. *Phi Delta Kappan, 69* (9), 643–647.

Raywid, M.A. (1990). Rethinking school governance. In R.F. Elmore and Associates, *Restructuring schools—the next generation of educational reform* (p. 155), San Francisco: Jossey-Bass Publishers.

Sato, N. & McLaughlin, M.W. (1992). Context matters: Teaching in Japan and the United States. *Phi Delta Kappan, 73* (5), 359–366.

Sergiovanni, T.J. (1990). *Value-added leadership.* Orlando, FL: Harcourt Brace Jovanovich, Inc., p. 21, 96–103.

Sirotnik, K.A. & Clark, R.W. (1988). School-centered decision making and renewal. *Phi Delta Kappan, 69* (9), 660–664.

Voices from the field (1991). Washington, D.C.: William T. Grant Foundation Commission on Work, Family, and Citizenship, and the Institute for Educational Leadership.

Weinholtz, D. (1991). *Restructuring an urban high school.* Bloomington, IN: Phi Delta Kappa Educational Foundation Fastback 323, 34–36.

Chapter 4

SCHOOL-BASED MANAGEMENT AND TEACHER ORGANIZATIONS: NEGOTIATIONS AND PARTNERSHIPS

School-based management may cause considerable change in the manner in which teacher organizations, especially those which are represented by unions, make decisions. Not only will the traditional roles of the superintendent of schools and the school district's management change as greater decision-making power is delegated to teacher and parent representatives at the individual school site level, but it will also cause either a delegation of teacher unions' leadership decision making power, or it will cause conflict between teacher union and SBM councils (Jacobson, 1990; Keith & Girling, 1991).

This chapter opens with an exploration of some of the historical experiences in decision making and collaborative designs utilized by school district administration and teacher organizations. Of course, differences historically existed in various school districts, and today differences continue to exist in various school districts. However, general patterns did exist; and these general patterns are worthy of discussion. The basics of Quality of Work Life programs are examined, and school district examples provided of such programs. The notion of win-win negotiations, and their inherent problems and logical connections are SBM are described. A discussion of the concept of SBM as a peer coaching and professional development vehicle and an outline of new accountability structures ends the chapter.

EARLY EXPERIENCES AND COLLABORATIVE DESIGNS

Although there was isolated teacher union activity in Wisconsin and New York City, for all practical purposes the extensive movement towards collective bargaining in the public sector; and, in many districts, adversarial union/management relations, had its beginning in 1962. Murphy

(1990) notes that at that time President Kennedy issued Executive Order 10988, entitled "Employee Management Co-operation in Federal Service" on 17 January 1962, giving federal employees the right to organize and bargain collectively. The presidential endorsement nudged along the cause of collective bargaining, so that by 1966 seven states had collective bargaining statutes on the books.

In the 1960s, 1970s and 1980s, teacher unionism became the mode because most states passed collective bargaining laws during this time period. It was during this time frame that the NEA (National Education Association) because of organizational competition from the AFT (American Federation of Teachers) became more adversarial in tactics and accepted the title of union. Prior to this conversion, the NEA insisted that it was a professional association and not a union (J.J. Herman & Megiveron, in press).

Prior to the passage of collective bargaining laws by most states, the relationship of the teacher organizations was vastly different than it is today. Also, the decision-making power was much more limited. Focusing on the largest teacher organization, the NEA, let's visit some of the precollective bargaining identifiers of this period.

- Administrators, as well as teachers, were members of the NEA. In fact, much of the leadership of the NEA consisted of those persons holding administrative titles. With the advent of collective bargaining, the NEA decided that administrators should be prohibited from membership.
- Superintendents of schools in many districts, either subtly or actively, pressured all administrators and teachers to join the NEA, and they took great pride in the poster which the NEA distributed indicating that their districts contained one hundred percent (100%) memberships. In fact, some teachers' lounges had thermometer-like charts, similar to those used in many communities for United Fund campaigns, indicating the daily percent of union membership.
- Teachers, in most districts comprised the majority of membership on school districts' curriculum committees and textbook selection committees. In essence, in those districts which did not have state mandated curricula or textbooks; teachers were the determiners of what was taught and how it was to be taught. For the most part, however, teacher decision making input was limited to the area of instruction. With the addition of administrator representation on some

of these committees, this activity constituted the primary method of collaborative functioning between teachers and administrators.
• Teachers had very little input into the salaries, fringe benefits or conditions under which they worked. Prior to collective bargaining, most salary and fringe benefit matters were recommended by the superintendent of schools and approved by the school district's board of education with no input into these matters by teachers or the teachers' organization. Occasionally, some school districts' superintendents of schools and boards of education would permit the teachers organization's president to make recommendations about salary and a few limited fringe benefits. If the teachers' organization's president proposed conservative cost items, and if she/he presented these as a request, rather than demands, the superintendents of schools and the boards of education would approve many of the requests.
• Superintendents of schools and boards of education would often request and expect teachers to freely give of their time to assist the boards in passing a tax referendum or a bond issue. In general, this activity was not truly collaborative in nature; teachers were expected to make phone calls, serve as drivers on election day, and serve as baby sitters while voters voted (J.J. Herman & Megiveron, in press).

In the 1960s a few districts involved their teacher organizations in a concept called Quality of Work Life that was being utilized by some of the major corporations in the United States. The U.S. corporations were concerned about the success of the Japanese corporations which were in competition with them, and they decided to visit Japan and discover the secret of the Japanese corporations' success. They took what they saw and brought it to their corporations under the title of QWL (Quality of Work Life) (J.J. Herman, 1982).

Those districts that implemented QWL, especially in districts which possessed teacher unions, found this collaborative effort had a very positive effect on the culture of the school district and its composite of school building. At the building level, groups of usually six to eight were organized, called Quality Circles, to identify and solve problems which existed at their work site. Another number of Quality Circles could be organized at each site (Herman & Herman, 1991).

Let's examine more closely this collaborative movement which preceded the movement of school based management. A description of the basics of QWL follows.

QUALITY OF WORK LIFE BASICS

Quality of Work Life programs operate under a variety of names such as Quality Circles, Employee Participation Circles, Job Enrichment Teams, Professional Development Teams, School Improvement Circles, and Working Groups. Whatever title is used, QWL: (1) is a *philosophy* that states people are good, they want to help themselves, their fellow employees, and their particular school organization to improve; (2) has a the *goal* of involving employees in improving the quality of their work environment, and, (3) is a *process* which involves employees in problem solving and in employee satisfaction activities through action programs which the employees develop to improve the quality of their work life (J.J. Herman, 1982). It should be stressed that QWL is always in a state of evolution as employees identify programs and problems, and as they develop action plans to achieved their desired results. Also, QWL will only work well if volunteerism is a building block of the structure. That is, any individual should be free to participate or not participate; and if the individual employee initially volunteers to participate and later wants to resign, this option is always open to all participants. The teachers' organization or union or other employee organization are also voluntary participants, and they may quit the SBM structure at any time they desire to resign (J.J. Herman, 1984).

Once a board of education, a school district's administration, and the teachers' organization or union accept the concept of QWL; details of the structure and processes under which QWL will operate have to be jointly and collaboratively decided upon before implementation begins (Herman & Herman, 1991). An example of the structure and processes utilized by a school district, West Bloomfield School District in Michigan, will illustrate some of the planning that should be completed before implementing QWL. It is interesting to note that QWL in the West Bloomfield School District involved six employee unions and all non-unionized groups as participants; and all individuals and groups were volunteers to the ECDC (Employees' Communication and Development Council), which was the name the employees chose for their QWL structure.

Board of Education Policy

The West Bloomfield School District's Board of Education recognizes that the competency and satisfaction of all its employees affects the quality of the schools' programs. In seeking to obtain the greatest degree of competence and satisfaction, assessment and evaluation of the needs of employees shall be identified in terms of:

1. district-wide operations,
2. subgroups within the district, and
3. individual employees.

The Board desires to establish a systematic process for the assessment of employee needs, the development of programs to meet these needs, and the measurement of results.

Furthermore, the Board desires to support a climate in which the district's employees participate in such a process, especially as it relates to:

1. planning for staff development,
2. solving problems, and
3. improving communication.

Therefore, the Board supports a program for staff development and it recognizes its obligation to provide funds to carry out such a program as an integral part of the total school district's operation.

The Board of Education directs the Superintendent of Schools to implement a staff development and employee involvement program for all employees of the school district.

POLICY ADOPTED.

Implementing Rules and Regulations

1. The Superintendent shall establish an advisory committee consisting of representatives of all employee subgroups within the school district. Participation in the advisory committee shall be voluntary.
2. The program shall encompass employee training needs as well as conditions relating to the quality of employees' work life.
3. The program shall not infringe upon the rights established under existing collective bargaining agreements.
4. Programs shall attempt to serve the needs of the total district organization, employee subgroups, and all employees of the school district.

Following the adoption of a board of education policy and the development of the implementing rules and regulations, the ECDC members met and developed the bylaws under which the ECDC would operate.

West Bloomfield School District's Employees' Communication and Development Council Bylaws

The Employees' Communication and Development Council shall be an on-going committee; advisory to the superintendent, representing all employees, and responsible for assisting in:

1. planning staff development,
2. solving problems,
3. improving communications

for the purpose of making the West Bloomfield School District a better place to work, live, learn and GROW.

Participation in the Employees' Communication and Development Council is limited to employees of the West Bloomfield School District.

Participation in the Employees' Communication and Development Council shall be voluntary.

The Employees' Communication and Development Council shall act in an advisory capacity, promoting rather than directing.

The Employees' Communication and Development Council welcomes all ideas from all employees.

The Employees' Communication and Development Council does not take the place of the legitimate roles of other groups in the school district such as employee bargaining groups, Curriculum Council, Communications/Governance Councils, Administrative Councils, and other groups.

REPRESENTATION

Two (2) representatives from each employee group, including at least one (1) representative from each work site.

Two (2) representatives at large may be added if the committee deems it necessary.

One (1) Superintendent's administrative designee, ex officio member.

One (1) Board of Education, ex officio member.

EMPLOYEE GROUPS

West Bloomfield Schools Association of Educational Secretaries

AFCME School Aide Bargaining Unit, Local 1284, Council 25

West Bloomfield Cafeteria Employees' Association

West Bloomfield Education Association

West Bloomfield Schools Team Management Association

AFSCME Custodial-Maintenance Bargaining Unit, Local 1384, Council 25

AFSCME Transportation Bargaining Unit, Local 1386, Council 25

Non-unionized Secretarial-Clerical Employees

Non-unionized Administrator-Supervisor Employees

WORK SITES

West Bloomfield High School, Orchard Lake Middle School, Abbott Middle School, Ealy Elementary School, Doherty Elementary School, Green Elementary

School, Scotch Elementary School, Roosevelt Elementary School, and West Bloomfield School District's Bus Garage.

REPRESENTATIVE ROTATION

Terms: September–August

Each employee group will be requested to select two (2) representatives by May 1 of each year for a: (1) Three (3) year term, and a (2) Two (2) year term.

After the second year, all terms will last two (2) years.

Work site and at-large representatives will be appointed by the chairperson for a one (1) year term.

ROLES AND RESPONSIBILITIES

Superintendent's Administrative Designee shall:

1. Keep and distribute minutes,
2. Monitor budget, keep within the allocation, and process expenditures,
3. Arrange for meetings,
4. Communicate information,
5. Maintain records, and
6. Accept agenda items, and prepare the agenda under the direction of the ECDC Chairperson.

OFFICERS:

Chairperson shall:

1. Develop agenda,
2. Chair meetings,
3. Appoint sub-committees,
4. Call meetings,
5. Act as spokesperson for ECDC,
6. Appoint work site and at-large representatives.

Assistant Chairperson shall:

1. Replace the chairperson in his/her absence.

Secretary shall:

1. Take minutes, and
2. Do necessary correspondence.

The Employees' Communication and Development Council will elect its officers in May of each year from the selected employee representatives who have served at least a one (1) year term on the Council. The terms of office to be one (1) year from September through August.

MEETINGS

Regular meetings will be held from 3:00–5:00 p.m. the first working Thursday of each month.

Special meetings may be called by the chairperson.

The chairperson will notify members at least five (5) working days in advance of special meetings.

Business will be conducted using simplified *Roberts Rules of Order.*

All meetings will be open.

AMENDMENTS

Amendments to the Bylaws may be proposed by any member of the committee and acted on by a simple majority of those present

When reviewing the structure of the West Bloomfield School District's ECDC, it is clear that the potential for many positive advantages exist in this collaborative venture. Some of the most important potential advantages include those listed below.

- The primary advantage of QWL is that the structure utilizes the intelligence of every employee in improving the school district's work climate and culture. This, in turn, improves the school climate and culture for students; and it lets each employee know he/she is respected, cared for and valued.
- It opens communications vertically and horizontally about goals, problems, challenges, and desires as viewed by all employees and by all employee and management groups. It allows for top-down, bottom-up, and horizontal openness.
- Important by-products, such as less absenteeism, less grievances and gripes, productivity increases, and high quality operational strategic and operational planning usually result.

Another collaborative teacher and union/management development is one called win/win negotiations. This development has been especially important in school districts which have experienced serious adversarial relations between the teachers' organization or union; and the administration and boards of education of the school districts.

WIN/WIN NEGOTIATIONS

Win/win collective bargaining implies a nonadversarial, mutual problem solving, collaborative approach between the union and the management of a school district. The key elements which make collaborative, win/win negotiations possible include: (1) trust building, (2) clear and continuous communications, (3) avoidance of a *one-upsmanship* strategy,

(4) mutual problem solving, (5) open communications, (6) respect for others, (7) a desire to improve oneself, the organization, and the entire school district, and (8) a desire for union and management to work together to achieve results that assist the individuals, the employees, the union, the management, and the school district (J.J. Herman & Megiveron, in press). To achieve this collaborative, win/win state, the individuals and the parties to collective bargaining and negotiations must realize that it is a long-term, day-by-day process (Nyland, 1987). It is not a quick fix, nor is it something that will be accomplished by a public relations effort or by pleasant-sounding, hollow utterances by either the union or management.

Empowering teacher representatives to work in a collaborative environment with the board of education's administrative representatives is a big step towards bettering teacher employees' satisfaction and towards improving the culture of any school district, especially those districts that have historically witnessed adversarial union/management relations and win/lose master union contract negotiations (J.J. Herman, 1985).

A simple example of the differences between win/win negotiations and adversarial negotiations can be illustrated by two brief scenarios dealing with teacher salary increases. Scenario #1 deals with an adversarial approach to this, and Scenario #2 deals with a win/win approach to the identical issue.

Scenario #1: The initial union's bargaining team proposal is for a fifteen percent (15%) raise, even though they would settle for five percent (5%), and they will hold tough for (7%). The board of education's negotiating team, realizing that the teachers' union always inflates its initial demand, offers an initial 2 percent (2%) raise. In reality, the board of education has decided it can afford a four percent (4%) increase. After months of adversarial bargaining and perhaps some negative publicity and attempts to discredit the other party, the master contractual agreement is settled at four and one-half percent (4½%).

Scenario #2: Members of both the union's and the board of education's negotiating teams have acquired great respect and trust for one another. Together, as a collaborative unit, they collect data on what comparative school districts are paying their teachers; and they analyze the school district's current and projected budgets, they study the cost-of-living index for their geographical area, they study the effort that the district's taxpayers are making in comparison to other districts, and they establish some criteria for making a decision.

This approach is one of collaborative problem solving based upon data, trust, and rationality. In the end, both parties agree that a 4½ percent raise is reasonable, is fair to the teachers, is fair to the taxpayers, is fair in comparison to other school districts in the geographical area, and will not require the diminishing of funds to meet any of the other needs of the school district.

The key to a successful win/win approach to all aspects of the collective bargaining process, and especially to the negotiation of a master contractual agreement, is for both parties to focus on the interests of each party—not on the positions. Interests are needs, desires, concerns, and fears. Behind the stated positions lie shared and compatible interests, as well as conflicting interests (J.J. Herman, 1991). The key to reaching a compatible and collaborative agreement is that of putting yourself in the shoes of the other party. When mentally in the other parties' shoes, answer the questions of *why?* and *why not?* to each issue that separates the positions of the parties. Once the other party's interests have been considered, ask for detailed information supporting that interest. Eventually a collaborative approach to problem solving will resolve any conflict of positions, and the interests of both parties will be served.

If the union and management can collectively bargain and if they can negotiate a contract on the basis of joint study and collaborative action; within an environment of trust, caring, respect, and mutual problem solving; the benefits of this win/win approach will not only accrue to the teachers, administrators, board of education members, union and management, and the community at large; but it will mostly accrue to the benefit of the students who will attend schools which possess an exceptionally positive learning climate. For after all, the only reason for schools to exist is to educate the young well; and the climate in which they learn is a powerful determiner of the students' attitudes towards schools and learning.

The earlier movements towards QWL (Quality of Work Life) and win/win collective bargaining, in districts which have used one or both of these techniques, will assist in a smooth transition to school-based management. However, even in those districts which have previously utilized these techniques, adjustments to the standard operating procedures will still have to be made (Cohen, 1990).

INHERENT PROBLEMS AND LOGICAL CONNECTIONS

Both Quality of Work Life programs and win/win collective bargaining can serve as strong building blocks as a district enters into school-based management, as a precedent has been set for collaborative and trusting communications and decision making. In those districts which have a history of QWL and/or win/win collective bargaining relations, SBM can be seen as the next logical step in the empowerment of teachers and other employees (J.J. Herman & Megiveron, in press). But, even in these districts, there will be adjustments to be made as the areas of decision making are broadened and as more decision making responsibilities and accountability are delegated from the central district level to the school site level.

In those districts attempting SBM which have no history of collaborative decision making and where, historically, all decisions have been of the top-down variety, major adjustments in the standard operating procedures and in the school district's culture will have to be made—many times with serious conflict resulting during the transition period to bottom-up, site-based decision making (Heller & Pautler, 1991). These dramatic adjustments will have to be made as the district implements SBM, whether it is done by legislative mandate or by voluntary action.

Let's explore the possible adjustment to be made and the inherent problems involved in initiating and maintaining school-based management in: (1) districts which have experienced some form of collaborative working relationships between teachers and administrators, and between union and management, and (2) districts which have a tradition of adversarial union and management relations which also affect the relationships between teachers and administrators in the school districts.

Connections and Problems of Implementing SBM in School Districts with a History of Collaborative Decision Making

The major adjustments to be made in the districts which have a history of collaborative decision making include:

- Providing parents with an equal voice on the school-based councils.
- Allowing many final decisions to be made at the school site level, rather than in conjunction with the central district level.
- Having the board of education adopt policies which support SBM, and causing them to modify policies which conflict or detract from the SBM structure and processes.
- Taking much of the accountability from the board of education, the

superintendent of schools, and the central administration; and placing it clearly with the principal and the SBM council.
- Negotiating, in a friendly and collaborative manner, those items wherein final decision making shall: (1) remain at the district level, (2) be delegated to the school site level, or (3) be made by joint decision between the central district and school site levels.
- Adjusting union master contractual agreements over time to fall in line with the decisions that are to be delegated to the SBM school site councils.
- Providing training in communications, problem identification, problem analysis, collaborative planning, conflict resolution, strategic and action planning, and presentation of recommendations, when necessary, to SBM council members who do not have the experience in collaborative decision making and team building; or who do not possess the skill areas required to function effectively as a member of a SBM council (Hess, 1991; J.J. Herman & Megiveron, in press).

Connections and Problems of Implementing SBM in School Districts with a History of Adversarial Union/Management Relations

Although Quality of Work Life and win/win negotiations diminished, to some degree, the power of school district administrators, the board of education, and the teacher union's leaders (in school districts which have officially recognized unions who are empowered to collectively bargain with management); neither of these movements come close to causing the upset in power and working relations that will be faced by a teachers' union which has operated in an adversarial manner, as the school district enters into an SBM structure and process.

For example, the Quality of Work Life structure generally contains bylaws stating that QWL activities cannot conflict with or replace any activities which are reserved to the union under a collective bargaining master contractual agreement. On the other hand, school-based management structures and processes, especially if they involve parents, taxpayers, and some of the community's power figures, have the potential to seriously impact the environment within which the union works and within which collective bargaining is conducted (David, 1990). This potential, if acted upon in fact, may cause serious conflict within the school district and lessen the power of union leaders, the board of education, and the school district's central administrators.

The initiation of school-based management may also impact both the existing and future board of education policies, and the existing and future master contractual agreements which are negotiated between the union and the board of education (Lewis, 1989). These master contractual agreements may be impacted during the process of negotiations, and they may be impacted during the daily operations as both parties attempt to manage a previously negotiated master contract (Lifton, 1992). For, in reality, many of the areas which are included in traditionally ratified master contractual agreements become the decision-making purview of a third party—the school-based management councils or committees (Bacharach, Shedd, & Conley, 1989).

IMPLEMENTATION OF SBM AS PEER COACHING AND AS A PROFESSIONAL DEVELOPMENT VEHICLE

Although neither staff development and training nor peer coaching are prerequisites to the implementation and maintenance of SBM, they certainly add positive dimensions to SBM (Steinberger, 1990). Staff development and training will assist all members of the SBM councils to become more efficient and effective in their council's work. Peer coaching also can assist in building strong relationships among the members of the SBM council, and it should cause a *winning* SBM team to develop.

Peer Coaching

If we think of peer coaching as a *growth process* wherein one or more individuals assist one or more other individuals to acquire skills, knowledge, or effective behaviors which complement the total SBM council and which improve upon the efficiency or effectiveness of the SBM council's work and upon the degree of satisfaction felt by each member of the council; it is most likely that a team building result will take place. In addition, each person shall possess one or more growth partners who will continually assist them in the process of being the best SBM council's contributor that they can become.

Whether staff development or training comes from the growth partners or it is supplied by another source, it is likely that staff development and training opportunities should be provided to SBM councils and to individual council members on an as-needed basis. Most likely, this training will be most effective if offered at the building site level (McClure, 1991).

Although many skills and knowledges can be approached through staff development and training activities, the prime candidate areas for SBM staff development and training should, as a minimum, include the following:

- *Communications* such as "I" messages, active listening, negotiating meaning, paraphrasing, and nonverbal scanning.
- *Collaborative relations* which includes team building and collaborative problem solving.
- *Planning skills* which include strategic and operational planning, tactical planning, and action planning. These skills should include problem or program identification, the establishment of goals and specific objectives, the methodologies of evaluating outputs and outcomes, the collection and analysis of data, and the monitoring and recycling of the plans (Levine, 1991).

UNION CHANGE, DECENTRALIZATION, AND SHARED DECISION-MAKING IMPLICATIONS

With regard to restructuring, the national unions have not taken oppositional stances, but rather have moved to different positions of support. The American Federation of Teachers' stance has been one of more direct support and movement towards the professionalization of teachers; the National Education Association has gradually changed from initial opposition to early reforms to a posture of encouraging restructuring at the local affiliate level. Their Mastery in Learning Project is a school-based improvement model in which 27 resource-supported cooperating schools operate collaboratively under an assumption that decisions about learning and instruction are to be made by the faculty. Another NEA effort, the Teams Approach to Better Schools, supports 70 projects focusing on developing school-based, shared decision making. Learning laboratories in each of the fifty states have been established to implement improvements in such areas as cooperative decision making (Lewis, 1988). The AFT's posture has been to support a more unilateral reform; the creation of an opportunity for chartered autonomous "schools within schools", bargained for with the local districts. These schools must meet several AFT criteria, one of which is participative management and governance. Additionally, the AFT's Center for Restructuring was created in 1988, and it formed the Urban District

Leadership Consortium in partnership with personnel in urban districts where participatory decision making is underway (McDonnell & Pascal, 1988).

NEW ACCOUNTABILITY STRUCTURES

It is appropriate, at this juncture, to trace the changes in accountability structures as districts have: (1) operated under a traditional, autocratic top-down model, (2) introduced QWL (Quality of Work Life) structures and processes into their decision making operations, (3) adjusted to the impact of teacher and other employees' unions and collective bargaining legislation, and (4) initiated SBM into the school districts. The reader is referred to Figures 7.1 through 7.8, in Chapter 7, which illustrate these changing relationships (QWL is not included, since only a limited number of districts implemented QWL structures).

In the historical, traditional model of accountability, which was very autocratic and top-down in nature; the accountability structure was thus:

- The *board of education* adopted policies, and they held the *superintendent of schools* accountable for operating the district well within the policy structure adopted by the board of education. The superintendent of schools developed a series of implementing rules and regulations related to each of the policies adopted by the board of education. At this level the board of education's individual members were held accountable by the people who elected them or by the mayor or city council who appointed them to their board of education's posts. The superintendent was held ultimately responsible for operating the district within the board of education's policies, and she/he was held ultimately responsible by the board for the quality of the day-to-day operation of all activities of the school district.
- The *building principals* and any central office administrators and supervisors were held accountable by the superintendent for operating within the board of education's policies and the school district's rules and regulations which were promulgated by the superintendent. Of course, all functionaries of the school district were also held accountable for operating within any applicable federal and state level laws.
- The *teachers and other site level employees* were held accountable to their principal or other immediate supervisor for operating within the federal and state laws, the board of education policies, and the district's rules and regulations. In addition, the teachers and other site level employees were held accountable to their principal or other immediate supervisor for operating within the building level rules promulgated by their immediate supervisor or principal (Conley, Schmidle, & Shedd, 1988).

When collective bargaining legislation was passed in those states which possessed collective negotiations laws permitting collective bargaining by public employees, the accountability relationship was modified, and it became convoluted and confusing to many members of the public and to many administrators, teachers, and board of education members (Eberts & Stone, 1984). The public, the board of education members, the administrators, and many of the employees still held to the traditional paths of accountability; and they had difficulty adjusting to this change. But, indeed, the change took place, and added a second party element to the decision-making and accountability structure. As boards of education and teachers' and other employees' unions negotiated master contracts which outlined the authority of the board and the unions and which also spelled out many of the conditions under which the management of the district was to take place, two major difficulties arose: (1) boards of education and school district administrators now had to manage the district and be accountable for the laws generated by the legislature under the specific state's collective bargaining legislation, (2) a written, and, many times, lengthy and detailed document spelled out the role of the union's leadership which allowed this leadership to impinge upon many of the prerogatives of the board of education, the superintendent of schools, the central office administrators and supervisors, and the building principals and her/his administrative and supervisory assistants (Kennedy, 1984). Some of the items included in the negotiated and ratified master contractual agreement between the board of education and the union not only caused a change in the roles of decision makers; but the contract, oftentimes, was in conflict with previously adopted board of education policies and the district's rules and regulations related to personnel decision making areas.

With the introduction of school-based management, there now enters a fifth party into the decision making and accountability equation. The district now has decision making done by: (1) the board of education, (2) the superintendent and her/his central administrative and supervisory staff, (3) the principals and her/his assistant administrators and supervisors, (4) the teachers' and other employees' unions, and (5) the SBM councils or committees (Lifton, 1992; Steinberger, 1990). Depending on whether or not the district enters SBM by legislative mandate or by voluntary action, and depending upon the degree to which various decision making categories are delegated to the site level, and depending upon whether or not parents, community members, nonteaching employees or others are included as members of the SBM councils or committees; it is quite obvious that the accountability structures become both more confusing and more focused. McDonnell and Pascal (1988) have pointed out that three conditions must be met if the AFT and NEA restructuring efforts described earlier are to expand into a discernible union trend: (1) that reform policies cannot be substituted for traditional contractual items, such as wages and working day (these agreements, may indeed be solidly concurred-upon prerequisites to professional autonomy bargaining discussions); (2) that not all union members may desire to more fully participate in governance, given the range of age and attitude across the current teacher cohort; and, (3) that consideration must be given to the potential packaging possibilities of bargaining agreements which include enhanced professionalism as negotiation points. Some of the agreements of restructuring and reform may need to be implemented outside of the master contract (Levine & Eubanks, 1992).

The accountability for decision making becomes more confusing because of the interface, with the possibility of conflict between two or more decision-making bodies. It becomes more focused, in most cases, because SBM usually delegates considerably more decision-making power to the school site level; and the accountability to that level is greatly increased by actual definition or by implication of the delegated decision-making power (David, 1990).

It is clear that in those districts that possess all categories of decision makers who believe in people, who trust people, and who want to empower people; the major philosophical commitment exists. Actions which allow this philosophical position to be embraced at the action level, however, will take collaborative efforts of all parties over a long period of time as the structure and processes to implement SBM in each school district and at each school site will evolve. For it should be clear to all that SBM is an evolutionary structure and process; and that it is not a revolutionary structure and process.

SUMMARY

This chapter focused on the role change and decision making shifts involved when employee organizations and school district management confront SBM implementation. The historical experiences of both sides' decision-making and collaborative designs were explored as a backdrop. The basic characteristics of Quality of Work Life, a distinctive collaborative effort, were illustrated in a school district structure and process example. A collegial structure still in effect in the cited district was described to demonstrate the potential for positive collaboration and SBM-types of ventures, including school culture and communications enhancements.

Another collaborative labor/management interaction, win/win negotiations, was described as a nonadversarial, mutual problem solving, collaborative approach between the union and the management of a school district. Key elements were provided and scenarios presented to illustrate this SBM-complementary collaboration. The key to success in win/win is to focus on the agendas of each party in order to discern shared and compatible interests. Quality of Work Life and win/win collective negotiations will assist in a smooth transition to SBM. The inherent problems and logical connections in the transitional stages of SBM can be mitigated if these building blocks are in place.

The standard employee relations operating procedures of the district will be affected, regardless of the level of previous collaboration, during any shared decision-making transitional process. Possible areas of adjustments included SBM council involvement, site decision making and accountability, policy adoption which supports SBM, a union master contract agreement which defines the territorial limits of SBM, and the provision of shared governance facilitation skills. All of these areas have the potential to seriously intrude upon traditional union-reserved activities, and may become especially disruptive in a district which has a history of adversarial relations.

The professional development vehicles of peer coaching and staff development were presented as having the potential for adding positive dimensions to SBM, as were some national union models for restructuring. The SBM-impacted changes in accountability structures, traditionally autocratic and top-down, were discussed, particularly the changes impacting board, superintendent, principals, teachers, and other employees. The new-player status of SBM, with its jurisdictional overlap of areas traditionally reserved (and, usually, clearly spelled out) for management and union negotiation, will create another dimension in that arena and will cause a realignment of their traditional decision making authority divisions.

EXERCISES

1. Reflect upon your recall (or the chapter's description) of the general patterns of collective negotiations in public schools during the preceding decades. How have they impacted the current climate of labor management relations in education?

2. What would be a workable Quality of Work Life structure in your district? Analyze the feasibility of implementation of the described ECDC model in your own setting.

3. Consider the state of management and employment relations in your district; are they win/win or adversarial in nature, and why?

4. If SBM were to be implemented in your district, which existing union/employee organization structures would be affected? What would be the outcome, and how could such implementation be facilitated?

REFERENCES

Bacharach, S.B., Shedd, J.B., & Conley, S.C. (1989). School management and teacher unions: The capacity for cooperation in an age of reform. *Teachers College Record, 91* (1), 97–105.

Cohen, M. (1990). Key issues confronting state policymakers. In R.F. Elmore and Associates, *Restructuring schools—the next generation of educational reform* (pp. 268–270), San Francisco: Jossey-Bass Publishers.

Conley, S.C. and Bacharach, S.B. (1990). From school-site management to participatory school-site management. *Phi Delta Kappan, 71*(7), 539–545.

Conley, S.C., Schmidle, T., & Shedd, J.B. (1988). Teacher participation in the management of school systems. *Teachers College Record, 90,* (2), 259–280.

David, J. (1990). Restructuring in progress: lessons from pioneering districts. In R.F. Elmore and Associates, *Restructuring schools—the next generation of educational reform* (pp. 237–240), San Francisco: Jossey-Bass Publishers.

Eberts, R.W. & Stone, J.A. (1984). *Unions and public schools.* Lexington, MA: D.C. Heath and Company.

Heller, R.W. & Pautler, A.J. (1991). The administrator of the future: combining instructional and managerial leadership. In S.L. Jacobson & J.A. Conway (Eds.), *Educational leadership in an age of reform* (pp. 140–141). New York: Longman.

Herman, J.J. & J.L. (1991). *The positive development of human resources and school district organizations.* Lancaster, PA: Technomic Publishing Company, pp. 153–162, 205–208.

Herman, J.J. & Megiveron, G.E. (in press). *Win-win, win-lose, and lose-lose collective bargaining.* Lancaster, PA: Technomic Publishing Company.

Herman, J.J. (1982). Improving employee relations with QWL. *Michigan School Board Journal, 29* (7), 10–13.

Herman, J.J. (1984). The quality of work life: Has it come of age? *Journal of NYSBA.* (August), 19–21.

Herman, J.J. (1985). With collaborative bargaining you work with the union—not against it. *The American School Board Journal, 172* (10), 41–42, 47.

Herman, J.J. (1987). Employee involvement through quality of work life programs: the key to satisfaction and productivity. *The Kentucky School Board Journal, 6* (3), 18–21.

Herman, J.J. (1991). The two faces of collective bargaining. *School Business Affairs, 57* (2), 10–13.

Hess, G.A., Jr. (1991). *School restructuring, Chicago style.* Newbury Park, CA: Corwin Press, Inc., pp. 70–71.

Jacobson, S.L. (1990). Reflections on the third wave of reform: Rethinking administrator preparation. In S.L. Jacobson & J.A. Conway (Eds.), *Educational leadership in an age of reform* (pp. 30–42). New York: Longman.

Keith, S. and R.H. Girling. 1991. *Education, management, and participation-new directions in educational administration.* Boston, MA: Allyn and Bacon, pp. 46, 308–311.

Kennedy, J.D. (1984). When collective bargaining first came to education: A superintendent's viewpoint. *Government Union Review, 5* (1), 14–26.

Kreptovics, J., Farber, K., & Armaline, W. (1991). Reform from the bottom up: Empowering teachers to transform schools. *Phi Delta Kappan, 73,*(4), 295–299.

Levine, D.U. (1991). Creating effective schools: findings and implications from research and practice. *Phi Delta Kappan, 72* (5), 389–393.

Levine, D.U. & Eubanks, E.E. (1992). Site-based management: Engine for reform or pipedream? problems, prospects, pitfalls, and prerequisites for success. In J.J. Lane & E.G. Epps (Eds.) *Restructuring the schools: problems and prospects* (p. 66). Berkeley, CA: McCutchan Publishing Corporation.

Lewis, A. (1989). *Restructuring America's schools.* Washington, D.C.: American Association of School Administrators, pp. 78–90.

Lifton, F.B. (1992). The legal tangle of shared governance. *The School Administrator, 1* (49), 16–19.

McClure, R.M. (1991). Individual growth and institutional renewal. In A. Lieberman & L. Miller, L. (Eds.) *Staff development for education in the '90s* (2nd ed.) (pp. 234–237). New York: Teachers College Press.

McDonnell, L. & Pascal, A. (1988). *Teacher unions and educational reform.* Rutgers, NJ: RAND Corporation, with the Center for Policy Research in Education.

Murphy, M. 1990. *Blackboard unions—The AFT & the NEA 1900-1980.* Ithaca, NY: Cornell University Press.

Nyland, L. (1987). Win-win bargaining pays off. *Education Digest. LIII* (1), 28–29.

Steinberger, E. (1990). Teacher unions handling tricky turns on the road to reform. *The School Administrator, 8* (47), 26–31.

Toch, T. (1991). Public schools of choice. *American School Board Journal, 178* (7), 18–21.

Chapter 5

SCHOOL-BASED MANAGEMENT AND THE PRINCIPAL: AUTHORITY, ACCOUNTABILITY, AND AUTONOMY

Effective school leaders do two things: they incorporate a problem-solving approach in their work with others, and they use group dynamics skills in their encouragement of school-based management teams (Aronstein and DeBenedictis, 1991). The authors are convinced that the school leader's level of skillfulness in applying those skills is the critical factor for success.

There is a constant theme, both in the early and continuing body of literature on school-based management, about the centrality and key player role of the school principal. William E. Brock, a former U.S. Senator and current member of President Bush's Advisory Committee on Education, spoke of the significance of school-based management in a *NASSP Bulletin* interview (Koerner, 1991b). He feels that it is the overriding factor, in consequence and importance, to be done in principal preparation for the twenty-first century. "A fundamental rule of management is never to separate accountability from responsibility and authority. Well, we have done that. We have give principals and teachers the responsibility, but not the authority, and that's just simply lousy management" (p. 55). Brock speaks further of the need to restore authority to the principal, and to constitute the principal's management team—of teachers—within the school, not from the central office. Responsibility, authority, and accountability can be combined if principals, teachers, and parents have the resources to run their schools; and, in so doing, will "unleash American education at its best" (p. 55).

Consideration is given in this chapter to the impact of school-based management on various dimensions of the school principalship: role and function, the relationship with teachers and other professionals and with community, strategies for successful implementation, and implications for training.

FOCUS ON THE PRINCIPAL'S ROLE

In an earlier broad study of school-based management, Clune and White (1988) examined the changes in the role of the principal, emphasizing the centrality of that figure and its extension in three directions — closeness to the educational process, closeness to the staff as mediator of shared governance, and an elevation in the district chain of command, more empowered and charged with extended responsibility and accountability. Principals are also held accountable for achieving school objectives as outlined in a school-site plan, and are the fosterers of emerging relationships in shared governance. The extension and expansion of the principal's authority into budgetary, curricular, and personnel areas is coupled with the requirement for shared decision making in those areas.

In focusing on the restructuring of schools, Lieberman and Miller in 1990 reflected upon both those procedural elements which worked, and those principles which mattered. The role of the principal in a school-based management context will be transformed when school schedules, staff meetings, budgeting, decision making opportunities, and structures for work begin to change. The emerging administrative profile is one of leader of leaders, or a cultural leader who achieves ends through empowerment and personal persuasion. They cite Clark and Meloy (1990) as identifying an array of values — including democracy, group authority and accountability, variability, generality, interactivity, individual and collective self-discipline and control, and group commitment and consensus — as the emerging underpinnings of school leadership. Lieberman and Miller investigated the questions raised by values through studying a group of principals engaged in restructuring their schools. Despite differing contexts, the principals had in common a sense of the importance of: the management function — the overseeing of operational details, the troubleshooting service, the need to listen and counsel, the importance and strategies needed for successful change, and the upholding of a collaborative culture. They were commonly engaged in the initiation of change and in the opening of discussion to a broad range of participants, even though that initial quest for common vision and consensus was conflictive and difficult. In a similar interview, Koerner (1991a) asked several nationally-honored principals to share their thoughts on the meaning of restructuring. They perceived a pending role change, seeing restructuring as a shift in control from the centralized power structure to the people most affected by the school, and felt, while principals still must be decision makers and organizers, they must also be bridge builders among local groups. Principals must involve parents and teachers in decisions that affect the student.

Developing Leaders for Restructuring Schools (1991) is a report and prescription which examined school restructuring and its implications. It spoke of the need to reinvent leadership—the role of the principal must change, it says, to that of coach and facilitator, not manager of buildings and of status quo. A restructured school calls for a leader at the nexus of a variety of impacting factors; one who must "forge connections and create interdependencies" (p. 28), and, by empowering others, fix in them a sense of direction and the responsibility for its achievement. In the language of SBM, it is noted that "the daily tasks of leadership and decision making must be informed by a deep commitment to collaborative action and shared decision making" (p. 33). Taylor (1991) spoke of the transitions required in SBM implementation, noting that his role as principal had changed from "steering committee facilitator to governance committee member with a shared voice, rather than the key leadership role" (p. 24).

In 1992 the National Association of Secondary School Principals' Commission on Restructuring offered a comprehensive redefinition of the principal role. Elements and specific implementation strategies of restructuring were developed by the Commission in an outline for initiatives. One of the elements was Collaborative Leadership and Management; specific SBM-related strategies include:

- Administrators and staff work together to provide leadership. (Teaming; delegating; shared decision making)
- Good group dynamics and modern management techniques are employed by the leadership team. (Shared decision making; conflict resolution; listening skills, etc.
- An effective communication process is used to promote the school's objectives. (School-site management; group process networking) (p. 11).

The Commission also recommends that restructuring school districts should "devolve authority to schools and to teachers" (p. 14) by giving schools authority over staffing and materials budgets, and by providing incentives for principals to involve teachers in site decisions. The new role of administrator as facilitator of teachers was emphasized, as was the provision of support and assistance through the release of time for school decision making.

PRINCIPAL RELATIONSHIPS IN SCHOOL-BASED MANAGEMENT

The concept of teacher empowerment drives much of the literature about principals and school-based management. There has been consideration in the literature of the interactions and perceptions of both SBM players in the teacher-principal relationship. In 1987, *Leaders for America's Schools* recommended that collegiality be fostered; that teachers and administrators share in planning, implementation, evaluation, and in learning together. In 1988 Stimson and Applebaum applied classic power theory to the SBM/empowerment teacher-principal relationship. They investigated positional power (drawn from position in the organizational structure) and personal power (drawn from the individual's characteristics) of principals as perceived by the principals themselves and by their staff. The implications supported the proper exercise of personal power to serve teacher satisfaction and the need for "power sharing" (p. 314), which encourages people at all levels of the organization to be involved in decision making, without feeling manipulated. Teachers are best influenced by involving them in decision making; employing personal power and using power as a shared resource resulted in both a sense of teacher ownership and an enhancement of teacher self-esteem. Lieberman (1988) noted that principals respond to teacher leaders in a variety of ways; in the best of situations, they acknowledge the value of peer-assistance and expertise, and recognize the depth of staff collegiality that occurs with shared knowledge. The worst scenario occurs when a loss of personal control is feared, and when a staff avoidance syndrome is the outcome, particularly on matters concerning curriculum and instruction.

In 1989 Clemons focused on the role of the assistant principal in SBM and on the likelihood that the effectiveness of assistant principals will be raised as a result of implementation. The increase in principal responsibility as a result of SBM will cause, Clemon feels, a displacement of many nontraditional functions, which will accrue to the role of the assistant principal. Serving as a member and principal liaison with school council decision-making subcommittees is one example. NASSP's Council on Assistant Principalship (1991) likewise emphasizes this role change, redefining the dimensions of the job to include participation on the school administrative decision-making team or site-based management council. A proactive stance as an instructional leader, especially in terms of curricular and budgetary involvement, is desirable for these professionals, especially in view of their likelihood for promotion to principal positions.

In 1990 Sergiovanni reflected on school improvement as achieved through leadership, and examined the effects of teacher empowerment on principals. If the school leader has a "principal teacher" mentality, and sees the job as simply possessing broader responsibilities than other teachers, then "having better trained and more involved and responsible colleagues to supervise enhances importance and prestige" (p. 109)—a collegial model found in other professions, such as law and medicine. However, if the principal is both viewed and self-perceived as a boss/manager with distinctly differentiated duties, the notions of teacher leadership and empowerment will challenge that sense of authority. Sergiovanni compares the former model as one closer to that of the executive, who is concerned with "broad administration of affairs, ensuring fidelity to agreed-upon values and goals, building commitment, and motivating others. Managers are concerned with directing people and monitoring people and events" (p. 110). In 1990 Lieberman and Miller also addressed the perception issue, pointing out that "the authentic inclusion of teachers in schoolwide decision making depends as much on principals' attitudes and beliefs as on their possession of certain process skills" (p. 762). As middle-level managers shaped by a history of bureaucratic structures, principals may experience difficulties in organizing and engaging their faculties in collegial relationships—they will move through developmental stages of relinquishing traditional views. In schools with strong cultures of collaboration, "teachers and administrators frequently observe each other teaching and provide each other with useful evaluations.... Teachers and administrators plan, design, research, evaluate, and prepare teaching materials together.... Teachers and administrators teach each other the practice of teaching" (p. 762).

Nardini and Antes (1991) considered principals' perceptions of teacher attitudes towards reform initiatives. They report that principals believed that teachers reacted quite positively to more school autonomy, and that, on the whole, they believe that teachers are most positive about reforms that "chip away at a top-down management model" (p. 19). Teachers strongly supported as reforms more teacher decision making, and more autonomy at the school level. All of the highly teacher-rated reforms had to do with changing the way the system works, especially in terms of decentralizing school decision making. Taylor and Levine (1991) also addressed the principal-teacher relationship, decrying the zero-sum game power theory, and commenting that simply empowering teachers is insufficient for school improvement. "Schools must develop 'balanced' authority relationships, through which leadership and support from the central office and the principal help execute decisions reached through the empowerment of teachers, while teachers' initiatives simultaneously enhance administrators' efforts to attain educational goals" (p. 396). The increased demands of time for collaboration and the sophisticated demands of current curricular and instructional theory application may be inherent barriers to teacher cooperation; it is critical, therefore, that the principal address these "hardships" of change in facilitating the process of teacher decision making.

Lucas, Brown, and Markus (1991) examined principals' perceptions about SBM and teacher empowerment by hypothesizing that school leaders may not be ready to share authority if it is perceived as related to job success and security. They discovered that principals may not wish to empower teachers in certain areas; the willingness to share authority was influenced by the amount of perceived administrator authority in a particular area. There was more willingness, for example, to share control of curriculum than of budgetary or staffing decisions. They concluded that the degree to which principals are willing to share decision-making rights with teachers is directly proportional to the perception of their own discretion and decision making. Further principal/teacher perspectives on restructuring and shared decision making were provided in 1992 by Stein and King. They point out that the focus in school reform and restructuring should be school effectiveness, not the distribution of power. The principals who relinquish budgetary and hiring prerogatives gain, in return, the time to be instructional leaders, thinkers, enablers, and facilitators. Poplin, in 1992, considered the new role of the school leader as one of looking toward the growth of teachers; in the same journal issue, Leithwood addressed transformational leadership as addressing three fundamental goals, one of which was helping staff members develop and maintain a collaborative, professional school culture. They described principals as assisting teachers in building and maintaining collaborative professional cultures, involving staff members in collaborative goal setting, and reducing teachers' isolation by creating joint planning time. New staff selection was characterized by choices which supported existing mission and priorities. These leaders shared power and responsibility with others through delegation of power to school improvement teams.

PRINCIPAL SBM STRATEGIES FOR SHARING LEADERSHIP

Barth in 1988 spoke of a shared leadership model he had exercised as a practitioner, and which may be a style currently practiced as a perceived version of school-based management; collegial decision making and delegation were the norm, as long as curricular, achievement, and student stability remained basically unaltered. The process of SBM implementation and teacher empowerment could begin with his description of shared leadership in a community of leaders. As an initial step towards shared leadership, Barth recommends that principals *articulate their vision* for their school to their staff and community; a risky endeavor, given the exposure of convictions and clarity of thought implied in the venture. *Relinquishing responsibility,* the second step, seems equally risky, given the concern for principal accountability and a potential sense of loss of control. *Entrusting,* a third step, involves that relinquishment of authority to teachers with no subsequent reclamation of it, regardless of consequences. The *involving of teachers in decision making* must afford real opportunities for staff members to address genuine problems, not simply provide maintenance for a principal-designed solution. The *wise assignment of responsibilities* involves, not the more common reliance on exceptionally capable teachers, but the careful matching of problems to the interests and particular motivations of many individuals. Such a widespread model of shared problem solving can include far more teachers than a small cadre of trusted staff members, and can provide the process for exposing more teachers to challenging situations—an intersection of staff development and leadership. *Sharing responsibility for failure* provides for an outcome of communal experience, collegiality, and higher morale; "as much can be gained from stumbling together as from succeeding" (p. 641). *Attributing success to the teacher* for leadership accomplishments provides the recognition and accolade so rarely experienced by teachers; good principals are as often hero-makers as heroes. *Believing in teachers* is a parallel step to the Effective Schools' high expectations concept; leadership tendencies of teachers are more likely to emerge in such a climate. *Admitting ignorance* can be a principal technique to broaden school leadership through the issuing of invitations to teachers to problem solve, without the discouraging accompaniment of a principal's competitive or know-all attitude. It creates a sense of community and mutual commitment, rather than task assignment.

This model of shared decision making has been demonstrated by several high schools in New Hampshire and Massachusetts, with a governance structure much like that of the New England town meeting. Teachers and students work with school administrators on policy development; the principal has one vote and a veto option, which can be overridden by a two-thirds majority vote. Likewise, the example of isolated Alaskan schools, staffed by three or four collegial and cooperative adults, and the example of parochial and Quaker private schools' culture of participatory leadership provide models where teachers play an active role in decision making.

In 1989 Karant considered the principal role-impacted and related issue of teacher supervision as practiced in the new environment of empowerment, suggesting that research highlighted in her case study of mentor/principal models. She feels that supervision can be dynamic in empowered situations (instead of mutually exclusive) if administrators are philosophically committed to the concept, and if sufficient implementation time is provided. Cherry (1991) also described the necessity for the principal to develop a foundation of ownership; and stressed that the attitude of the principal in this undertaking was critical. School ownership (and, by inference, shared decision making) is built one teacher at a time. The need for principal support for teacher growth, ownership, and empowerment was considered by White-Hood in 1991 in examining principals who fully "exist" in their school, and create a commitment to change through a "way of being" (p. 19). She identified major themes of shared leadership, and recommended them as principal strategies. Leaders aspiring to change their style to one of sharing should:

- Familiarize themselves with literature and familiarize themselves with the challenges and opportunities of SBM
- Reflect upon the instructional leader role and on visioning for excellence, and continue to revise both role and vision
- Determine strategies for involving others and communicate with stakeholders and key leaders—staff members, parents, and students
- Invite stakeholders to a personal educational platform
- Be authentic and caring, sharing self and vision, and build a spirit of collaboration and trust

A similar list of behaviors and strategies was suggested by Collins and Fisher in 1991, in viewing those considerations for site administrators prior to SBM implementation and those considerations which deal with the school's adaptation of such implementation. They suggest that, initially, the school leader and planning team members become knowledgeable regarding SBM, include co-administrators in the process, identify student achievement as the primary goal, assist the development of district policy concerning SBM, put to rest the question of principal accountability (pointing out that collaborated decisions are less frequently challenged), and play a role in the developmental process of providing district training for school-based management. Once such a structure is established, each school and community must:

1. Identify the level of readiness for SBM
2. Involve parents and classified staff members
3. Ensure that all school community members are aware of and understand the management processes and roles.
4. Address the issue of governance; (the possibility of a principal veto, and the notion of council voting vs. consensus)
5. Ensuring the role of other school administrators
6. Clarifying the language of the SBM proposal, especially with regard to legal terms and interpretations
7. Define the mission and vision for the school and the SBM proposal
8. Guide the development of measurable objectives for the SBM proposal
9. Keep the proposal writing positive
10. Ensure that the timelines and workloads of administrators are understood
11. Combine SBM implementation timelines with existing timelines of other elements
12. Understand the variety of decision making interests within a school and community

Dufour and Eaker (1991) presented some specific areas of teacher empowerment that principals should consider: developing the curriculum, assessing student achievement, selecting instructional materials, and planning and presenting staff development programs, determining instructional styles and strategies, scheduling, hiring new staff, and mentoring. They likewise recommend the formation of small units or teams within the larger organization as one of the most effective spurs to innovation and ownership. Crafting these small coalitions and the building of teams can heighten the teacher's sense of joint involvement, contribution to decisions, responsibility, and power. They offered a variety of examples of team grouping structure: by grade or subject level, by similar teaching assignment, interdepartmentally, or in school-wide task forces. Administrators must insure that small groups have a significant focus or mission; surveys of teachers have consistently revealed that they while they wish to be included in decisions regarding substantive issues, they do not wish to be involved in every decision. Administrators must likewise insure that groups have the authority, as well as the responsibility, to provide solutions. Dufour and Eaker conclude by recommending that principals embark upon such change with more than staff acquiescence as commitment—that they (in the spirit of Peters' and Waterman's successful business practice findings) identify and empower champions—advocates from the teacher ranks who embrace the notion of shared decision making and of school-based management, and who are encouraged and nurtured as key partners in the process of bringing about change.

A more specific view of school-based management and shared leadership responsibility was provided in 1991 by Hallinger, who considered the formation of instructional teams in secondary schools. Given the notion that high school principals exercise instructional leadership by delegating responsibilities and by working closely with teams of administrators, supervisors, and teachers, he makes a case for decentralizing this leadership through the systematic use of teams to coordinate and monitor curriculum and instruction. The structure and complexity of the secondary school demand that the principal assume direct responsibility for selected (presumably, those with the most impact) leadership functions, and must therefore delegate partial or full responsibility for other such functions, thus diffusing the leadership role and creating a "leader of leaders" structure. In effect, shared decision making and decentralization are the logical structural responses to the constraining characteristics of the large, complex, political organization that is the contemporary high school. Principals can allocate task responsibilities to assistant principals, department chairs, supervisors, and teachers according to the various leadership functions. Teams can be organized in different configurations according to school need, with the skills' needs and talents—the shared decision making readiness level—of staff members in mind. A small high school may choose to function through one team composed of department heads and principal; a large school may utilize a central team with delegated subunit responsibility. Instructional leadership responsibilities can be allocated in different ways; the entirety of a leadership function, such as goal communication or instructional supervision, may be retained by the principal or may be dispersed across several leadership teams.

IMPLICATIONS FOR TRAINING

Successful implementation of school-based management, existing in a new leadership environment, will definitely demand a particular principal preparation program, one focused on context and process, rather than content. Thomson (1991) feels that this means that the principal will need to enhance the educational program with every possible resource, and that the integration of these enhancements will require skills that principals frequently do not acquire in traditional programs. Stover (1989) reported that some reluctance and sense of peril is frequently expressed when school based management is contemplated or proposed. Concerns about encroachment upon prerogatives and sensitivity to accountability issues are common, particularly in more experienced school leaders. Careers spent under traditional, authoritarian systems are not the optimum preparation for SBM's autonomy and collaborative planning. Adequate training, sensitivity to the changes demanded, and direct addressment of such issues as relationships with teacher organizations and central office personnel should accompany principal orientation and immersion in the SBM process.

Principals today must combine the skills of the specialist with the perspective of the generalist, working with diverse groups to integrate ideas aimed at solving a continuous stream of problems. This demands preparing school leaders to formulate goals collectively, to set and maintain direction with groups, and to jointly develop organizational procedures. Thomson notes, "All of this works best when leaders nurture in their constituencies a capacity to engage in this leadership task. Since autocracy undermines this initiative, building this capacity requires leaders who consult and listen and who respect and develop the human potentiality" (p. 298). A similar concern was expressed by Powell (1991); principals may attempt to retain significant leadership responsibilities, or may exercise veto power to reverse team decisions. "True shared leadership will not result until almost everything can be discussed and decided by the team" (p. 13).

The partnerships demanded by collaborative planning, particularly through school councils, will require a specific training and preparation of school leaders. Cherry (1991) and Brown (1991) referred to the need to cultivate staff leadership, and acknowledged that professional development activities must address that need. Murphy (1991) considered the specific area of parental involvement, noting that dealing with a variety of community and stakeholder constituencies represented on councils will require more political astuteness on the part of the principal, particularly as they manage situations on councils. Establishing social networks within their communities and displaying a knowledge of organizational development and planning are further examples of council-related principal skills. As school council decision-making purview expands into detailed areas of budget development and resource assignment, there will be demands placed on the principal to provide information, relate strategies to productivity, and to facilitate accountability design. The provision of appropriate supervision and instructional leadership under collaborative school management will require principal depth of knowledge in curriculum and learning theory, since the design and delivery of effective instructional programs will also be a concern of the council.

Decision-making school councils will expect, in essence, a leader who is skilled at the executive tasks of precisely assessing a complex situation, identifying potential action strategies, and, possibly, leading a group to problem resolution consensus.

SUMMARY

The chapter has focused on school-based management as it blurs the lines between dimensions and domains of principalship and teachers and other professionals, as they begin to work together as colleagues for the best interests of students. The impact of school-based management on various facets of the school principalship was considered.

Principal role and function were investigated; with emphasis on the profound change SBM would demand of traditional school leaders. There is a consistent theme in SBM literature which describes the building leader as the key player in the decentralization and restructuring process; the convergence point of all the other SBM players and the locus, quite frequently, of the SBM initiation itself. Personal power and empowerment were persistent terms throughout the section; principals in a restructured environment use these skills as they facilitate shared decision making through consensus building and through sheer expertise in communications and coalition-building. The more managerial and traditional dimensions of the role must be maintained or delegated as the leader becomes the facilitator of teachers in a redefined leadership role.

Principal relationships with other professionals in a school-based management environment most commonly focus on the administrator-teacher connection. It is a linkage strongly impacted by the perceptions and attitudes of the school leader, faced with relinquishing long-standing authority and responsibility. Teacher empowerment is the pivotal issue, with consideration given to the developmental stages which must accompany involving teachers in decision making and which must reflect the receptivity and comfort level of the principal. The view of the school leader as a teacher of teachers rather than a manager of process is recommended. Principals in SBM cooperatively interact with colleagues as they assist teachers in building and maintaining collaborative professional cultures and involve staff members in collaborative goal setting.

Principal strategies to successfully implement school-based management consistently include the setting of vision, mission, and the provision of comprehensive planning. Leaders must cultivate school ownership among a variety of constituencies, and must plan to deal with a range of readiness for shared decision making, particularly among staff members. Accommodations must be made for the transitions demanded by SBM, and for the clarification of governance and decision-making accountability. Different configurations of groups or teams, reflective of the needs of each individual school, were suggested as possible SBM substructures.

The implications for training in SBM are reflective of the role changes described; a new leadership environment demands a differentiated principal preparation and retraining program. The need for skills in goal setting, strategic and operational planning, and group process demonstrate the need for principals who are generalists rather than specialists, and whose depth of knowledge of curricular, instructional, and managerial theory and practice must exceed that of traditional school leaders.

EXERCISES

1. What changes in the role of the principal in a school-based management setting do you feel will be most difficult to achieve? Which would be most critical in successful SBM implementation in your district?

2. Assess the present readiness level of your school's teaching staff for assuming decision making responsibility in the three areas of budget, personnel hiring, and curriculum/instruction. What transitions might need to be provided for teacher subcommittees charged with authority in these areas?

3. Which SBM implementation strategies do you think would be

necessary for successful implementation in your district? What would be the most achievable changes in governance and accountability?

4. Assess your own communications and group process skills. What strengths do you possess, and, as a principal implementing SBM, what training needs would you have?

REFERENCES

Allen, L. & Glickman, C. (1992). School improvement: The elusive faces of shared governance. *NASSP Bulletin, 76* (542), 80–87.

Aronstein, L.W. & DeBenedictis, K.L. (1991). An interactive workshop: Encouraging school-based management. *NASSP Bulletin, 73* (537), 67–72.

Barth, R. (1988). Principals, teachers, and school leadership. *Phi Delta Kappan, 69* (9), 639–642.

Brown, R.E. (1991). Restructuring educational leadership programs. *NASSP Bulletin, 73* (537), 40–45.

Cherry, M. (1991). School ownership—the essential foundation of restructuring. *NASSP Bulletin, 73* (537), 33–39.

Clark, D.L. & Meloy, J.M. (1990). Recanting bureaucracy: a democratic structure for leadership in schools. In A. Lieberman (Ed.), *Collaborative cultures: creating the future now,* (pp. 3–23), Philadelphia, PA: Falmer Press.

Clemons, M.J. (1989). The assistant principal's responsibility in school-based management systems. *NASSP Bulletin, 73* (518), 33–36.

Clune, W.H. and White, P.A. (1988). *School-based management—institutional variation, implementation, and issues for further research.* Center for Policy Research in Education, pp. 19–20.

Collins, R. & Fisher, N. (1991). School-based management: practical strategies for administrators. *School-based management: Theory and practice.* Reston, VA: National Association of Secondary School Principals, pp. 8–13.

Conley, S.C. & Bacharach, S.B. (1990). From school-site management to participatory school-site management. *Phi Delta Kappan, 71* (7), 539–545.

DuFour, R. & Eaker, R. (1991). The principal as leader: Promoting values, empowering teachers. *School-Based Management: Theory and Practice.* Reston, VA: National Association of Secondary School Principals, pp. 47–52.

Hallinger, P. (1991). Instructional leadership teams in secondary schools: Developing a framework. *School-based management: Theory and practice.* Reston, VA: National Association of Secondary School Principals, pp. 41–46.

Karant, V.I. (1989). Supervision in the age of teacher empowerment. *Educational Leadership, 46* (8), 27–29.

Koerner, T. (1991a). Restructuring, reform, and the national goals: What do principals think?. NASSP Bulletin, *75* (533), 39–49.

Koerner, T. (1991b). Principals—what they can do to prepare for the 21st Century. *NASSP Bulletin, 75* (534), 49–66.

Leithwood, K.A. (1992) The move towards transformational leadership. *Educational Leadership, 49* (5), 8–11.

Lieberman, A. (1988). Teachers and principals: Turf, tension, and new tasks. *Phi Delta Kappan, 69* (9), 648–653.

Lieberman, A. & Miller, L. (1990). Restructuring schools: What matters and what works. *Phi Delta Kappan, 71* (10), 759–764.

Lucas, S., Brown, G.C., & Markus, F.W. (1991). Principal's perceptions of site-based management and teacher empowerment. *NASSP Bulletin, 73* (537), 56–62.

Murphy, P.J. (1991). Collaborative school management: Implications for school leaders. *NASSP Bulletin, 73* (537), 63–66.

Nardini, M.L. & Antes, R.L. (1991). The right reforms. *American School Board Journal, 187* (6), 17–18.

NASSP. (1990). *Restructuring the role of the assistant principal.* NASSP Council on the Assistant Principalship. Reston, VA: National Association of Secondary School Principals.

NASSP. (1992). *A leader's guide to school restructuring: A special report of the NASSP commission on restructuring.* Reston, VA: National Association of Secondary School Principals. pp. 7–14.

National Commission on Excellence in Educational Administration (1987). *Leaders for America's schools.* The University Council for Educational Administration, pp. 1–12.

National LEADership Network Study Group on Restructuring Schools (1991). *Developing leaders for restructuring schools.* Washington, D.C.: U.S. Department of Education, Office of Educational Research and Improvement, pp. 25–28, 33.

Poplin, M.S. (1992). The leader's new role: Looking to the growth of teachers. *Educational Leadership,* 49(5), 10–11.

Powell, N. (1991). School-based management in smaller secondary schools. *NASSP Bulletin, 73* (533), 11–15.

Sergiovanni, T. (1990). *Value-added leadership: How to get extraordinary performance in schools.* San Diego, CA: Harcourt Brace Jovanovich, pp. 109–110.

Stimson, T.D. & Applebaum, R.P. (1988). Empowering teachers: do principals have the power? *Phi Delta Kappan, 70* (4), 313–316.

Stover, Del. (1989). But some principals feel threatened. *The Executive Educator, 11* (1), 17.

Taylor, B.O. & Levine, D.U. (1991). Effective schools projects and school-based management. *Phi Delta Kappan, 72* (5), 394–397.

Taylor, E.E.II. (1991). Implementing school-based governance. *Schools in the Middle: Theory into Practice, 1* (2), 23–25.

Thomson, S.D. (1991). Principals for America 2000. *Journal of School Leadership, 1* (4), 294–303.

White-Hood, M. (1991). Meeting the need of students: Stories of shared leadership. *NASSP Bulletin, 73* (537), 19–22.

Chapter 6

SCHOOL-BASED MANAGEMENT AND THE CENTRAL OFFICE: FLATTENING THE PYRAMID

The issue of alteration of governance is at the heart of school-based management, and, as a restructuring measure, is the most fundamental and far-reaching reform measure of all. It represents a reversal of a more than a hundred years' of educational practice. Raywid in 1990 added a historical note to this governance issue:

> For almost a century, a steady trend has shifted educational control farther and farther from the classroom, its final point of application. With the adoption by schools of large-scale bureaucratic organizational practices came the rationale for controlling the teacher's work and, to the extent possible, for placing the most important decisions for the classroom in the hands of administrators.... That same organizational structure also served as a steady drain on the prerogatives of building administrators such as principals, as central administrators in district offices exercised more and more control (p. 182).

As the century ends, there has been mounting pressure, David (1991) commented, on school districts to restructure; the systemic change need is evident, being supported by research findings on how people and organizations change, and by the increasing gap between today's schools and the ones needed for the future. There have been few examples of successful school district decentralization; these districts, are, indeed, constrained to some degree by federal and state mandates. The pioneer districts described in Chapter 1 frequently were required to implement their school-based management models through waivers and exemptions as pilot projects. By and large, in most districts, the centralized pattern prevails. Policies on curricula and testing, the school calendar, hiring, purchasing, staff assignments, and building maintenance are controlled centrally, and teachers report knowing and caring little about how such decisions are made (Johnson, 1990). Many of the constraints on individual schools, are district/central-office created, and, in most of the literature on school-based management and restructuring, those constraints and the role of that central administration are the target of SBM change, whether named directly or readily inferred from the description of the proposed change. Sheingold (1991) reported that the central idea underlying many restructuring efforts dictates a very different relationship between the schools and the central office; many decisions must be pushed downward, and the central office can then play a supportive role. David's (1991) view of restructuring is similar; she recommends that educationally important decisions within broad goals must shift to the school site, and that district and state administrators must change their role correspondingly: from rule making and monitoring to providing resources and helping school faculties develop stimulating learning environments.

This chapter considers the role, function, and organizational pattern of the school district's central office, as a different relationship is being worked out with the schools. The inherent problems and solutions to central power dispersal and the transitions demanded by it are reviewed, and some large district models are presented (Stevenson & Pellicer, 1992). Implications and recommendations for SBM implementation focus on three key central office functions.

NEW ROLES AND ORGANIZATIONAL PATTERNS OF CENTRAL OFFICE PERSONNEL

A general view of empowering schools was provided by AASA (1990); a publication on educator and community empowerment listed suggestions for central office administrators to play key leadership roles in school-based, newly empowered structures; to serve as valuable sources of information as respected, experienced, and talented professionals:

- Involve staff in developing a vision for your schools.
- Recognize that all school staff members are professionals who are dedicated to helping students learn.
- Support innovation and risk-taking. Show you understand that improvement takes time.
- Ask principals and teachers for their suggestions on how to improve the schools.
- Hold high expectations — and fight for the resources required to meet those expectations. It may be as simple as getting a copy machine repaired ... or as complex as changing a state regulation. See it as your job to remove obstacles to school improvement.

- Listen. Regularly set up informal meetings to hear "how the system really works."
- Focus public attention on the accomplishments of students, teachers, and other school staff.
- Be visible. Visit schools and classrooms to see successes—and challenges—firsthand.
- Establish school-based management systems that allow individual schools a strong voice in budget, personnel, and other decisions that bear on education.
- Share the spotlight. Give credit to staff when good things happen. Let the community know the pride they should take in the high-quality staff of their schools.
- Remove roadblocks to getting needed supplies, ranging from paper to computers, and ensure responsiveness to maintenance concerns.
- Promote professional development for *all* staff" (p. 13–14).

A like viewpoint is that of a Rochester, New York central office administrator, reflecting upon the role changes demanded by that district's restructuring and decentralization. In forging new relationships with the schools, (Delehant 1990), the district's staff development director, observed that all resources which impact student performance were being directed to the schools, and that central office staff were being asked to review services and methods of delivery to ensure that they were compatible with and supported the schools' new SBM roles. Central office personnel now alternate and balance between being responders (facilitators) and initiators (directors) of services. There may be overlapping lines of authority in the early stages of SBM, as new structures and lines of responsibility are worked out; it is advisable to develop a tolerance for ambiguity. The most exciting aspect of the new environment, Delehant concludes, is that the central office administrator can anticipate becoming a creative problem solver, coalition builder, and entrepreneur.

Chapter 1 described pioneer districts implementing SBM, aided through the use of waivers that allow a school to overcome restrictions imposed by federal, state, and local regulations and policies. Taylor and Levine (1991) report that 14 of the schools in the Dade County SBM project have received such waivers, noting that central-level technical assistance and other resources may be then provided to these schools in support of school improvement designs.

Hirsh and Sparks (1991) quoted a superintendent whose message regarding the nature of his job and that of his staff was to assist in the attainment of long range goals: "Once we sign off on your mission and objectives.... it's our responsibility to provide you with the resources and support you need to get the job done. If you fail, we also have failed" (p. 16). The authors then spoke of this altered relationships between schools and central office staff as embodying a paradigm shift:

- Central and cabinet level administrators were coming to see change as a constant for continuous improvement.
- Central office departments were shifting from monitoring and regulatory agencies to service centers for schools.
- Day-to-day, central administrators were spending more time as planning facilitators and members of improvement teams (as in Muscogee, Georgia), either at the district or school level. They served as liaisons and brokers of central services (as in Richardson, Texas).

The authors had recommendations for central office staff in implementing a new vision of schooling via shared decision making:

- Do long-range, strategic planning (as described in Chapter 2), both at the district and the departmental level.
- Stay on the cutting edge; be the expert, and therefore, the informational and service source for the schools. Some central administrators are forming study groups to stay research-current and discuss applications to district issues.
- Be customer-driven and proactive; one district offered a monetary incentive to schools to purchase staff development support from a new matrix-designed, school-improvement-driven inservice menu.
- Be a friendly critic; provide your more unbiased and broad-base viewpoint to schools requesting assistance with the research/study process.
- Celebrate success and honor your customers.
- Generate new services to offer customized training needs of schools; the provision of integrated curricula for schools' curriculum innovations is an example.
- Refuse to do some things; requests for inappropriate or nonexistent services must be fielded.
- Develop facilitation skills; Jefferson County, Colorado's central office has a cadre of process consultants to assist schools.
- Help schools give something up; sites need aid in abandoning outdated paperwork/practices and auditing current ones for effectiveness and efficiency.

INHERENT PROBLEMS AND SOLUTIONS TO THE DISPERSAL OF CENTRAL POWER

Early in 1992 *The School Administrator* invited superintendents, a building principal, and teacher union and NEA representatives to describe attempts to solve the problem of defining the relationships—drawing the line—in shared decision making, between the school-based teams and the central office. McWalters (1992) of the Rochester City Schools commented that SBM, at the level of implementation, runs "straight into state statutes, local school board policy, administrative regulations, union contracts, and past practice" (p. 9). He reports that Rochester's aim in attempting to reposition the central office bureaucracy is to support, rather than block, innovation; and, in close judgment calls, to err on the side of school-based decision making. Information on an effective waivers process was shared by Doyle and Tetzloff (1992) regarding the Marshalltown, Iowa district shared decision-making plan. Abandoning a "laundry list" effort of deciding what school-based teams could or could not do, the district team determined that allowing waivers which were related to each school's goals, needs assessments, and collective vision was a more viable and less prescriptive way for schools to ask for relief from district policy, regulation, practice, or specific provision of the master contract. The process and procedure involves a school's documented and justified request for a waiver, which is then considered by the district team in an attempt to resolve the conflict without a waiver being granted. If not, a one-year waiver is granted, with monitoring and assessment done to determine if continuation is recommended. Consideration is given to the consensus status of the request, to ensure that anyone impacted has had input into the request; this concern for the collective aspects of any waiver's impact assures that there is both a building wide and district wide perspective on the process. The formal action necessitated by an approved request is then referred to the appropriate level; the superintendent or central office (for policy and regulation waivers), and the executive board of the union (for master contract waivers) are examples. Doyle and Tetzloff also offer twelve principles, sequentially ordered, for what must take place for effective school-based decision making to take place; several are particularly related to the central office role:

- Agree on the desired level of involvement and participation before beginning.
- Establish ground rules early to include how and by whom decisions will be made.
- Reduce barriers to collaborative decision making through renegotiation of union contracts, waivers from district and other policy, and flexibility in reporting systems.
- Monitor equity and excellence, and provide technical assistance to ensure that community needs are met.

Another school-based management method was shared by Torres (1992), whose Silver City, New Mexico district identified, at both school and district level, those areas participants were willing to share in and those they were willing to share with others. Areas easily negotiated were textbook selection, staff hiring, curriculum development, and distribution of funds within building budgets. Unresolved areas include staffing allocation patterns by building, the question of budgeting by membership or by need, interscholastic athletic programs, and extracurricular activities. To facilitate this process and to address the concern for accountability, a day-long "articulation" staff development activity was held, where representational teams of school personnel (each consisting of professional and classified staff and covering all levels in the district) shared ideas and established priorities in decision making.

TRANSITIONS DEMANDED BY SBM: LARGE DISTRICTS ALTER CENTRAL OFFICE STRUCTURE AND FUNCTION

In 1990 Hanson examined the experience of three of the nation's four largest school systems as they underwent SBM implementation. They vary by source and amount of authority redistribution. He selected four terms to describe the redistribution of authority, and considered the districts in light of those definitions, which refer to the *source* of the redistribution, such as the state legislature or local board, and the *amount* of authority redistributed:

- ***Deconcentration*** involves the transfer of tasks and work load to other units, but there is no real authority redistributed.
- ***Participation*** means that subordinates have more input into the decision-making process, but the decision-making right is retained by the superordinate.
- ***Delegation*** involves the actual transfer of decision making authority to a lower level in the hierarchy; this must, however, be executed within a firm policy framework.
- ***Devolution*** involves the shifting of authority to an autonomous unit which may then act independently; once devolution occurs, the authority is not retrievable.

Dade County in Florida in 1986 created a School-Based Management/ Shared Decision-Making Pilot Program with the cooperation of the teachers' union; the subsequent policy and legal language supporting the program became part of the master contract. While the district reports that school decision-making structures have changed dramatically, there is no genuine power delegated. Administrators have been approving budgetary, hiring, curricular, and other decisions emerging from school councils, but they are not obligated to do so (a model demonstrating *deconcentration* and *participation*); also, the present SBM agreement is contractual in nature and must be renegotiated.

The Los Angeles model, Shared Decision Making/School-Based Management, began after a union contact dispute, and is a two-stage process. Shared decision making began in 1989, with school-based management to follow. Each school council makes policy decisions about staff development, discipline, student activities, and certain budget items, in a *devolution* model. The focus is on policy and planning direction. A higher level central council will serve as the review board for the eventual individual, voluntary school plans and proposals for school-based management.

Hanson, in 1991, described the "Chicago Revolution," which began in December of 1988, when the governor of Illinois signed a bill to transform education. The grass-roots rebellion, massive restructuring came about as a result of public, business community, and parent frustration with an apparently unresponsive bureaucracy and with a school system in disarray. The 123-page Chicago School Reform Act included a set of goals, most significantly dealing with raising student achievement, attendance rates, and graduation rates (Hess, 1991). The most controversial part of the Chicago School Reform Act was the establishment, in a *devolutionary* model, of a local school council for each of the system's 540 schools. In a 1990 article, Hanson detailed the process:

- These 11-member councils (six elected parents, two elected teachers, two elected community representatives, one nonvoting high school student, and the principal) approve the school's budget, develop a School Improvement Plan, help choose texts and curricular materials, and recommend new teacher appointments. The majority of Council votes are in the hands of the parents.
- Each of the councils is authorized to hire and fire the principal based on four-year performance contracts. If a principal is not appointed, he/she may be placed on a waiting list for vacant teaching positions; and may ultimately, in the absence of a teaching job, be out of the Chicago education field.
- The Local School Council members receive training in budgeting, educational theory regarding each center's particular needs, and personnel selection processes and practices.
- Like most urban districts, Chicago was divided into administrative subdistricts; the new law created corresponding subdistrict councils, with powers similar to those of the Local School Councils and charged with the selection of a subdistrict superintendent. This individual is no longer a line officer and supervisor of principals; instead, the role is one of facilitating training, monitoring the school improvement process, and mediating disputes.

Hess's 1991 text on the Chicago experience notes that two provisions of the Reform Act placed a cap on administrative costs. A restructuring of the city school budget resulted in the freeing up of about $40,000,000 through a downsizing of the central administration, which was available for redistribution to local schools. An example of this is the reallocation to the schools of 95 percent of the Chapter I funds; the bypass of central administrative costs netted $30,000,000. Additionally, fiscal restructuring resulted in "supplemental/discretionary funds distributed to the schools; as a result of these various provisions, the average elementary school received about $90,000 in new discretionary resources for the first year of implementation." (p. 206)

Consideration must be given to the impetus for central office decentralization in Hanson's four cases. In Dade County and Los Angeles, a key ingredient was the willingness of the superintendent and of volunteer principals to engage in some dimension of power sharing. In Chicago, there was a situation of superintendent focus on power accumulation and bureaucratic expansion, and a confrontational, rather than collaborative, approach to employee unions. Following the financial collapse of the system in 1979 and an ongoing climate of fiscal strain, a business and civil rights group-funded Special Task Force on Education was formed; their first recommendation was to decentralize authority at the central office in favor of adding talent at the school and district level (Cooper, 1992). Improving the system's responsiveness by relocating decision making is an action which is strongly supported in the literature on restructuring. Whether the Chicago model can sustain its initial momentum and achieve true systemic change is yet to be seen. Hess pointed out that there are many dimensions which affect the success of this effort. One is whether the centralized governance structures are focused on supporting and encouraging school-based management. How central office units redefine their missions, whether attitudes among that central staff shift to one of a service perspective, and how hiring procedures are transferred to facilitate local school staffing decisions are examples. The most important of these measures is the reallocation of resources; if, as a prime example, the first year's $40,000,000 windfall is continued via other avenues and amounts of redistributed resources.

The Chicago School Reform Act has sought to change the nature of the central administration of the system "from a controller and director into a servant, and seeks to constrain its ability to exercise direct control over local schools" (Hanson, 1991, p. 209). This far-reaching reform plan, certainly one of the most radical and politically visible school-based management efforts, has a legal postscript. In December of 1991, Rothman reported that a court ruling has upended the plan; a case brought by school principals resulted in the court determining that the method for electing local school councils (the Reform Act's hallmark) was unconstitutional because it gave more weight (by numerical membership on the council) to parents than to others. The mayor then reappointed the council members, and the legislature, after a significant delay, adopted a measure aimed at correcting the original law to meet the court's objections.

As an additional perspective to the large district view, there is substantial international implementation of school-based management, particularly in Canada, Australia, and New Zealand. In the last, local schools have had the option to operate as free-standing entities, at liberty to contract in the private sector for such services as maintenance and housekeeping. Two other international examples are described, since they possess parallels to some of the concerns and experiences outlined in this chapter. Maeroff, in 1992, described a British program of "local management of schools," under which schools may decide to become independent of the local district and become directly responsible to and grant-supported by the central government (this is further detailed in Chapter 11). This secessionist plan allows for the newly-independent school to be emancipated from the local educational authorities and shifts funds from the local funding source directly to the school. Maeroff reported the British concern that widespread secession may cause a scaling down of the ability of the local education authority (LEA) to provide centralized services, and mentioned cases where opting-out schools had been stripped of supplies and physical resources by local authorities, claiming central ownership. Schools that do opt for this free-standing model must do so by a ballot of parents, must follow the new national curriculum, and are inspected through the same type of national system as are the local jurisdictional schools. This had been described as a weakening of the LEA system, since, under the proposals for local financial management, each school would receive an annual budget based on a formula related to numbers of students, ages, and socioeconomic weightings. Under the control of the head teacher, the budget will be overseen by the board of governors (similar to SBM school councils), in something of a corporate board fashion. The board/council will also have the responsibility for personnel appointments, funding for staff and for equipment and materials, as well as maintenance.

In 1990 Hanson described school-based management in Spain, where it has been functioning since 1985. The local school councils are now sharing power with the Ministry of Education and Science, and are highly teacher-dominated. As in Chicago, the councils can hire and fire the director (principal), but at *any* point in time; there is no contractual protection. The situation in both Chicago and Spain creates a politicization of the principal role; both have been the object of much controversy. In the British system of an option for solo standing and direct connection to the central government are the elements of a true secessionist model; it is conceivable that a given U.S. school district could evolve into a loose confederation of independent, school based sites, with little resources or support being given or obtained from the central office.

IMPLICATIONS AND RECOMMENDATIONS: FOCUS ON THREE KEY AREAS

One concern which in constantly raised in any consideration of decentralized authority is the nature of the required curricular, instructional, and administrative minimums presumably guaranteed to be retained at each school-based managed site; to keep the schools operating within the parameters of public policy. The enlarged decision-making role of the schools must not escalate local creativity to the point of loss of public accountability. Also, the lodging of the preponderance of authority in the schools should not abrogate student rights or unsecure access to a sound educational program. At present, there is an overlapping check and balance system, provided, to some extent by the central office, to ensure both guarantees (Raywid, 1990). The difficulty in determining the correct mix of local and central school-based jurisdiction and the drawing of lines of accountability and authority is clearly demonstrated in practice and is evident in the literature. Herman (1992) presented a model showing a continuum of resource decision making, to be used as a matrix road map in attempting to reach a consensus on who has what portion of the decision making power in such resource areas as purchasing or school plant modification. He described the range of the continuum as decisions to be classified as: totally school-based; negotiated and shared through consensus; and totally district-based. In 1988, Lewis, reporting on SBM practice and research, outlined a possible division of decision making responsibilities between the schools and the central office. Some decisions that might be made at the site level include:

- developing educational priorities for the building and the students
- developing new programs to meet the needs of the students
- developing scheduling to meet instructional goals
- allocating resources to best meet the needs of students
- selecting supplemental instructional materials
- selecting applicants from a pool of prescreened candidates

The school district level could continue:

- developing districtwide priorities
- developing grade level objectives and curriculum
- supervising capital expenditure
- selecting textbooks
- selecting principals
- screening job applicants

This list encompasses the key areas of central office impact, as described previously in Chapter 1; budget, hiring, and curriculum. Each of these areas of central office administration is considered briefly in the context of school-based management.

School-Based Budgeting

Budgeting planning and expenditure control are the areas of SBM action most frequently and primarily decentralized. Much of the literature in this area has focused on principal strategies to both create a workable budget and to obtain the consensus of the staff for its approval. A term frequently used is school-based budgeting (SBB). Hartley (1991) spoke of SSB as enabling a principal to comprehensively plan, with stakeholder input, and to both submit a site budget request and to administer an approved budget in a way that enhances student performance.

Honeyman and Jensen (1988) presented three options for allocating SBB decision-making responsibility: the principal acting alone; the principal sharing power with select administrators and department heads; and a more broadly representative committee making decisions. They describe a site budget process which includes the total costs for a school, including personnel salaries and nonsalary operating costs. Such a model would necessarily involve personnel decisions, and in the hands of the principal alone, would be very time-demanding. Almost any site budgetary model will demand time, whether from a budgetary committee, or from teachers as they prepare program budgets. The level of preparation to handle this type of responsibility is sophisticated, and there is no guarantee that all principals and staffs currently possess it. In 1989 Neal reported on Prince William County, Virginia's 12-person task force which undertook a study of school-based management, resulting in a pilot program of five schools. The principal, parents, and teachers at these schools were given their pro rata share of the district budget and left free to allocate funds as they saw fit, in the areas of personnel, instruction, and maintenance and operations. The amount provided per school was determined through review of previous individual budgets and divided up after funds were set aside for transportation, food service, and the central office. Some weightings were applied to allow for size and student factors. The school-based budget must abide by state regulations, accreditation standards, board policies, and administrative regulations (though waivers are available for the latter two). While there is central office review for major omissions or problems of the submitted budgets, only the superintendent and director of SBM can insist on changes. Neal described some lessons learned from the SBB decentralization process:

- Make a firm commitment, since there may be central level resentment over the dispersal of the budget function. Financial sabotage or out-of-line appeals to the school board are possible reactionary tactics. A clear superintendent and board commitment to SBM, and the inclusion of a director of school-based management who has the authority to resolve conflicts were steps taken by the district to prevent this.
- Seek a qualified consultant. Radical school reorganization requires some assistance; experienced advice and guidance are needed for such a complex process.
- Be willing to accept mistakes. A climate of cooperation and assistance will help to promote the budgetary initiatives and experimentation SBM should bring.
- Outline the central office's role. Though the administrative system will not disappear, some reassurance must be provided to the central staff.

In 1991, Herman and Herman described the role of the school business official in school-based management; in SBB, this individual may be called upon to both provide training and serve a fiscal troubleshooter for newly-empowered principals and staff. The school business official may also be needed to broker or decentralize into cost centers (also noted by Sanders and Thiemann in 1990) such support services as transportation or food service. This central office individual may be, at the outset of SBM, the staff member most intensively involved with the school sites, particularly in the areas of collaborative creativity with site committees and as oversight advisor to emerging school-designed budgets. One of the most critical areas in SBB, as shown in Lewis' (1988) list giving a logical division of financial authority, is the determination of site and nonsite budgetary costs. Decisions regarding school operations that require a degree of uniformity for purposes of efficiency, economy, or understanding, could be retained at the central level. Some support services such as transportation are so varied and diffused that they are not easily assigned to individual buildings; some are so large (such as purchasing of common supplies) that individual schools would benefit from economies of scale if they were left at a central level (Herman and Herman, 1991). Product quality information should also be maintained there, as schools may have neither the time nor the expertise, at least initially, to make informed purchase decisions.

Patterns of implementation range from minimal financial discretion, representing a small fraction of the budget, to financial levels of control such as eighty or ninety percent of the school budget, including teacher salaries. Incentives are sometimes added which include the return of operational or salary savings to the discretionary budget of the school. School-based budgeting is a topic of increasing significance in SBM, and an adequate treatment of recommendation and common practice is not possible in this broadly conceived text. The reader is referred to Greenhalgh's (1984) work on school site budgeting as a salient source of information, as well as to the increasing amount of later publication within the field.

School-Based Personnel Management

Involvement in hiring and assignment of employees is a key empowerment factor of SBM, and one of the most controversial. It can be viewed from a fiscal perspective, as a process of the allotment of teacher or employee equivalents per building and the subsequent expenditure of those equivalents (J.J. Herman, 1991) by the school SBM decision-making team. It can also be viewed realistically as the expenditure of only additional personnel units, as they are accrued, through a collaborative interview and hiring process. Kentucky's new SBM regulations require this, and preclude any SBM council action in employee transfer or termination. Depending on the district's past practice, support and training may be needed from the central office in either case, as individual school council or team members may be unskilled in the interview and hiring process. To maintain legal integrity, it may be desirable to keep the initial personnel screening process at the central level, as Lewis (1988) recommended. Employee actions which are due process-impacted and which may involve the individual school in questions of an employee's continuation of employment may be more safely left to the principal-central office connection. Peterson in 1991 pointed out that some uniformity of personnel quality should be maintained, so that schools do not neglect low-profile personnel services, such as media specialists and librarians, and to prevent any temptation to increase discretionary funds by understaffing or hiring inexperienced or part-time employees. Districts experienced in SBB allow schools to hire teachers on an average-cost basis, with the site paying a flat, predetermined rate for each teacher, regardless of the teacher's actual salary. Another dimension of SBM involvement in personnel matters is that of supervision and evaluation, functions that are normally principal and central-office supported, but which may be affected by teacher empowerment and collaborative peer coaching efforts.

School-Based Management and Curricular and Instructional Management

This is an area of decentralized decision making which is most commonly given to schools after budgeting and personnel matters have already been released, yet it is, by common practice, the area of central office responsibility which is familiar to most teachers and principals. Many districts have a history of intensive involvement of site personnel in curriculum development and revision, in instructional projects, and in selection of methods and materials, particularly textbooks. It is also an area which is heavily impacted by state quality control through required courses of study and curricular and instructional regulation. Federal influence in this area, particularly in categorical fund programs, is substantial. It is possibly, then, an SBM implementation area of more perceived sensitivity and critical nature than hiring or budget making.

A clear theme in SBM research and recommended practice is the development of each school's curricular and instructional plans which are a customized and enhanced version of the district's goals and objectives, but which may vary significantly from site to site. Chopra (1991) speaks of the optimum model of this "synergistic" (p. 24) curriculum design as combining the most positive elements of a standardized curriculum with the most positive elements of a school-based curriculum. It is accomplished by collaborative curriculum planning (already a commonality in many districts), the provision of training in effective instruction and leadership for both teachers and principals, and an increasing dependency on the central office staff as a sources of curricular and instructional expertise. Streshley (1992) stresses a similar process, aimed at obtaining significant levels of curriculum ownership and at revealing submerged student problems and raising faculty awareness of special needs. Ambroisie and Haley (1991) echo this synergistic model, emphasizing the role of the principal in SBM curricular matters and noting that the elimination of the central office K–12 content expert is too drastic a venture in school restructuring; a level of broad-based curricular perspective should be maintained, even though some centralized positions may be redistributed at the building level. Larger districts may wish to dramatically change the K–12 supervisory line positions, redefining them as supporting staff positions and reassigning them to serve as consultant groups at the request of the schools.

The ultimate concern about curriculum and instruction responsibility being lodged at each site level is the need to ensure, within district guidelines, a minimum quality program and a reasonable distribution of higher cost and more administratively complex programs, such as special education. If each school exercises curricular and instructional entrepreneurship, then very distinctively different programs may evolve at each school; each one's fidelity to the common district core of academic goals and objectives must be demonstrated to the parents and community, and, possibly, for accreditation purposes, to other governing bodies and agencies. Presumably, a school's demonstrated excellence and evidence of satisfactory accountability for student outcomes should ultimately be sufficient to release a school from close district curricular scrutiny. There will be a transition period, however, until the differing SBM curricular distinctiveness effect of a system of unique schools becomes more common and more accepted.

These three areas of traditional central office involvement are the action agendas for SBM implementation. Conflict and difficult transitions may be inherent in a phase-in process of decentralization, given the legal, stewardship, and statutory compliance-driven concerns each area generates.

Conclusion

The future of the central office function in a school-based and decentralized environment has no clear consensus, at this time, in the literature or in broad practice. Its target status within the SBM process creates a vulnerability, despite the recommendations and suggestions for reconceptualized roles and functions described in this chapter. The inversion of the central pyramid is not just a bandwagon notion, NASSP commented in 1991, quoting from a principal interview on restructuring, reform, and the national goals. There is a widespread perceived need to divert resources from nondirect services to direct services impacting students; in other words, as in the Chicago example, to reduce the administrative staff at the central office. However, total decentralization is as extreme a model as is a totally centralized structure. Certainly much of the needed expertise in budgeting, hiring, curricular and instructional matters, and provision of staff development services is held at the central level; the staff there are key players when the process of school-based management begins. Much experimentation and consideration of optimum governance and school-support services arrangements are needed, yet are only beginning to be broadly implemented within the larger context of school-based management practice.

SUMMARY

This chapter has been concerned with the unique and highly impacted role and function of the central office in the context of school based management. A historical perspective began the chapter, briefly outlining the centralization trend of the last half of the century, and the current restructuring emphasis on shifting authority and responsibility to the school site.

A section on new SBM roles and organizational patterns of central office personnel summarized the continuing theme of current research and thought about the site support function and resident-expert status of central office personnel. New roles of responder, facilitator, interventionist, and coalition builder were mentioned as part of a paradigm shift in central office administration. The inherent problems and solutions to the dispersal of central power were examined; waiver policies and procedures, early determination of decision making boundaries, and the redrawing and articulation of overlapping areas of responsibility.

The transitions demanded by SBM were illustrated by the experience of three of the nation's four largest school systems. The redistribution of authority and the amount of power dispersed were considered in the Dade County, Florida, Los Angeles, and Chicago school systems. There are significant differences from system to system, particularly in the various points of SBM instigation; a district-initiated, voluntary status in the former two and a sweeping legislative change in the latter. Such items as personnel selection and budgetary discretion were investigated in these systems and in two international school systems: Great Britain and Spain.

Implications and recommendations for the function and changing role of the central office in an SBM climate were provided through a focus on three key areas of district level responsibility; budget development, personnel management, and curricular and instructional management. There is a consensus within the literature and a strong field rationale to decentralize all three areas; difficulty occurs when the details of shared function must be worked out. The need to give maximum latitude to the schools must be balanced against legal, financial, compliance, and optimum resource use practicalities. A final note reflected upon the future of the central office function in a school-based management environment.

EXERCISES

1. What changes do you see in the roles of your central office personnel in a school-based management setting? How would the central office's present structure and lines of authority look as a result?

2. What are the talents possessed by the present central office personnel which would enhance their function as support providers and initiators?

3. Compare the experience of Chicago and of Dade County in school-based management implementation. What advantages and disadvantages exist in each model?

4. What would be the most workable and readily acceptable model of school based budgeting in your district? What areas would be the most difficult to resolve?

5. What areas of personnel administration would be most easily decentralized in your district? What is the readiness level of principals and teachers in skillfully selecting new employees?

6. What curricular and instructional functions would be most easily decentralized in your district? What would happen if each school were free to create their own curriculum and distinctive instructional programs?

REFERENCES

AASA. (1990). A new look at empowerment. *AASA Leadership for Learning.* Arlington, VA: American Association of School Administrators.

Ambroisie, F. & Haley, P.W. (1991). The role of the curriculum specialist in site-based management. *NASSP Bulletin, 75* (537), 73–81.

Bruce, M.G. (1988). All is change in Britain's schools. *Phi Delta Kappan, 69* (9), 691.

Chopra, R. (1991). Synergistic curriculum design: Its time has come. In NASSP's *School-based management: theory and practice* (pp. 24–27), Reston, VA: National Association of Secondary School Principals.

Cooper, B.S. (1992). A tale of two cities: Radical school reform in Chicago and London. In J.J. Lane & E.G. Epps (Eds.) *Restructuring the schools: problems and prospects* (p. 88). Berkeley, CA: McCutchan Publishing Corporation.

David, J.L. (1991). Restructuring and technology: Partners in change. *Phi Delta Kappan, 73* (1), 37–40.

Delehant, A.M. (1990). A central office view: Charting a course when pulled in all directions. *The School Administrator, 8* (47), 14–19.

Doyle, R. & Tetzloff, P. (1992). Waivers provide relief, allow improvements. *The School Administrator, 1* (49), 10–11.

Greenhalgh, J. (1984). *School site budgeting: Decentralized school management.* Lanham, MD: University Press of America, Inc.

Hanson, E.M. (1990). School based management and educational reform in the United States and Spain. *Comparative Education Review, 34* (4), 523–537.

Hanson, E.M. (1991). *Educational administration and organizational behavior.* Boston: Allyn and Bacon, pp. 383–387.

Hartley, H.J. (1991). Decentralized school-site budgeting: Some guidelines. In NASSP's *School-based management: theory and practice* (p. 64–69), Reston, VA: National Association of Secondary School Principals.

Herman, J.J. (1991). *School-based management: Methods of maximizing site level decision making related to staffing and budget expenditures.* Manuscript submitted for publication.

Herman, J.J. (1992). *School based management: Sharing the resource decisions between the central and school-site levels of a school district.* Manuscript submitted for publication.

Herman, J.J. & Herman, J.L. (1991). Business officials and school-based management: Roles, opportunities, and challenges. *School Business Affairs, 57* (11), 34–37.

Hess, G.A., Jr. (1991). *School restructuring, Chicago style.* Newbury Park, CA: Corwin Press, Inc., pp. 23–25, 29, 99–100, 106–111, 119–120, 206–209.

Hirsh, S. & Sparks, D. (1991). A look at the new central-office administrators. *The School Administrator, 8* (48), 16–19.

Honeyman, D.S. & Jensen, R. (1988). School-site budgeting. *School Business Affairs, 54* (2), 12–14.

Johnson, S.M. (1990). Redesigning teachers' work. In R.F. Elmore and Associates, (Eds.) *Restructuring schools—the next generation of educational reform,* San Francisco: Jossey-Bass Publishers, 138.

Lewis, A. (1989). *Restructuring America's schools.* Washington, D.C.: American Association of School Administrators, p. 178.

Maeroff, G. (1992). Focusing on urban education in Britain. *Phi Delta Kappan, 73* (5), 355–358.

McWalters, P. (1992). Handing accountability and authority to schools. *The School Administrator, 1* (49), 9–10.

NASSP. (1991). Restructuring, reform, and the national goals: What do principals think? *NASSP Bulletin, 75* (533), 39–49.

National LEADership Network Study Group on Restructuring Schools,. (1991) *Developing leaders for restructuring schools.* Washington, D.C.: U.S. Department of Education, Office of Educational Research and Improvement, pp. 25–28, 33.

Neal, R.G. (1989). School-based management lets principals slice the budget pie. *The Executive Educator, 11* (1), 16–19.

Peterson, D. (1991). The challenge of school-based budgeting for business officials. *ASBO Accents, 11* (12), 4–5.

Raywid, M.A. (1990). Rethinking school governance. In R.F. Elmore and Associates (Eds.), *Restructuring schools—the next generation of educational reform* (pp. 182, 191–192), San Francisco, CA: Jossey-Bass Publishers.

Rothman, R. (1991). Education vital signs: Main events. *The Executive Educator, 13* (12), A3–A5.

Sanders, K.P. & Thiemann, F.C. (1990). Student costing: An essential tool in site-based budgeting and teacher empowerment. *NASSP Bulletin, 74,* 523, 95–102.

Sheingold, K. (1991). Restructuring for learning with technology: The potential for synergy. *Phi Delta Kappan, 73* (1), 17–27.

Stevenson, K.R. & Pellicer, L.O. (1992). School-based management in South Carolina: Balancing state directed reform with local decision making. In J.J. Lane & E.G. Epps (Eds.) *Restructuring the schools: problems and prospects* (p. 131). Berkeley, CA: McCutchan Publishing Corporation.

Streshly, W. (1992). Staff involvement in a site-based curriculum development model. NASSP Bulletin, 76 (540), 56–63.

Torres, H. (1992). Wrestling with what to include in SBM. *The School Administrator, 1* (49), 14.

Chapter 7

SCHOOL-BASED MANAGEMENT AND THE SUPERINTENDENT: CHANGE CATALYST AND ACTIVE PARTICIPANT

In traditional terms, a board of education employed a superintendent of schools to be its CEO, and it held her/him responsible for the total day-to-day operation of schools within the policy guidelines promulgated by the local school district's board of education. However, school districts added numerous additional administrators; business managers were added to handle and control the income and expenditure functions of the school district; directors of instruction were hired to oversee curriculum development and the instructional supervisory functions of the school district; directors of personnel were added to oversee all employee related hiring, placement, record-related, and other employee related matters; and directors of buildings and grounds were added to oversee all matters related to school plants, school sites, and school-owned property.

As school districts continued to grow and legislation caused additional functions to be added to the schools, additional hierarchical layers of administrators and management types were added. Some of the additional positions which were added in medium and large-sized school districts were employed under such titles as: athletic director, guidance director, special education director, food service manager, transportation manager, maintenance manager, custodial manager, and director of staff development. During the time period when school districts continued to grow in numbers of pupils and complexity of functions, individual school buildings grew in size, and many assistant principals and other supervisory or management specialists were added to the individual school building level (Guthrie & Reed, 1991).

Also, during the 1960s and 1970s many states adopted laws which permitted collective bargaining in the public sector. This trend added, in many cases, to the board of education's policies which previously guided the operation of the local school district, a *do-it-by-the-book* (master contract agreement between union and management) mentality to the operation of school districts (Keith & Girling, 1991).

It is within this complex environment that school-based management enters as another structural and process entity to be added to the decision making elements already in existence in local school districts. It is also within this evolving and as-yet-to-be-defined growth stage of organizational development (Herman & Herman, 1991) that the superintendent of schools must function, and she/he must function effectively if the school district is to become and remain productive, efficient, and effective.

To lead into the discussions of the transitions and new role perceptions related to the superintendent of schools as districts opt for school-based management, it is important to graphically review the complexities within which the superintendent of schools: (1) has historically functioned, (2) is currently functioning, and (3) will have to probably function in the near future (Schlechty, 1990). Obviously, the entire area of federal and state laws, which are in an accelerating pattern of proliferation, would have to be added to the graphics presented in order to provide a complete visual structure of the environment within which the superintendent of schools functions.

Now that we have, in words and in graphic representations, outlined the parameters within which the superintendent of schools has, is, and potentially will operate; let's turn to the topical discussions to be covered in the remainder of this chapter. The topics remaining to be addressed are: (1) the transitions and new role perceptions related to the superintendent of schools in districts which initiate school-based management, (2) the superintendent of school's symbolic leadership functions and support demands, (3) implications for realignment of interactions with the school board and central office personnel, (4) new relationships with building principals and teachers, and (5) common national and state patterns of school-based management implementations.

TRANSITIONS AND NEW ROLE PERCEPTIONS RELATED TO THE SUPERINTENDENT IN DISTRICTS WHICH INITIATE SCHOOL-BASED MANAGEMENT

The superintendent of schools traditionally has been perceived as the CEO of the school district's board of education; and she/he has been traditionally held accountable for all the day-to-day activities of the school

FIGURE 7.1

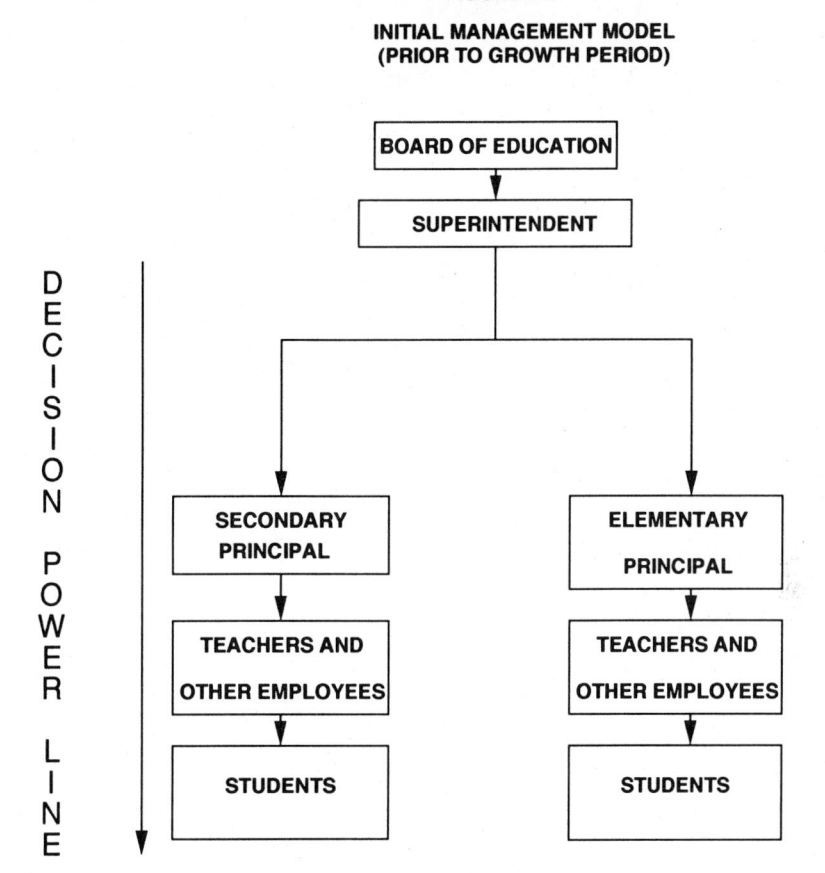

**INITIAL MANAGEMENT MODEL
(PRIOR TO GROWTH PERIOD)**

```
                        ┌──────────────────────┐
                        │ BOARD OF EDUCATION   │
                        └──────────┬───────────┘
                                   ▼
                        ┌──────────────────────┐
                        │    SUPERINTENDENT    │
                        └──────────┬───────────┘
                     ┌─────────────┴─────────────┐
                     ▼                           ▼
D           ┌─────────────────┐         ┌─────────────────┐
E           │    SECONDARY    │         │   ELEMENTARY    │
C           │    PRINCIPAL    │         │    PRINCIPAL    │
I           └────────┬────────┘         └────────┬────────┘
S                    ▼                           ▼
I           ┌─────────────────┐         ┌─────────────────┐
O           │   TEACHERS AND  │         │  TEACHERS AND   │
N           │ OTHER EMPLOYEES │         │ OTHER EMPLOYEES │
            └────────┬────────┘         └────────┬────────┘
P                    ▼                           ▼
O           ┌─────────────────┐         ┌─────────────────┐
W           │    STUDENTS     │         │    STUDENTS     │
E           └─────────────────┘         └─────────────────┘
R

L
I
N
E
▼
```

DECISION POWER LINE

district, as well as being held accountable to the board of education for seeing that all district activities conform to the letter and intent of the adopted school board policies. In addition, the superintendent of schools has been historically perceived as the school district's ultimate *boss*.

With the growth in size of school districts and with the addition of numerous administrators, supervisors, and managers, the superintendent of schools became the coordinator, director, and monitor of management functions. With the proliferation of federal and state laws and state departments' of education mandates, the superintendent of schools assumed the additional responsibility for assuring that the district not only operate within school board policies; but, also, she/he was held accountable for overseeing that all employees operated within the letter and intent of federal and state laws and within the letter and intent of state departments' of education mandates (Brown, 1990).

FIGURE 7.2

INITIAL MANAGEMENT CONTROL DOCUMENTS

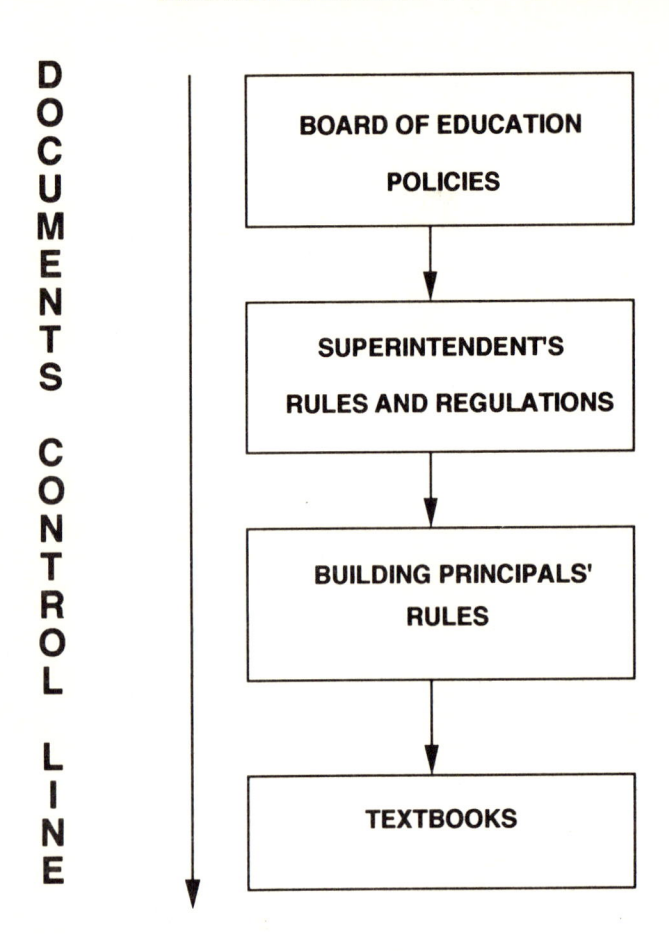

```
DOCUMENTS CONTROL LINE
    │
    ▼
┌─────────────────────┐
│ BOARD OF EDUCATION  │
│      POLICIES       │
└─────────────────────┘
           │
           ▼
┌─────────────────────┐
│   SUPERINTENDENT'S  │
│ RULES AND REGULATIONS│
└─────────────────────┘
           │
           ▼
┌─────────────────────┐
│ BUILDING PRINCIPALS'│
│        RULES        │
└─────────────────────┘
           │
           ▼
┌─────────────────────┐
│      TEXTBOOKS      │
└─────────────────────┘
```

With the advent of collective bargaining, in those states which passed laws permitting or mandating school districts boards of education to bargain collectively with officially recognized employee unions until a master contract agreement was reached, the superintendent was required to assume an additional area of responsibility (Cloyd, 1990). Even though the superintendent had specialists to assist in this area, much of the ultimate responsibility for the negotiation of a *good* master contract rests on the superintendent's shoulders.

Finally, in those districts which have been mandated to initiate school based management by the state legislature, as in Kentucky, or have been

FIGURE 7.3

LARGE DISTRICT GROWTH PERIOD MANAGEMENT MODEL

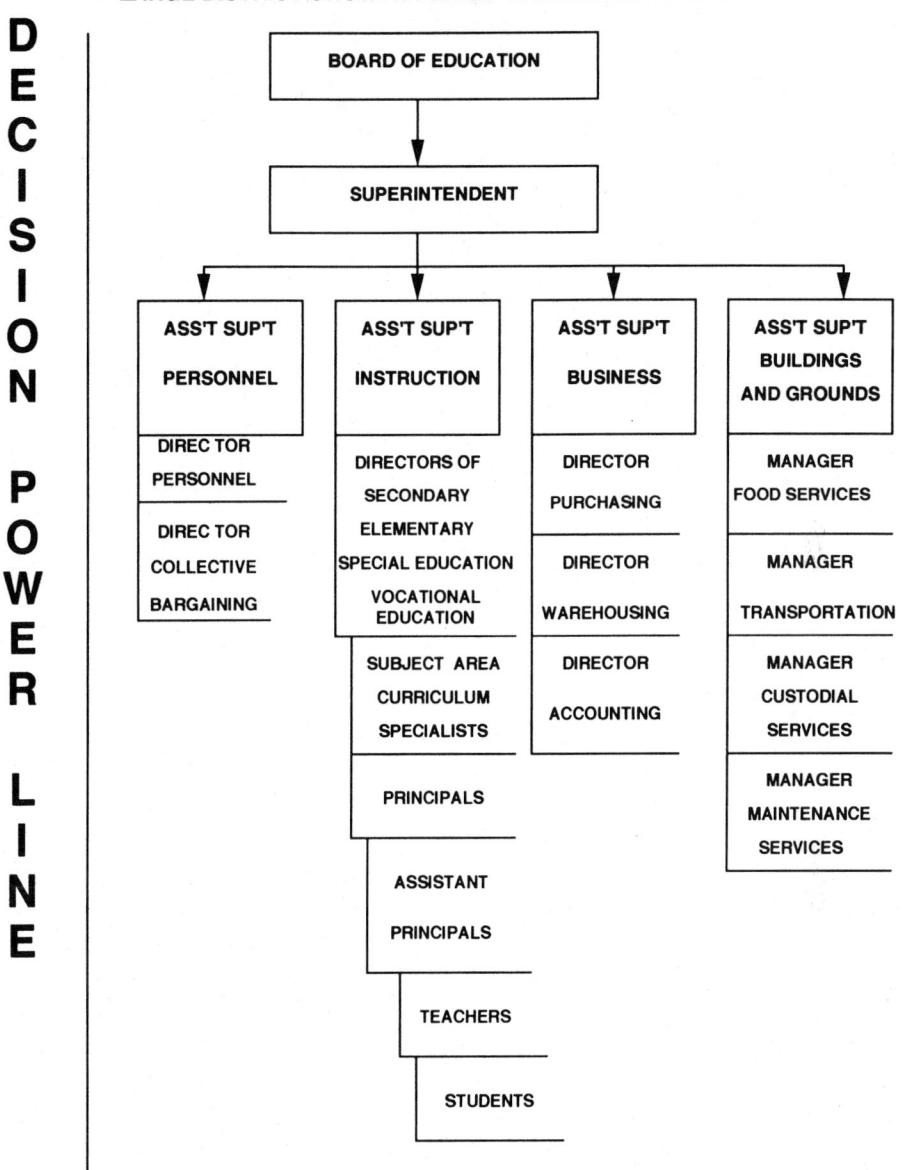

DECISION POWER LINE ↓

```
                        BOARD OF EDUCATION
                                │
                                ▼
                          SUPERINTENDENT
        ┌───────────────┬────────┴────────┬───────────────┐
        ▼               ▼                 ▼               ▼
   ASS'T SUP'T     ASS'T SUP'T       ASS'T SUP'T     ASS'T SUP'T
   PERSONNEL      INSTRUCTION         BUSINESS       BUILDINGS
                                                     AND GROUNDS
```

ASS'T SUP'T PERSONNEL	ASS'T SUP'T INSTRUCTION	ASS'T SUP'T BUSINESS	ASS'T SUP'T BUILDINGS AND GROUNDS
DIRECTOR PERSONNEL	DIRECTORS OF SECONDARY ELEMENTARY SPECIAL EDUCATION VOCATIONAL EDUCATION	DIRECTOR PURCHASING	MANAGER FOOD SERVICES
DIRECTOR COLLECTIVE BARGAINING		DIRECTOR WAREHOUSING	MANAGER TRANSPORTATION
	SUBJECT AREA CURRICULUM SPECIALISTS	DIRECTOR ACCOUNTING	MANAGER CUSTODIAL SERVICES
	PRINCIPALS		MANAGER MAINTENANCE SERVICES
	ASSISTANT PRINCIPALS		
	TEACHERS		
	STUDENTS		

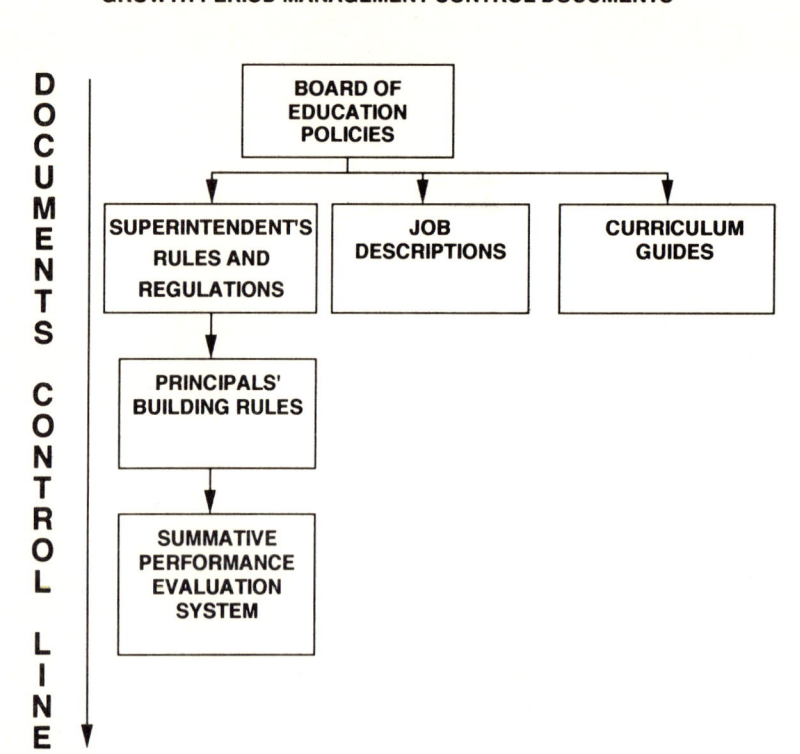

FIGURE 7.4

GROWTH PERIOD MANAGEMENT CONTROL DOCUMENTS

```
D
O
C
U   ┌─────────────┐
M   │  BOARD OF   │
E   │  EDUCATION  │
N   │  POLICIES   │
T   └──────┬──────┘
S    ┌─────┼─────────────┐
     ▼     ▼             ▼
C  ┌──────────────┐ ┌──────────┐ ┌────────────┐
O  │SUPERINTENDENT'S│ │   JOB    │ │ CURRICULUM │
N  │  RULES AND   │ │DESCRIPTIONS│ │   GUIDES   │
T  │ REGULATIONS  │ │          │ │            │
R  └──────┬───────┘ └──────────┘ └────────────┘
O        ▼
L  ┌──────────────┐
   │  PRINCIPALS' │
L  │BUILDING RULES│
I  └──────┬───────┘
N        ▼
E  ┌──────────────┐
   │   SUMMATIVE  │
   │  PERFORMANCE │
   │  EVALUATION  │
   │    SYSTEM    │
   └──────────────┘
   ▼
```

mandated via another source, as in Chicago; or in those districts which have voluntarily entered the restructuring process and structure called school-based management, the superintendent of schools has, whether she/he desired it or not, been delegated the responsibility for overseeing the implementation of SBM in the school district. In fact, the Kentucky Reform Act of 1990 mandates that all individual school buildings will have school-based decision making in place within five years; and for the first year, if there is no single school to volunteer to initiate school-based decision making, the superintendent of schools in that district is mandated to select an individual school to implement it (Miller, Noland, & Schaaf, 1990).

The superintendent of schools will be ultimately held responsible for seeing that all of these diverse decision making elements operate in harmony and in concert in a manner that will assist, or, at least, not hinder, the education of students and the operations of the entire school district. Indeed, we believe the current day superintendent of schools

FIGURE 7.5

COLLECTIVE BARGAINING PERIOD MANAGEMENT MODEL

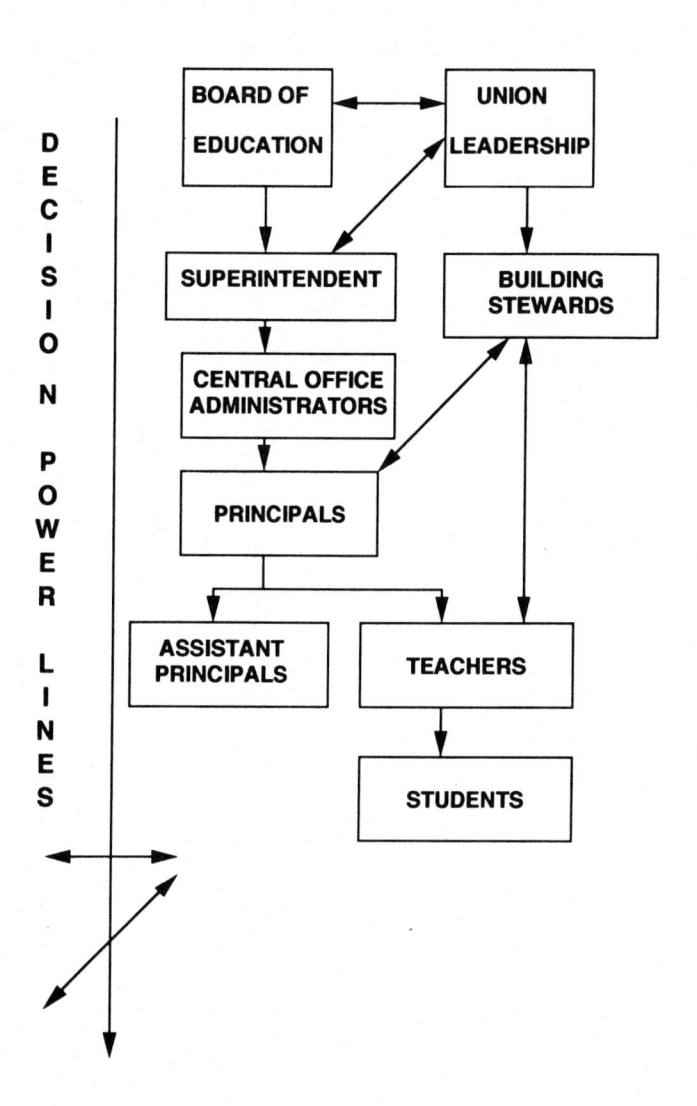

```
                    BOARD OF  ←→  UNION
D                   EDUCATION     LEADERSHIP
E                       │    ↗       │
C                       ↓  ╱         │
I                   SUPERINTENDENT   │
S                       │         BUILDING
I                       ↓         STEWARDS
O                   CENTRAL OFFICE
N                   ADMINISTRATORS
                        │        ↗
P                       ↓      ╱
O                   PRINCIPALS
W                   ╱       ╲
E                  ╱         ╲
R              ASSISTANT    TEACHERS
               PRINCIPALS      │
L                              ↓
I                           STUDENTS
N
E
S
```

who works in a district with multiple unions, a board of education, numerous specialized management employees, and school-based management building level committees (comprised of a principal, teacher representatives, parent representative, and perhaps other categories of representatives) can only be described as a person who is the coordinator of a *function* entitled superintendency. She/he can no longer fill the role

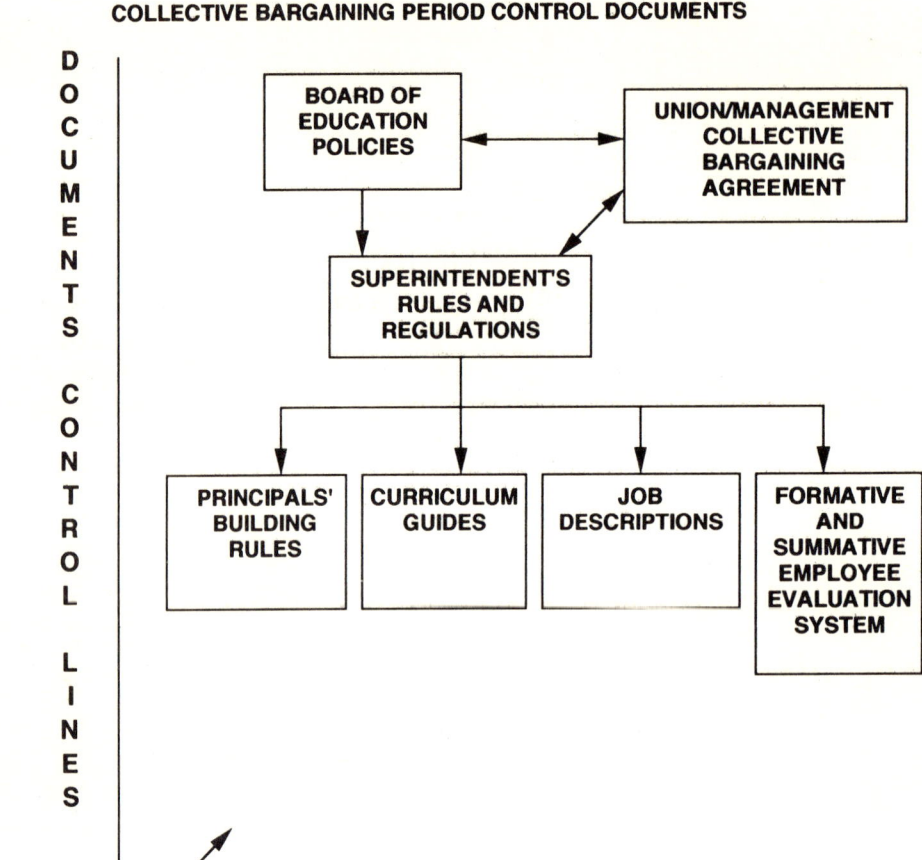

FIGURE 7.6

COLLECTIVE BARGAINING PERIOD CONTROL DOCUMENTS

of the *ultimate boss* (Prasch, 1990). A major problem with this functional change is that many superintendents were trained under the old hierarchical and autocratic system; and they do not know how, nor do they desire, to operate under this new and substantially more *flattened* decision making structure and substantially more *open* decision-making process (Murphy, 1989).

School-Based Management and the Superintendent   123

FIGURE 7.7

**SCHOOL-BASED MANAGEMENT POTENTIAL
MANAGEMENT MODEL**

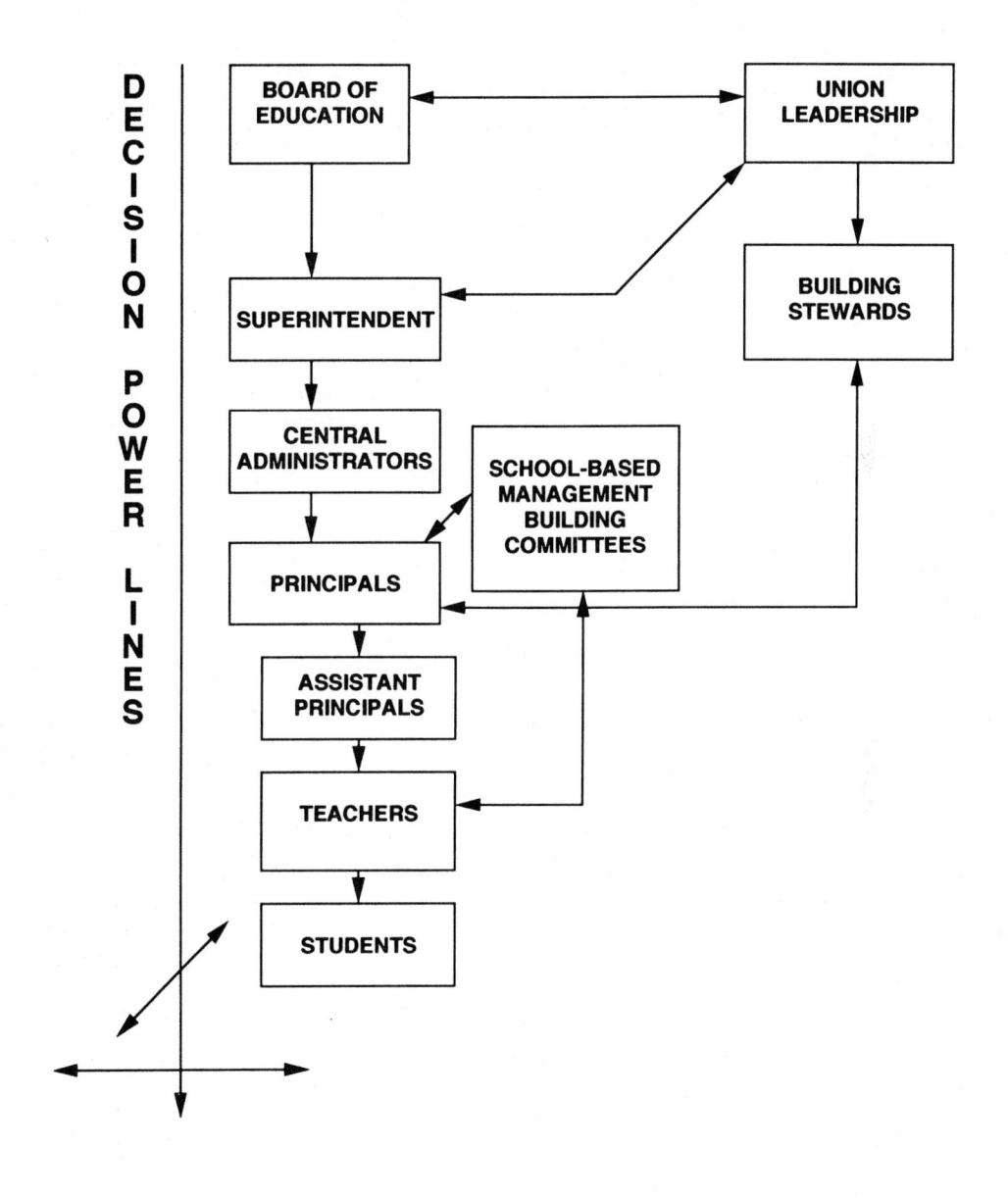

FIGURE 7.8

SCHOOL-BASED MANAGMENT PERIOD POTENTIAL CONTROL DOCUMENTS

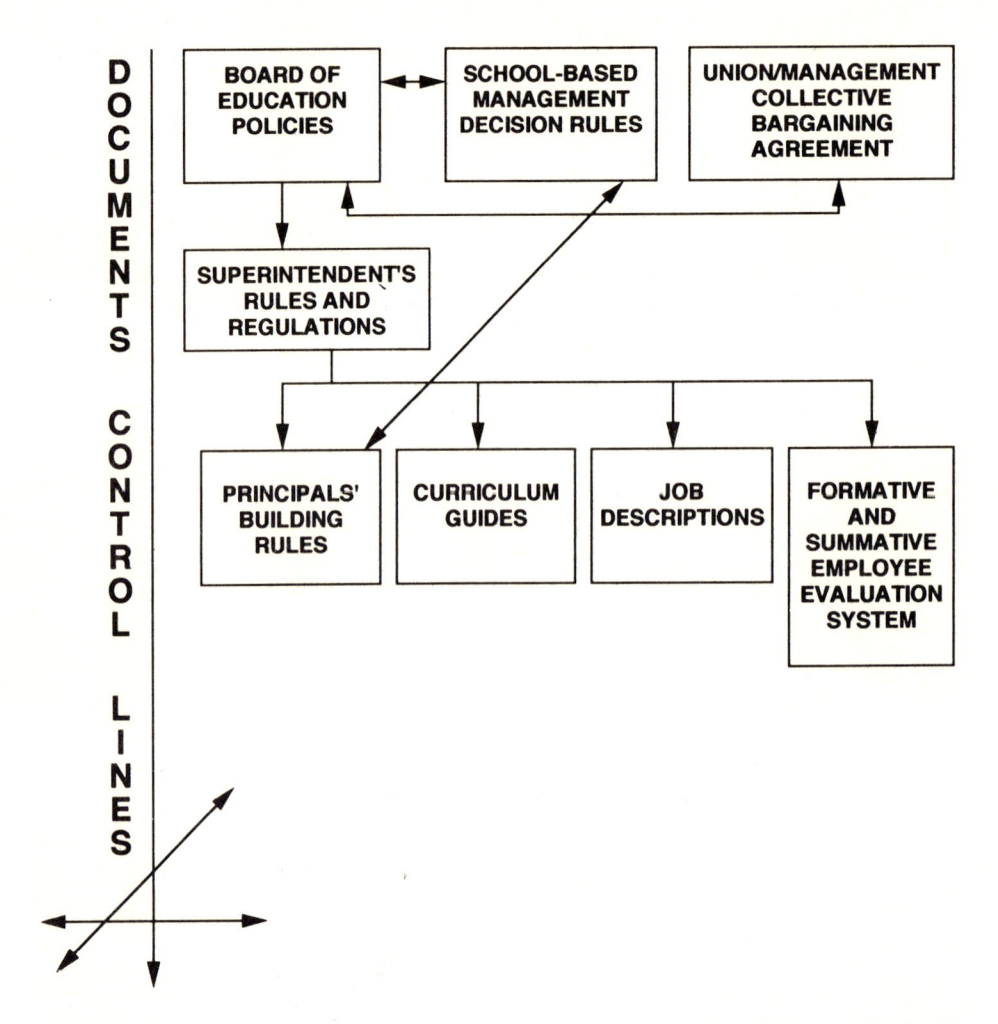

In three separate publications by the American Association of School Administrators, which were written a few years apart, authors attempted to outline the major responsibilities and functions of those women and men who are filling the role of superintendent of schools. Although they have addressed the issue, the publications are not a close fit when applied to the current environment within which superintendents find themselves.

In 1982, the American Association of School Administrators listed a series of competencies. These were entitled competencies for school leaders, and they are listed below in parentheses following a statement of each specific task.

- Design and establish a school climate with attainable goals (organizational, motivational, leadership and interpersonal skills).
- Understand and employ political skills for support of education (public relations, communication of position, negotiation).
- Develop a systematic school curriculum (understand cognitive development, development of indicators for instruction).
- Plan and implement an instruction management system (monitor student achievement).
- Manage finances, materials and human resources (Hoyle, English, & Steffy, 1985).

In the 1985 American Association of School Administrators' publication entitled: *Skills for Successful School Leaders* (Hoyle, English, & Steffy) eight specific skill areas were listed and elaborated upon. These eight skill areas were, by implication, necessary for a superintendent of schools to be successful.

- Skills in designing, implementing and evaluating school climate.
- Skills in building support for schools.
- Skills in developing school curriculum.
- Skills in instructional management.
- Skills in staff evaluation.
- Skills in allocating resources.
- Skills in educational research, evaluation, and planning.

In 1990, the American Association of School Administrators published a revised edition of their publication *Skills for Successful School Leaders* (Hoyle, English, & Steffy, 1990). In this publication, the authors addressed numerous subheadings under the eight skills that they listed in their 1985 publication of the same title. It is interesting to view the chapter titles and subheadings to determine all the knowledges and skills that supposedly, by implication, should be possessed by individuals who are to be highly successful in the role of the superintendent of schools. The eight skill areas with the subheadings under each skill are duplicated from the chapter headings of this publication.

- **Skills in Designing, Implementing, and Evaluating School Climate.**

    Evaluating school climate; climate theory base; Theories X, Y. and Z; motivation theory; job enrichment and career ladders; climate and student achievement; climate improvement skills; designing and implementing school climate improvement programs; human relations, organizational development and leadership skills; school climate improvement models and skills; collaborative goal setting and action planning; organizational and personal planning and time management; participatory management; variations in staffing; climate assessment methods and skills; improving the quality of relationship among staff and students to enhance learning; multicultural and ethnic understanding; group process, interpersonal communication, and motivation skills.

- **Skills in Building Support for Schools.**

What "public relations" is; creating a public relations program; steps in developing a public relations plan; the school public relations officer; the art and the science of public relations; analyzing; planning; communicating; evaluating; a few words about publics; internal communication; the role of the mass media; the meaning of news; dealing with the media; education and the art of politics; coalition building; identifying community power structures; winning at the polls, tips for winning at the polls; the art of lobbying; a few words about coalitions; collective bargaining; communicating and projecting an articulate position for education.

- **Skills in Developing School Curriculum.**

Skills of systematic curriculum development; planning/future methods to anticipate occupational trends; the taxonomies of instructional objectives; curriculum mapping; theories of cognitive development and curriculum; development/application of valid and reliable performance indicators; the matter of curriculum quality control; use of computers and other technologies; and development and use of available cultural resources.

- **Skills in Instructional Management.**

A model of an instructional management system; curriculum design and instructional delivery strategies; instructional and motivational psychology; alternative methods of monitoring and evaluating student achievement; management of change to enhance the mastery of educational goals; application of computer management of the instructional program; cost effectiveness, and program budgeting.

- **Skills in Staff Evaluation.**

Evaluating administrators and supervisors; evaluating principals; growth plan; evaluating teacher performance; characteristics for any teacher evaluation system; developing LBO/R teacher evaluation forms; indicators of teaching effectiveness; ghosts of principals past; and evaluating other staff members.

- **Skills in Staff Development.**

Interaction of staff development with organizational development; system and staff needs assessment; using clinical supervision as a staff improvement and evaluation strategy; other approaches to staff development; and assessing individual and institutional sources of stress.

- **Skills in Allocating Resources.**

Budgeting, accounting, facilities planning, maintenance and operations; other challenges; plant operations and maintenance costs; emerging concerns; financial planning and; cashflow management; personnel administration; pupil personnel and categorical programs; legal concepts, regulations, and codes for school operations; litigation concerning religion and prayer; litigation regarding finance and school resources; collective bargaining; student rights and problems; employee rights; sexual discrimination; school desegregation; rights of handicapped pupils; analytical techniques of management; decision theories; and financial concepts and applications.

- **Skills in Educational Research, Evaluation, and Planning.**

Research: definition, problems, and value; research designs and methods include gathering, analyzing, and interpreting data; descriptive and inferential statistics; computer program statistical package for the social sciences (SPSS); program evaluation, planning, and futures methods; selection, administration, and interpretation of evaluation instruments.

Another view of the necessary leadership skills is presented by the National Association of Secondary School Principals, based upon many years of experience with their leadership assessment centers. In 1985, NASSP identified the following eight skills.

- Problem analysis—data collection and analysis.
- Judgement—critical evaluation and decision making.
- Decisiveness—acting when a decision is needed.
- Organizational ability—planning and scheduling personnel and resources.
- Leadership—guiding others to act.
- Sensitivity—awareness of other's needs.
- Stress tolerance—performing under pressure.
- Communication—speaking and writing skills.

Based upon twenty years of experience as a superintendent in various types of schools districts in multiple states and based upon a very large number of consulting situations with a wide variety of school districts, the authors agree that the AASA listings fit the functions of *superintending*. This implies multiple functionaries who are available to assist the person who is entitled superintendent of schools. If, however, we are looking specifically at the desirable (and, perhaps, required) skills possessed by those individuals who operate as the superintendent of a local school district, the NASSP listing appears to be more pragmatic.

While acknowledging the AASA and NASSP work in this area, the authors, based upon their years of experience as public school administrators and as consultants to school administrators, offer their own set of desired operational skills and beliefs that the individuals filling the role of superintendent of schools should possess. If we were to consider the function of superintending, utilizing many other administrators and supervisors, the list would be considerably lengthened.

DESIRABLE PRAGMATIC SUPERINTENDENT'S SKILLS AND BELIEFS CHECKLIST

I am able to, or with representative stakeholders, clearly define a *vision* of "what should be" in the future for my school district.

I am able to clearly define and describe the "what is" state of my school district.

I am able, with the help of others, identify the *needs*, which are discrepancies between the "what is" state of the school district and the "what should be" desired future state.

I am able to mobilize the employees and stakeholders to work in a collaborative manner to arrive at the "what should be" desired future state for the school district.

I am able to develop strategic and operational plans; or, at the very least, employ someone with this expertise with whom I can work to make certain we stay on the right path as we work to achieve our desired future "what should be" state in the school district.

Even though sometimes I feel like I would like to be an autocrat, I will most of the time accept the fact that I must work in a collaborative manner with employees, students, parents, community members, and numerous employee and community groups; and I am able to successfully do this.

I remember and know how to effectively give credit to others for their good work. I continue to do this even though I may not be a recipient of such behavior.

Whether I like it or not, I must be a role model for the students, employees and the community. I realize that it comes with the job.

I can balance my decisive and individual decision making, when I necessarily must act in this manner, with an ability to act as a mediator to assist others in resolving conflict in a positive manner.

I unquestionably possess excellent writing and verbal communications skills, and I utilize them daily with board members, employees, students, parents, community members, and state and federal agency employees or politicians.

I have the ability to hire good people, and I have faith that they will do their jobs well. In other words, I trust them.

I care about people, but mostly I make certain that everyone who deals with the children and youth in our school district demonstrates a caring attitude.

I have the ability to analyze external and internal variables to discern trends, also, I can promote action to take advantage of positive trends and take actions which will negate or lessen the impact of negative trends.

I hold high levels of aspiration for my achievement, and I strongly attempt to make certain that the desire for high level achievement exists among the students and employees of the school district.

I have the skills to monitor the district's programs and employees' contributions.

I have a realization that I must maintain my physical, mental, and financial health in order to be the best superintendent that I can be.

I enjoy the responsibilities and functions placed upon me as a superintendent of schools, because I feel I am contributing positively, in my way, to the future of the children and youth entrusted to the charge of the employees of the school district.

I have a commitment to look for other categories of employment or retire if I ever do not enjoy the position of superintendent of schools or if I ever feel that I am not making positive contributions to the welfare and education of children and youth.

Now that we have thoroughly explored the skills and beliefs that, hopefully, are possessed by those individuals serving as superintendents of schools, let's elaborate a bit on the symbolic leadership functions of current day superintendents. Also, let's explore the types of support demands placed upon the superintendents when the district which is considering implementing school-based management.

THE SUPERINTENDENT'S SYMBOLIC LEADERSHIP FUNCTIONS AND SUPPORT DEMANDS IN A DISTRICT CONSIDERING IMPLEMENTATION OF SCHOOL-BASED MANAGEMENT

In a district that is considering school-based management, the superintendent of schools must provide the leadership model which: (1) keeps an open mind about investigating the value of SBM, (2) involves a variety of stakeholders in investigating the potential value to the school district of implementing SBM, and, (3) expresses a willingness to share some of the personal power she/he possesses with others as more decisions will be made at the local building level by employees, parents, and others.

The superintendent, in addition, to her/his personal support for implementation if SBM is desirable; adds requisite support to the budgetary structure, provides time allocation of personnel, and works with the school district's board of education to develop the policy and implementing district rules and regulations which will promote SBM (Lewis, 1989). She/he will develop school-based budgeting, and will work with the building SBM committees as a resource.

Having outlined the overview leadership modeling and resource allocation responsibilities of the superintendent under a school-based management restructuring model, let's investigate some of the specific details that should be explored before deciding to implement SBM. To investigate the potential of SBM to the school district, the superintendent may, by her/his own volition, choose to initiate discussions with the school board, employees and community representatives, and encourage them to investigate the potential of SBM for their school district (Tewel, 1991).

If the superintendent is convinced that a greater variety of stakeholders should be involved in serious decision-making responsibilities; and if the superintendent believes that more decision making should take place at the individual school building level, then the superintendent will exercise her/his leadership and support by involving the board of education members, administrators, teachers, students, and community representatives to a comprehensive investigation of school-based management (Ingwerson, 1990). The stakeholders investigating SBM can arrive at answers to a series of key questions that will assist them in making a *go* or *no go* decision for their school district as related to SBM. However, before the superintendent involves a wide variety of stakeholders in a comprehensive investigation of SBM, she/he should personally address a series of questions, such as those listed below.

SCHOOL–BASED MANAGEMENT INTERROGATORY CHECKLIST (A REFLECTIVE AID TO BE USED BEFORE JUMPING HEADLONG INTO SCHOOL-BASED MANAGEMENT)

(Answer "yes" or "no" to each question)

1. Do you really believe in shared decision making?
2. Are you willing to take full responsibility (accountability) for your decisions?
3. Have you decided which stakeholders should be given the power to make final decisions?
4. Have you decided which stakeholders will be given a role in the decision-making process?
5. Have the central decision makers reached agreement with the building decision makers on the policies, procedures, and methodologies to implement the process of school-based management?
6. Have the local decision makers been given maximum decision-making power and flexibility related to staffing, instruction, and operational budget decisions?
7. Have you allowed sufficient time to reflect on all important decision areas before establishing a date to implement?
8. Do you realize that this may cause an additional workload to be placed on the principal and the school building's employees?
9. Have the local decision makers clearly defined, in operational terms, what they mean by school-based management; and have they developed the bylaws and policies which are necessary for implementation?
10. Have you determined the outcome measures that will be assessed to decide whether or not your locally designed program of school-based management is working well, or whether or not it requires modification?
11. Are the roles of the central personnel and the building personnel crystal clear in each area of decision making?
12. Is it clear, on the continuum of possible decision making possibilities, which decisions are totally school-based, which are totally district-based, and which are shared?
13. Have you budgeted time and money to conduct training or staff

development programs for those persons who are to become involved with school-based management for the first time?

14. Have you decided upon methods to perform formative and summative evaluations?

15. Will each school be able to develop its own school-based management procedures, or will there be a district structure applied to all school buildings within the school district?

16. Do you have realistic expectations of what school-based management can do, and do you realize that it is not a "cure all" for everything that is happening in the schools?

17. Do you realize that this is not a "quick fix", and that it will take considerable time and effort to implement and improve the process that you initially use?

18. Do you realize that over a long time period, not only will the decision making process change; but that there will be a dramatic (hopefully, positive) change in the entire culture of the organization?

19. Are you prepared to collect "hard" and "soft" data to make a yearly report of the degree of success of the school-based decision process in your school building?

20. Do you really believe that the process of school-based management will improve the effectiveness and efficiency of your school and your school district, or are you involved simply because it is the thing to do?

21. Do you believe that school-based management will improve communication, trust, and collaboration between the school building and school district levels?

22. Do you believe that school-based management will create a greater feeling of ownership and greater support from the employees and the community-at-large?

23. Do you really like and respect people, and are you willing to depend on them to help you make important decisions?

24. Do your employee union leaders and your board of education members buy into school-based management?

25. Do you believe that dispersed leadership is the best type of leadership, and do you believe that school-based management nurtures and stimulates new leadership at all levels of the organization?

26. Do you realize that school buildings and school districts are open systems (as opposed to closed systems), and that school-based management is a process that improves the schools' ability to become more open?

27. Do you believe in "loosely coupled" organizations?
28. Do you believe that school-based management can promote continuous school renewal?
29. Do believe in promoting entrepreneurial efforts?
30. Again, do you really believe and trust people, and are you willing to share your decision-making power?
31. What types of training will you provide the school-based management team related to:
    a. Communication skills?
    b. Planning skills?
    c. Decision-making skills?
    d. Problem-solving skills?
    e. Other skill areas?
32. What specific procedures will you put in place to arrive at decisions related to:
    a. Staffing?
    b. Budget?
    c. Instruction?
    d. Building level governance?
    e. Other? (J.J. Herman, 1990)

Now that we have discussed the transitions, and new role perceptions of the superintendent related to SBM; and we have dealt with a series of threshold questions that should definitely be addressed *before* SBM is initiated into any school district, consideration must be given to the potential changes that must be considered related to the persons, who in the traditional school district hierarchy, occupy positions above and below the position of the superintendent of schools. We begin with a discussion of the implications of SBM implementation at the school board and central office administrative and supervisory levels.

IMPLICATIONS FOR REALIGNMENT OF INTERACTIONS WITH THE SCHOOL BOARD AND CENTRAL OFFICE PERSONNEL

Once the specific structure of the school-based management councils or teams has been decided upon (they usually involve a minimum of teachers, parents, and the building principal), and once the areas and degree of decision making that has been delegated to the school building level (which could include decisions related to finance, personnel, instruction, operations, and governance); the school board has two major changes to make: (1) the school board should adopt policies promoting the structure and processes to be utilized in the local school district's scheme for school-based management; and, (2) it will have to condition itself and the individual school board members to not interfere, and to avoid trying to influence decisions that have been delegated to the local school building level (Neal, 1991).

Depending on the specific authorities delegated to the local school-based management councils, each central office group's specialized employees will have to make appropriate adjustments in their roles (Harrison, Killion, & Mitchell, 1989). If broad-based authority and responsibility are delegated to the school building level functionaries, the power and line responsibility roles of the central office administrators and supervisors will be substantially lessened. If, for example, the business manager does not agree with the expenditure pattern of a local school building's decision makers, and the decision is within the locally delegated authority, the business manager cannot impose her/his will upon that school's decision makers. If the hiring of employees has been delegated to the local level, the personnel administrators will change from final decision makers to roles of helping to locate and attract potential employee candidates, from which the local school's decision makers will make employment selections. The same type of adjustments will have to be made by central office administrators and supervisors who are assigned responsibilities in the areas of instruction, transportation, custodial and maintenance, food services, and operations (Prasch, 1990). This topic is addressed more completely in Chapter 6.

NEW RELATIONSHIPS WITH BUILDING PRINCIPALS AND TEACHERS

Under the usual structure and processes utilized during the operation of school-based management, the principal and teachers are given a great deal of additional decision-making power. The teachers have a major say in budgetary decisions at the local building level; and they have a large say in who is hired, the work schedule, the instructional delivery and testing systems, the equipment and supplies which are provided, and the methodologies utilized to evaluate students, programs and themselves. More direct communication and interaction begins to occur between the teacher and the central office staff, and, particularly, with the superintendent (Ingwerson, 1990). The principal under SBM has the advantage of working and leading the local school building's employees and parents in much greater depth and breadth of decision making. This is possibly something that the principal has desired for a long time. On the other hand, the principal, rather than the superintendent, will be the person primarily held responsible for the quality of the results of the local decisions that were made (NASSP, 1992). This can be unsettling for a principal who has not been previously held accountable for major local school building decision making; and, indeed, if the results are unfavorable and highly visible, the principal may lose her/his job. This is especially true since, in most school districts, principals are in a nontenured position.

Nevertheless, the challenging and novel SBM-instigated interactions between principals and teachers, as described in Chapters 3 and 5, are mirrored in the new SBM interactions demanded of the superintendent and principal. If support and autonomy are prerequisites for principal instructional leadership (J.J. Herman, 1991), then the superintendent must initiate and facilitate those conditions for her/his individual school leaders. The nature of the relationship between the superintendent and the district principals must become more directly connected and synergistic in order to create the correct climate for SBM (Fielding & Schalock, 1986; Neal, 1991).

COMMON NATIONAL AND STATE PATTERNS OF IMPLEMENTATION

As school districts became larger in size and more complex in programs and responsibilities, superintendents had to acquire additional knowledge and skills. As collective bargaining and numerous state and federal mandates impacted the school districts, the superintendents of schools had to again acquire additional knowledge and skills. Now the new interloper called school-based management has entered the environment; and, whether or not the superintendents wish to embrace it, they will, once again, have to acquire additional knowledge and skills. Also, they will have to change the traditional way in which they carry on the school district's business. For some this will be impossible; for many, this will be difficult, but attainable. Lewis (1989) considered, on a national level and common practice basis, the strategies needed by superintendents as they implement shared SBM and decision making, particularly through the creation of individual site teams. Recommendations included: the provision of time for meetings; the giving of importance to the planning team and products; the presence of the superintendent as the strongest and most vocal supporter of SBM; the superintendent and board's personal involvement; and the need for patience and the monitoring of process and results. Likewise mentioned were some concepts and commonalities addressing a number of local superintendency leadership issues, such as continuing district support, training, new fiscal practices, the allowance of time for policy change, the need to provide schools with access to new information, and the intense requirement for enhanced communication in such an inclusionary process as SBM.

IMPLICATIONS FOR TRAINING AND ROLE CHANGE

There is an obvious requirement to bring assistance, in the way of training, to these persons who are undergoing major changes in their roles because of the implementation of SBM within their school districts. The training necessary to adjust to this drastically changed superintendent work environment probably will differ with individual superintendents. Preparation and retraining for SBM are areas which can be addressed by a variety of sources: (1) individuals currently employed as superintendents, (2) national, state, and regional superintendents' associations, (3) universities (especially for the training of the next generation of superintendents), and (4) all other organizations who have a stake in assisting in the improvement of the management of schools. Many such organizations and groups have initiated that training, and it has become an integral part in innovative and revamped preparation programs (Barnett et al., 1992; Schmuck, 1992). There are national level recommendations for such training, further described in Chapter 11. One example of this is the recommendation of the Education Commission of the States (1991) to provide leadership policies which address changed roles and responsibilities, especially in ensuring that professional development assistance is available to help staff change their roles, particularly as SBM creates the need for collaboration and intervention in adjusting to new responsibilities.

Such change, both in decision-making attitude and in sheer collaborative skill aptitude, must be provided for incumbent school leaders approaching a school-based management implementation. It should also be included in competency training provided in administrator preparation programs. Given common research and field response on the inadequacy of current administrative training, such content and skill areas as group decision-making models and processes, collaborative strategies, team development, and employee empowerment are possibly absent in many existing preparation and retraining programs. As collaborative process training they do, of course, exist in university business and management preparation programs and in private sector executive and employee training. Many innovative school administrators do access such training through these avenues.

Application of these shared-governance prerequisites to the field should occur in the training process. They could be adapted and incorporated into existing preparatory curricula and into diagnostic centers to assist both the administrative intern and the experienced practitioner. Superintendents will need field-specific, customized training for meaningful attitudinal change and subsequent successful implementation of school based management (J.L. Herman, 1991).

Murphy (1989) speaks to the changes in power, persuasion, and direction of the superintendent in a school-based management setting, noting that "superintendents need to pay more attention to the unheroic dimensions of leadership if they are to promote local autonomy and professionalism. . . . they must also work with others to develop a shared vision and to find the common ground. . . . they must not only persuade, but also listen carefully and consult widely before making decisions; they must not only wield power, but also depend on others and develop caring relationships; they must not only exercise leadership, but also nurture the development of leadership throughout the school district" (p. 810).

In 1991, J.L. Herman considered a comparison of an original study's findings on superintendents' instructional leadership skills and competencies with common practice in school-based management and shared governance, intending to point out areas of overlap and, perhaps, potential interdistrict conflict. The original study was undertaken to identify salient instructionally-related characteristics of exemplary school district leaders; the findings understandably reflect the traditional areas of superintendent and central office responsibility. Many of those identified characteristics, as displayed in this chapter's superintendent site team nurturance strategies, would seem to support and facilitate shared governance and school-based management. However, the original study's outcomes regarding superintendent perception and attitude about success in instructional incidents reflect a preference for independence of action and self-reliance. If solo entrepreneurship and decision-making ownership is a preferred superintendency managerial style, then substantial change will be required to implement shared governance, particularly so when considering the critical leadership and initiative role of the superintendent in SBM.

School-based management demands, to a certain extent, a voluntary divesting of power and control; superintendents may perceive that they are not only expected to be an initiator and catalyst for shared governance, but that they are expected, simultaneously, to be the architects and facilitators of their own abdication. Profound role change occurs during the process of empowerment and decentralization. If shared governance and school-based management are to become common practice on a national scale, whether by legislative fiat, as in Kentucky, or by school district initiative and innovation, their contexts of empowerment and improvement require a fundamental change in school district management functions and in, particularly, superintendent leadership purview (J.L. Herman, 1991).

SUMMARY

A brief description of the expansion of the public school administrative hierarchy provided background for the complex organizational environment within which SBM must operate. A similar perspective was offered on the complex milieu within which the superintendent of schools must function. Eight management models were provided, mapping lines of decision power documents control, which operate within the situations of district growth, collective bargaining, and offered a visual perspective of potential SBM decision making power.

The transitions and new role perceptions related to SBM were explored, demonstrating the district function coordination effort on the role, the impact of the collective negotiations leadership role, and the newly emerging SBM shared leadership dimension of that function.

Some current perspective of the practitioner-based school leadership function was provided by a review of information from AASA and NASSP, as an outline of skills and competencies. Likewise offered were a set of desired pragmatic operational skills and beliefs for superintendents. The symbolic leadership functions and support demands made on superintendents in districts which are considering SBM include openness, a sharing of power, and provision of support. A readiness checklist was provided as a caveat for superintendents to consider prior to SBM implementation.

The implications of SBM on the superintendent's interactions with the board and central office personnel were elaborated upon, describing possible situations which could arise if there were disagreements between central and local levels over decisions made. Common national and state patterns of SBM implementation were described, focusing on the new expectations of the superintendent in a decentralized setting. The implications for training include the need for group decision-making models and processes, collaborative strategies, team development, and employee empowerment. School-based management demands, to a certain extent, a voluntary divesting of power and control; major superintendency role change occurs during the process of empowerment and the sharing of governance.

EXERCISES

1. If yours is a small size district (5,000 students or less), compare your line-staff structure and control to Figures 7.1 and 7.2. How would it differ with respect to an SBM readiness growth stage?

2. If yours is a large size district (25,000 students or more), compare your line-staff structure and control to Figures 7.3 and 7.4. How would it differ with respect to an SBM readiness growth stage?

3. If yours is a district in between in size, which of the two sets of models would be most applicable with regard to decision power and document control line?

4. Compare your collective negotiations (or employee relations) process with that outlined in Figures 7.5 and 7.6; create a similar model for your district.

5. With regard to Figures 7.7 and 7.8, what adjustments would be necessary for your district to achieve a similar flattening of decision power and document control lines?

6. Use the Interrogatory Checklist to assess your personal and organizational readiness for SBM implementation.

REFERENCES

Barnett, B.G., Caffarella, R.S., Daresh, J.C., King, R.A., Nicholson, T.H., & Whitaker, K.S. (1992). A new slant on leadership preparation. *Educational Leadership, 49* (5), 72–75.

Brown, F. (1990). The language of politics, education, and the disadvantaged. In S.L.

Jacobson and J.A. Conway (Eds.) *Educational leadership in an age of reform* (pp. 88–98). New York: Longman.

Cloyd, S. (1990). Involving school board members in negotiations. *School Business Affairs, 56* (12), 24–27.

Education Commission of the States (1991). *Exploring policy options to restructure education.* Denver, CO: Education Commission of the States, pp. 21–23.

Fielding, G.D. & Schalock, H.D. (1986). *Promoting the professional development of teachers and administrators.* Eugene, OR: Center for Educational Policy and Management and ERIC Clearinghouse on Educational Management, pp. 55–58.

Guthrie, J.W. & Reed, J.R. (1991). *Educational administration and policy.* Boston, MA: Allyn and Bacon, pp. 85–86.

Harrison, C.R., Killion, J.P., & Mitchell, J.E. (1989). Site based management: The realities of implementation. *Educational Leadership, 46* (8), 5–58.

Herman, J.J. & J.L. (1991). *The positive development of human resources and school district organizations.* Lancaster, PA: Technomic Publishing Company, pp. 25–26.

Herman, J.J. (1990). School based management: A checklist of things to consider. *NASSP Bulletin, 74,* (527), 67–71.

Herman, J.J. (1991). Prerequisites for instructional leadership. In J.W. Keefe & J.M. Jenkins (Eds.) *Instructional leadership handbook* (2nd ed.) (pp. 99–100). Reston, VA: National Association of Secondary School Principals.

Herman, J.L. (1991). *Instructional leadership skills and competencies of public school superintendents: Implications for preparation programs in a climate of shared governance.* (ERIC Document Reproduction Service No. ED 328 980).

Hoyle, J.R., English, F.W., & Steffy, B.E. (1985). *Skills for successful school leaders.* Arlington, VA: American Association of School Administrators, p. 3.

Hoyle, J.R., English, F.W., & Steffy, B.E. (1990). *Skills for successful school leaders* (2nd ed.). Arlington, VA: American Association of School Administrators, pp. 15–18, 49–50, 83–85, 113–115, 135–149, 153, 171–172, 215–217.

Ingwerson, D.W. (1990). A superintendent's view: Learning to listen and trust each school faculty. *The School Administrator, 8* (47), 8–11.

Keith, S. & Girling, R.H. (1991). *Education, management, and participation.* Boston, MA: Allyn and Bacon, p. 309.

Lewis, A. (1989). *Restructuring America's schools.* Washington, D.C.: American Association of School Administrators, p. 184.

Miller, M.H., Noland, K., & Schaaf, J. (1990). *A guide to the Kentucky Education Reform Act.* Frankfort, KY: Legislative Research Commission.

Murphy, J.T. (1989). The paradox of decentralizing schools: Lessons from business, government, and the Catholic Church. *Phi Delta Kappan, 70* (10), 808–812.

NASSP. (1985). *Performance-based preparation of principals: A framework for improvement.* Reston, VA: National Association of Secondary School Principals.

NASSP. (1992). *A leaders' guide to school restructuring.* Reston, VA: National Association of Secondary School Principals, pp. 16–17.

Neal, R.G. (1991). *School based management: A detailed guide for successful implementation.* Bloomington, IN: National Educational Service, pp. 22, 58.

Prasch, J. (1990). *How to organize for school-based management.* Alexandria, VA: Association for Supervision and Curriculum Development, p. 18–22.

Schlechty, P.C. (1990). *Schools for the 21st century.* San Francisco, CA: Jossey-Bass Publishers, pp. 127–129.

Schmuck, P.A. (1992). Educating the new generation of superintendents. *Educational Leadership, 49* (5), 66–71.

Tewel, K.J. (1991). A case study in reform. *American School Board Journal, 178* (10), 30–33.

Chapter 8

SCHOOL-BASED MANAGEMENT AND THE SCHOOL BOARD: ALTERING TRADITIONAL GOVERNANCE AND POLICY

Historically, the roles of the school boards in this country have included: (1) the establishing of policies within which the school district's operations functioned, (2) the hiring of a superintendent of schools and officially approving all employees to be hired, (3) the setting of a budget and approving of all expenditures, and, (4) the ratifying of contracts with suppliers, contractors, and employee unions. Although many of the hiring and financial matters were delegated to the superintendent and her/his staff members, the board of education retained final approval control (Guthrie & Reed, 1991).

With the transition to school-based management, the board of education still retains the official roles, but it modifies the procedures and daily operations for conducting the school district's business. With the advent of SBM councils, much of the actual (not final or legal) decision making is placed at the individual school site. Also, the school-site decisions are made by a group of newly empowered persons, usually including teachers, parents, and the principal of the individual school building (Goldman & Dunlap, 1990).

What, then, are the transitions and new role functions required of boards of education as the district embraces school based management? The remainder of this chapter will be dedicated to answering this question.

TRANSITIONS AND NEW ROLE FUNCTIONS DEMANDED BY SBM

On a legal level, very little change is required unless the school district falls within a state where the legislature has mandated school-based management and it has spelled out specific requirements of boards of education. However, in all districts which have voluntarily or by mandate adopted SBM, the operation of the district's decision making process has changed (Hill, Bonan, & Warner, 1992). These changes may involve the manner in which employees are selected, the manner in which budgets are developed and expenditures processed, the manner in which instructional decisions are made, and the manner in which daily operational and governance decisions are handled (Murphy, 1989).

The most dramatic changes in operational decision making leading to school based management are those which are required in Kentucky. In 1990, the Commonwealth of Kentucky's legislature passed the Education Reform Act of 1990. Those mandated changes in doing business are related below.

Kentucky Law: KRS Chapter 160, Sections 12, 14, and 15

Section 12: Professional Development.

1. A consortium shall receive the district's professional development funds during 1991–92 through 1994–1995.
2. After July 1, 1995, an individual school district can withdraw from the consortium and receive its own professional development funds.

Section 14: School-Based Decision Making.

1. By January 1, 1991, the school board shall adopt a policy for implementing the school-based decision making approach, and policies related to KRS 160.340 must be amended to further implement this approach related to professional development activities (sections 2 & 3 of HB 940).
2. Each participating school shall form a school council composed of 2 parents, 3 teachers and the principal or administrator. Can add more, but the proportion must be the same. Parents cannot be related to any school employee.
   a. Teachers shall be *elected* for 1 year terms by a majority of teachers.
   b. Parents shall be "selected" by the members of the PTO of the school; or, if none exists, by the largest organization of parents formed for this purpose.
   c. The principal or head teacher shall chair the council.

The Council's and Principals' Responsibilities Include:

(1) Set school policy to provide an environment to enhance students' achievement and meet the goals of Sections 2 and 3 of this act. The principal shall be the primary administrator and instructional leader of the school; and, with the assistance of the total school staff, shall administer the policies established by the school council and school board.
(2) All staff *may* be participants. The staff shall divide into committees according to their areas of interest. A majority of each committee's members shall "elect" a chair to serve a one year term. Each committee shall submit its recommendations to the school council for consideration.

(3) The council and each committee shall determine the agenda and frequency of meetings. The meetings shall be open to the public with the exceptions provided in KRS 61.810.

(4) Within the funds available from the school board, the council *shall* determine the number of persons to be employed in each job classification at the school, and can make personnel decisions on vacancies. It cannot recommend transfer or dismissals.

(5) The council *shall* determine which instructional materials and student support services shall be provided in the school.

(6) From a list of applicants recommended by the superintendent, the principal *shall* select personnel to fill vacancies, after consultation with the school council.

(7) To fill a principal vacancy, the school council *shall* select from among those persons recommended by the superintendent, and the superintendent "shall" provide additional applicants upon request.

(8) The council shall adopt a policy to be implemented by the principal in these additional areas:

> (a) Determination of curriculum, including needs assessment, curriculum development, alignment with state standards, technology utilization, and program appraisal within the local school board's policy.
>
> (b) Assignment of "all" instructional and non-instructional staff time.
>
> (c) Assignment of students to classes and programs.
>
> (d) Determine the schedule of the school day and week subject to the beginning and ending times and school calendar set by the school board.
>
> (e) Determine the use of school space during the school day.
>
> (f) Plan and resolve issues regarding instructional practices.
>
> (g) Select and implement discipline and classroom management techniques; including the roles of students, parents, teachers, counselors and principals.
>
> (h) Select extracurricular programs and determination of policies relating to student participation based on academic and attendance requirements, program evaluation and supervision.

3. The Local Board Policy on School-Based Decision Making "shall" also Address:

> a. School budget and administration (discretionary funds; activity and other school funds; funds for maintenance, supplies and equipment; and accounting and auditing).
>
> b. Assessment of individual student progress, including testing and reporting of student progress to students, parents, the school district, the community and the state.
>
> c. School improvement plans, including the form and function of strategic planning and its relationship to district planning.
>
> d. Professional development plans developed pursuant to Sections 12 and 13 of this act.
>
> e. Parent, citizen and community participation including the relationship of the council with other groups.

f. Cooperation and collaboration within the district and with other districts, public agencies and private agencies.

g. Requirements for waiver of district policies.

h. Requirements for record keeping by the school council.

i. A process for appealing a decision made by a school council.

j. In addition, the school board "may" grant to the school council any other authority permitted by law.

4. The school board "shall" make liability insurance available to all members of the school council when performing duties as school council members.

5. After the effective date of this act, any school in which two-thirds (2/3) of the faculty vote to implement school-based decision making may do so.

6. By June 30, 1991, each school board shall submit to the Chief State School Officer, the name of at least one (1) school which has decided to implement school-based management. If no school so votes, the school board "shall" designate one (1) school to implement it.

All schools shall implement school-based management by July 1, 1996. However, by a majority vote of the faculty, a school performing above its threshold level requirement, as determined by the Department of Education, may apply to the State Board for exemption from this requirement.

7. The Department of Education shall develop sample guidelines to assist local boards in the development of their policies, and it shall provide professional development activities to assist schools in implementing school-based decision making.

8. A school that chooses to have a different school-based model than the one outlined, can request an exemption by describing the model, submitting it through the board of education to the Chief State School Officer and the State Board for approval (Miller, Noland & Schaaf, 1990).

It is quite clear from this legislation that the operational decision making in Kentucky's schools and in its school districts changed as of July 1, 1991. Also, it is clear that the boards of education in Kentucky have had to adopt policies and modify existing policies, where necessary, to promote and implement school based management; as every school building in every district is required to implement SBM by July 1, 1996. This certainly is not going to allow business as usual to continue in the schools of the Commonwealth of Kentucky. Further consideration of this topic is provided in Chapter 10.

NEED FOR BOARD LEADERSHIP AND SUPPORT

As boards of education, either voluntarily or by legislative mandate, enter into school-based management, the collective board of education and the individual board members have two important roles to play. First, they should be salespersons for SBM when they talk to the media, to the community members, or to the employees of the school district. Second, they should adopt a series of board policies that provide the leadership guidance to the entire structure and the processes required to implement a healthy and effective SBM operation within the school district (Mitchell, 1990).

The adoption of implementation policies should be conducted in public meetings, and they should be discussed in multiple board of education meetings before final adoption. In each district that is attempting to implement school-based management the board of education should provide a sound policy structure for that implementation (Doyle & Tetzloff, 1992). Again, the Kentucky experience shall be used to provide an example of a set of implementation policies. The policies adopted by Kentucky's Hopkins County School System's Board of Education on December 17, 1990, provide a comprehensive example of implementation policies adopted by one board of education.

SCHOOL-BASED DECISION-MAKING POLICIES FOR THE HOPKINS COUNTY SCHOOL SYSTEM

Introduction to SBM Policies

Current research on "effective schools" indicates that if students are to receive the maximum benefits from schooling, the focus must be on the basic skills of English, reading, writing, grammar, computation, communication, and thinking and learning skill improvement; and that most decisions relating to this have to be school-based. Further, research indicates that the building principal is the key figure in the development and monitoring of a vision which will lead to high achievement. Professional employees want students to "be the best they can be," and they realize that community involvement and support are critical.

It is important for site-based councils to maintain their extended ownership to all of those affected by their decisions. Therefore, we must constantly be aware and remind one another that the movement to school-based decision making at the building level is to involve all constituencies in the effort to fulfill the philosophy, mission statement, goals, objectives, and adopted beliefs of the school system developed on behalf of the children we all serve—to improve student learning, performance, and achievement.

Implementation of School-Based Decision Making

INSTRUCTIONAL IMPACT: PROCESS MONITORING AND ACCOUNTABILITY

The board approves the implementation of the SBDM process model. It extends to the council of those schools the authority to create curricular/instructional/program designs that meet the unique learning needs of the children served. The council shall inform the local board of education before implementation of new curricular/instructional programs. They must be consistent with and fulfill the *Mission Statement* of the Hopkins County School System and the legislation of the State of Kentucky.

The visions and implementation strategies shall be arrived at through a process of *consensus* involving council members with input from the school/community members who would be most affected by the curricular/instructional/program changes. All staff at any school shall be encouraged to be participants in SBDM.

Once consensus has been reached in the subcommittee, the decision will become policy *only* when the council has formally voted to implement the decision. It takes a majority of the council members to make policy. All policy decisions shall be reflected in the minutes showing the vote of each council member.

The authority extended to individuals should not be construed as having the meaning that traditional district decisions will no longer be made. The process being endorsed by the Board is an evolutionary change, not a revolutionary change. This process only extends to SBDM schools the minimum authority set forth in HB 940.

Consensus is used only at the subcommittee level. It is defined as the judgement arrived at by most of those concerned where everyone agrees to support the decision even though it may not be their first choice. Everyone agrees that he/she has had sufficient opportunity to influence the decision and can state the decision.

Instructional Input: School Based Decision Making (SBDM)

Definitions: *School-Based Decision Making (SBDM)* is a model for school improvement that allows for building level shared decision making. It is the vehicle through which research on what constitutes effective schools will be implemented.

Effective School is an individual school building where SBDM is in effect and which incorporates the characteristics of an effective school that are listed as follows:

consensus on explicit instructional goals and values as related in the Mission Statement,

the belief that all children can learn,

district level support for school improvement,

ongoing, school wide staff development training,

individual school autonomy and flexibility,

collaborative, collegial instructional planning,

a focus on basic skills acquisition,

an emphasis upon higher order cognitive skills,

high expectations for student achievement,

teacher responsibility for instructional and classroom management decisions,

teacher/parent accountability and acceptance of responsibility for student performances,

a safe, orderly, and disciplined school climate, and

strong instructional leadership.

Instructional Input: Process Elements of School Based Decision Making

Each SBDM school will incorporate the fulfillment of the process elements that are listed as follows:

1. school-based visions of excellence and implementation strategies must fulfill the mission statement of the school district;
2. the school-based subcommittee MUST represent a balance of all school and community constituencies when appropriate; the subcommittee will be formed at the discretion of the school-based council;
3. implementation strategies must flow from the vision statement and support the carrying out the mission statement of the school system;
4. school based councils must fully utilize the resources available to analyze their school's present situation, to explore resources and assess

options for reaching their vision, and to evaluate implemented plans on at least an annual basis;
5. the school based council is responsible for carrying out its own implementation strategies; and
6. no member of the school-based council has veto power.

SCHOOL COUNCIL: MECHANICS AND STRUCTURE

Voting

After an indication of interest in SBDM, the professional association's building representative shall notify the principal. The principal shall set the date, time and place of a meeting for the purpose of voting on entering SBDM. This meeting shall be held not less than 5 school days and not more than 10 school days from the principal's or head teacher's receipt of notification.

Voting is restricted to one vote per school calendar month.

Notice of the meeting shall be provided to all teachers assigned to the school at least 5 school days in advance of the meeting.

The principal shall chair the meeting at which the vote is taken. Voting shall be by secret ballot. Ballots shall offer teachers the opportunity to vote for or against entering SBDM. The principal and one teacher chosen by the faculty shall count the ballots and announce the results at the conclusion of the meeting. The principal shall forward the results of the vote to the superintendent; the superintendent will present the results to the board.

If two-thirds of the total teaching faculty vote for SBDM, the school will enter SBDM. The principal shall organize the elections to select teacher and parent representatives for the school council as specified in the Board Policy on Election of School Council Members.

If none of the schools decide to go in SBDM, then the board shall make the decision as to which school will go into SBDM.

For the purpose of policies relating to SBDM, "teacher" is defined as all certified staff assigned to the school; except the principal, assistant principal, or head teacher. Itinerant teachers shall vote at their designated home school and may serve on the council of their home school.

Home school is defined as the school where the itinerant teacher spends the most time.

Repeal

After an indication of interest to repeal SBDM, the professional association's building representative shall notify the principal. The principal shall set the date, time, and place of a meeting for the purpose of voting on the repeal of SBDM. This meeting shall be held not less than 5 school days and not more than 10 school days from the principal's or the head teacher's receipt of notification.

Voting is restricted to one vote per school calendar month.

Notice of the meeting shall be provided to all teachers assigned to the school at least 5 days in advance of the meeting.

The principal shall chair the meeting at which the vote is taken. Voting shall be by secret ballot. Ballots shall offer teachers the opportunity to vote for or against repealing SBDM. The principal and one teacher chosen by the faculty shall count the ballots and announce the results at the conclusion of the meeting. The principal shall forward the results of the vote to the superintendent and the board.

A vote of the majority of the teachers shall be required to repeal SBDM.

Any school voluntarily voting to enter SBDM under the provisions of board policy may repeal that vote only until June 30, 1995.

Any school performing above its threshold level requirement as determined by the Kentucky Department of Education under DRS 158.6455 may apply to the State Board for Elementary and Secondary Education for exemption from SBDM.

Any school that requests such exemption shall inform the superintendent and the board.

Alternate Models

A school may develop an alternate form of SBDM under the process outlined in HB 940, Section 14, Subsection 7, Page 43.

Election of School Council Members

Following a two-thirds vote in favor of SBDM, the principal shall give appropriate notice of elections of teacher and parent members to the school council.

Procedures for holding elections for teacher council members shall be the same as those governing the election to determine if the school will adopt SBDM. Teachers may nominate themselves or another teacher.

Nominations shall be made in writing to the principal no later than 5 days before the election. The principal shall prepare a ballot containing the names of all qualified teachers nominated. The principal shall chair and oversee the meeting to elect teacher members to the council. Balloting will continue until three (3) teachers are elected. Teachers must be employees of the district and currently assigned to the school where they are elected as council members. Election shall be by majority vote of all teachers assigned to the school. Notice of the election of parent council members shall be provided by the principal to the parents and to the president of the school's parent-teacher organization. The notice shall state that the parents who are members of the parent-teacher organization may vote to elect the parent council members. The date of the meeting shall be set in cooperation with the president of the parent-teacher organization. If the school does not have a parent-teacher organization, then the principal shall set the date and time for a meeting of parents to elect parent council members. The principal shall provide notice of this meeting to parents.

The meeting to elect parent council members shall be held after normal working hours at a time and place convenient for parents to attend. The principal shall notify the local newspaper of the date, time, and place of the vote in a manner that gives sufficient time for the newspaper to provide notification to the community.

Election of parent members to the council shall be by a majority of the voting, qualified parents who are present at the meeting. Parents may nominate themselves or another parent. Nominations shall be made in writing and submitted to the principal no later than 5 school days prior to the date scheduled for the election. The principal shall prepare a ballot containing the names of all qualified parents nominated. Voting shall continue until two (2) representatives are elected. Separate ballots shall be taken until two (2) parents receive a majority of the votes of the members present.

Parent council members shall be a parent, stepparent, foster parent or legal guardian of a student enrolled in the school, and shall not be a relative of an employee of that school. Relative shall mean father, mother, brother, sister, husband, wife, son, daughter, aunt, uncle, son-in-law, or daughter-in-law.

Terms of school council members shall begin on July 1 and end on June 30 of the following year. Annual elections for the following year's term shall be held during the preceding May on a date set by the principal.

Teacher and parent council members are eligible for reelection.

Council vacancies shall be filled at a special called election and shall follow the guidelines set forth in this policy. A vacancy is created when a teacher is no longer assigned to the school, a parent no longer has a child enrolled in the school or a member of the council has missed three (3) meetings of the council without council approval or without a written resignation of the council member.

School Council Authority

The council is a corporate policy making body. Outside of a legally called council meeting, no council member, other than the principal, has decision making or administrative authority conferred by office on the council. The principal is the school's primary administrator and instructional leader.

School Council Meetings

The first meeting of the council shall be called by the principal; the council shall set its own meeting schedule.

All meetings of the council are open to the public and subject to the open meetings law.

Meetings shall be held at times convenient to working parents. No council meeting shall be held during the scheduled instructional day. Advance notice of meetings shall be given to parents, teachers, and the media.

A written agenda shall be prepared and copies made available to the public at all meetings of the council. The agenda of each council meeting shall provide the opportunity for interested persons to address the council.

In order for a legal meeting of the council to take place, a quorum of the council consisting of the principal, one parent and one teacher and at least one additional parent or teacher, as a minimum, shall be present.

The principal shall be the chair of the council and shall be responsible for securing minutes that record the council's actions. Minutes shall be approved by the council, kept in a permanent file, and open to public inspection. A copy of the minutes of each council meeting shall be forwarded by the principal to the superintendent who shall keep the board informed of council actions.

Roberts Rules of Order (newly revised) shall be the guide for conducting all council meetings.

School Council Relationships

Councils shall encourage parent, citizen, and community participation in council meetings and in school activities.

School Council Policies

No policy shall be adopted by a council at the meeting in which the policy is introduced. Section 14, Subsection (2), (j).

The council shall adopt policies which provide an environment that enhances student achievement and helps the school meet the mission and goals established by law and by the Hopkins County Board Policies.

In the development and application of school policies, as permitted by statute, schools operating under SBDM shall comply with board policies, including, but not limited to those prohibiting discrimination based on age, race, sex, color, religion, national origin, political affiliation, marital status, or handicap.

Appeal of Decisions

Appeals from decisions of the council may be made by any resident of the district, parent, student, or employee of the school.

Prior to being appealed, the issue must first be presented in writing to the council for reconsideration. Issues for council consideration shall be delivered to the principal who shall bring the matter before the council at its next meeting. If the matter is not satisfactorily resolved within ten (10) school days from the date the issue is presented to the council, an appeal may be submitted in writing to the superintendent.

If, within ten (10) school days of receiving the appeal, the superintendent has not been able to satisfactorily resolve it, a further appeal may be made in writing to the board. The board shall act on the appeal within forty (40) school days of the board meeting when the appeal was made. A final appeal may go to the Commissioner of Education.

Actions of the council will be reviewed on appeal based on whether the council's action was arbitrary, violated district policy, exceeded the authority of the council or was otherwise unlawful under state or federal law.

School Budget

The board shall appropriate to each school an amount of funds equal to or greater than that specified in KAR to purchase instructional materials, supplies and equipment.

The school shall, in expending allocated funds, comply with all state and board budgeting, purchasing and reporting laws, regulations, policies and procedures. Board purchasing procedures shall be followed in the expenditure of these funds. Expenditure of these funds shall be accomplished only by completing a central office purchase order.

The allocation of instructional materials, supplies and equipment is the total financial resource available to that school in those categories of purchase for the fiscal year. The school shall not expend or commit to the expenditure of any funds in excess of funds allocated.

All state allocated funds managed by the school but not expended by the end of the fiscal year shall accumulate in the account of the school and be available to the school for future expenditure.

The superintendent shall prepare and provide the school a monthly statement of current financial status of funds allocated for purchasing instructional materials, supplies and equipment. This statement shall include the beginning unencumbered balance for each category of authorized expenditure, an itemized listing of purchase orders paid, and itemized listing of purchase orders authorized but not paid, and the end-of-the-month unencumbered balance of funds allocated.

In schools where SBDM has been implemented, the school council shall determine the expenditure of funds allocated for purchasing instructional materials, supplies and equipment. In schools where SBDM has not been implemented, the principal of the school shall determine the expenditure of these funds.

References: KRS 160.345 (2) (h) and KAR.

School Purchasing

Subject to KARs, the board shall allocate to each school an appropriation as dictated by the Kentucky State Board of Education's administrative regulations.

The council shall determine, within available resources, the instructional materials and student support services to be provided in the school.

In order to comply with state accounting and bidding requirements, all purchases of goods and services shall be made in conformity with board policy.

State law, at present, does not permit schools to bid their supplies separate from the total bid of the school system. Therefore, all schools in SBDM shall refer their purchase requests of goods and services to the board for inclusion in the bidding process.

School Hiring

After receiving notification of the financial allocation for the school from the board, the council shall determine, within funds allocated, the number of persons to be employed in the school in each job classification. The council shall not have the authority to recommend transfers and dismissals.

From a list of applicants recommended by the local superintendent, the principal at the participating school shall select personnel to fill vacancies, after consultation with the school council. Requests for transfer shall conform to any employer-employee bargained contract which is in effect. If the vacancy to be filled is the position of principal, the school council shall select the new principal from among those persons recommended by the local superintendent. Personnel decisions made at the school level under the authority of this subsection shall be binding on the superintendent who completes the hiring process. The superintendent shall provide applicants upon request.

When a new facility is constructed causing the consolidation of several schools, the existing SBDM council of those schools that will make up the new school, shall select one teacher from each council to serve as a committee to name the principal of the newly formed school from a list provided by the superintendent. Schools not having SBDM will select one teacher, by secret ballot, to serve on this committee.

A vacancy is created in the position of principal by the resignation, removal, transfer, retirement, death of the current principal, or one created by a new facility.

When the position to be filled in the school is other than that of principal; the principal, after conferring with the council, shall fill the position from a list of nominees provided by the superintendent. Should the school council decide not to fill a teaching position that becomes vacant, the superintendent will provide in the budget to the council, the amount of money of a Rank III Teacher with zero experience, for its discretionary use.

Training of School Council Members

The majority of the school based council members shall receive the minimum training by the State Department of Education and any additional training individual school councils deem necessary.

Waiver of Board Policies

The principal on behalf of the school council may submit to the superintendent a written request to waive board policy.

The superintendent shall present the request to the board along with a recommendation to approve or deny the request. The council shall have the opportunity to address the board directly to support its request.

The decision to approve or deny the request shall include, but not be limited to, a consideration of the following:

1. The legality of waiving board policy.
2. If the district's mission statement and goals will be advanced by the waiver.
3. If student outcomes will be promoted.
4. If district uniformity is required in the circumstances under consideration; and/or
5. If the larger interests of the public will be served.

Within forty (40) calendar days from the date on which the superintendent presents the waiver request to the board, the board shall rule on the request.

If the request for waiver is denied, the grounds for denial will be recorded in board minutes.

Other Board Policies

All board policies shall be reviewed and amended, as necessary, to conform to the requirements of KERA 90.

Accountability

By October 15 of each year, each council shall submit, in writing to the board, its measurable goals and objectives for the school year. The goals shall be related to the mission statement of the district and the goals listed in HB 940, Part I, Sections 2 and 3.

By October 15 of each year, each council shall submit, in writing, its plan for achieving the district's mission statement, its goals and objectives, and the method for evaluating the achievement of the plan.

By June 30 of each year, each council shall submit, in writing, its annual evaluation report to the board.

A performance based testing program based on the capacities listed by the Commonwealth of Kentucky, will be used to evaluate the educational program.

> References: HB 940, Part I, Sections 2 and 3.
> KRS Chapter 158
> HB 940, Part I, Section 13
> KRS 160.290

Assessment of Student Progress

District assessment of students' progress shall be conducted annually. The instrument to used is the CTBS Fourth Edition. It will be given to students in grades one through ten, with the exception of certain Special Education students who should be excluded because of handicapping conditions. Special Education students shall be evaluated according to the specifications in each child's IEP. The SBDM council at each school may provide for further assessment of students by appropriate and effective methods as determined by the council (Hopkins County Board of Education, 1990).

It is clear in the case of the policies (which in reality include a combination of policies, bylaws, rules, and procedures) adopted by the Hopkins County School District's Board of Education, that this board attempted to clarify and put in place adopted statements which implement the detailed Kentucky Reform Act of 1990. Of course, the policy structure established by each school district involved in school-based management will vary with the comprehensiveness of the SBM structure and processes, either entered into by legislative mandate or by voluntary action. Each district is a unique entity and each SBM implementation is evolutionary in nature (Simpson, 1991).

In each district's case, however, the board of education should adopt supportive policies, and it should modify those existing policies which inhibit or negatively affect the implementation of SBM. In addition, the board of education and the individual board members should show visible support for the SBM movement in their discussions with others and in their formal actions as a board of education (Education Commission of the States, 1991).

Visible board support is especially important during the initial, transitional phase, when moving from the traditional decision-making process within the school district to one which empowers new individuals to make significant decisions, and one which delegates much decision making to the individual school building site level (AASA, 1988; Harrison, Killion, & Mitchell, 1989). In fact, a unified board of education support is crucial to the successful probability of implementing SBM. For, eventually, the standard operating procedures, the roles played by traditional decision makers, and the entire culture of the school district and its component individual school buildings are likely to change.

IMPLICATIONS FOR PROVIDING RESOURCES AND FOR RESTRUCTURING RELATIONSHIPS WITH THE SUPERINTENDENT, PROFESSIONAL STAFF, AND WITH INDIVIDUAL SCHOOLS

Not only does the board of education have to show visible support for the implementation of school-based management, it also has to: (1) provide the necessary resources to accomplish a sound implementation, and (2) be mindful of and adjust to the changing roles and the new decision paths required by SBM. The provision of resources may involve delegating responsibility and funds to the local school site level for such purposes as instructional programs, training, and the purchase of supplies and equipment. Further, it may involve delegating decisions to the school site level related to schedules and the employment of personnel (AASA, 1990; Cohen, 1988).

The greatest change in the relationships with the superintendent, the central staff, the individual school building's principal, and the school-based management council is that of a quantum shift in decision making authority and power (Neal, 1991; Prasch, 1990). Assuming that the SBM structure and the numerous implementation details are not legislatively mandated, as in the case of Kentucky, the district's decision makers will have to decide which decisions (and to what degree each of those decisions) are totally kept at the central level, which are totally delegated to the school building site level, and which are to be shared decisions between the central level and the school site level. Obviously, the structure decided upon will identify the changes in the decision making power of all parties involved.

A sample exercise which lists those areas of decision making that should be resolved are listed in Figure 8.1.

FIGURE 8.1
AREAS OF SCHOOL-BASED DECISION MAKING POSSIBILITIES

Directions: Place an "X" in the appropriate column for each of the areas of possible decision making.

		District Level	Building Level	Shared
1.	Staffing	____	____	____
2.	Staff development and training	____	____	____
3.	Instructional programs	____	____	____
4.	Purchasing of equipment and supplies	____	____	____
5.	Governance policies	____	____	____
6.	Transportation services	____	____	____
7.	Co-curricular and athletic programming	____	____	____
8.	Guidance and counseling services	____	____	____
9.	Custodial services	____	____	____
10.	Food services	____	____	____
11.	Maintenance services	____	____	____
12.	Budgeting	____	____	____
13.	Accounting	____	____	____
14.	Substitute teacher services	____	____	____
15.	Instructional and clerical aides services	____	____	____
16.	Secretarial services	____	____	____
18.	Collective bargaining provisions	____	____	____
19.	Other possible areas of decentralized (school based) decision making	____	____	____

COMMON IMPLEMENTATIONS AND RECOMMENDATIONS

In a study of the process of restructuring in several districts (Davis, 1988), there emerged definable themes of SBM implementation, which, by the nature of their implied traditional policy change and resource allocation, would involve school boards in both the described broad initiatives and in the more detailed process of launching the innovation:

- The goal of restructuring through site-based management is long-term, comprehensive change guided by a conception of schools as stimulating workplaces and environments.
- School staff need the skills, authority, and time to create new roles and environments appropriate to their situations.
- Restructuring through site-based management requires building new coalitions of support and new conceptions of accountability.

Extending these themes are the common SBM implementations were listed in Chapter 1, and which also imply, by their nature, board compliance and facilitation: the pioneer districts:

- began with schools that volunteer
- supported with waivers from constraints
- involved staff in developing goals/actions
- made cooperative agreements with unions
- gave schools staffing and materials budgets
- provided incentives for principals to involve teachers in site decisions
- developed and demonstrated new models during the summer
- used multiple measures of accountability, including those defined by the schools
- provided professional growth for principals and teachers in management, clinical supervision, and instruction
- provided time for staff to work with colleagues make site decisions
- sought supplementary sources of funding (Lewis, 1989).

The major thrusts of these implementation areas are policy-related and require board procedural alignments and facilitations that support a decentralized system. There are larger implications for board action, as described in Chapter 2's strategic planning prerequisites, and as exemplified in this chapter's description of an SBM-aligned board policies. In its more comprehensive and recommended ideal form, the implementation of school based management is a restructuring effort, which is very much board-driven and/or supported (Candoli, 1991). The approval and support, both in policy-making and in demonstrated leadership and collaboration, of the board is an essential, if not the critical, component of school-based management implementation (Prasch, 1990).

SUMMARY

SBM will require some modification of procedures and daily operations, but board members will still retain official and legal roles. The transitions and new role functions for individuals operating in an SBM environment are primarily located at operational levels below the action level of the board. The chapter provided a dramatic example of operational decision making change in its description of the Kentucky Education Reform Act; by its provisions, local boards will need to adopt new policies and modify existing ones to facilitate shared decision making. A sample of aligned local Kentucky school board policies was also provided, to demonstrate the requirement for compatibility of language and policy intent and to display the local district language detail and articulation with the state law. The SBM implementation need for board leadership was stressed, since board members should be salespersons for decentralization. Unified board of education support is crucial to the successful probability of implementing SBM.

The greatest SBM-caused change in school district relationships is that of a quantum shift in decision making authority and power; the district's decision makers will have to decide which decisions are totally kept at the central level, which are totally delegated to the school building site level, and which are to be shared decisions between the central level and the school site level. A sample exercise to that effect was provided. The definable themes of SBM implementation, which, by the nature of their implied traditional policy change and resource allocation, involve school boards in both broad initiatives and in the more detailed process of launching school based management, especially in the provision of resources.

The major thrusts of most SBM implementation areas are policy-related and require board procedural alignments and facilitations which will support a decentralized system. That approval and support, both in policy-making and in demonstrated leadership and collaboration, of the board is an essential component of successful school based management implementation.

EXERCISES

1. Which typical policy changes demanded by SBM implementation would be the most difficult for your board to accept? Why?

2. Complete the exercise *Areas of School-Based Decision-Making Possibilities*, with your district in mind. What can you conclude from the results?

3. Which of the common SBM implementations, requiring board support, do you judge to be most doable in your district, and why?

4. Describe some ways in which some elements of SBM could be achieved without your district's board sponsorship or approval.

REFERENCES

AASA. (1988). *School-based management* (AASA Stock Number 0221-00209), Washington, D.C.: American Association of School Administrators, National Association of Elementary School Principals, and National Association of Secondary School Principals, pp. 12–13.

AASA. *A new look at empowerment.* (1990). (AASA Stock Number 021-00278). Washington, DC: American Association of School Administrators.

Candoli, I.C. (1991). *School system administration: A strategic plan for site-based management.* Lancaster, PA: Technomic Publishing Company, p. 220.

Cohen, M. (1988). Restructuring the education system: Agenda for the 1990's. In *Results in Education,* Washington, D.C.: National Governors' Association Center for Policy Research, pp. 14–19.

David, J.L. (1988). *Restructuring in progress: Lessons from pioneering districts.* Center for Policy Research in Education. New Brunswick, NJ: Rutgers University.

Doyle, R. and Tetzloff, P. (1992). Waivers provide relief, allow improvements. *The School Administrator, 1* (49), 10–11.

Education Commission of the States (1991). *Exploring policy options to restructure education.* Denver, CO: Education Commission of the States, p. 27.

Goldman, P. & Dunlap, D. (1990, October). *Reform, restructuring, site-based management, and the new face of power in schools.* Paper presented at the Annual Meetings of the University Council on Educational Administration, Pittsburgh, PA.

Guthrie, J.W. & Reed, R.J. (1991). *Educational administration and policy* (2nd ed.). Boston, MA: Allyn & Bacon, pp. 77–79.

Harrison, C.R., Killion, J.P., & Mitchell, J.E. (1989). Site based management: The realities of implementation. *Educational Leadership, 46* (8), 5–58.

Hill, P.T., Bonan, J.J., & Warner, K. (1992). Uplifting education. *National School Board Journal, 179* (3), 21–25.

Hopkins County Board of Education (1990). *School based decision making: Policies for Hopkins County School System.* Reprinted with permission.

Lewis, A. (1989). *Restructuring America's schools.* Washington, D.C.: American Association of School Administrators, p. 144–145, 148.

Miller, M.H., Noland, K., & Schaaf, J. (1990). *A Guide to the Kentucky Education Reform Act.* Frankfort, KY: Legislative Research Commission.

Mitchell, J.E. (1990). Share the power. *American School Board Journal, 177* (1), R 5–6.

Murphy, J.T. (1989). The paradox of decentralizing schools; lessons from business, government, and the Catholic Church. *Phi Delta Kappan, 70* (10), 808–812.

Neal, R.G. (1991). *School based management: A detailed guide for successful implementation.* Bloomington, IN: National Educational Service, p. 81.

Prasch, J. (1990). *How to organize for school-based management.* Alexandria, VA: Association for Supervision and Curriculum Development, pp. 12, 17.

Scholes, G.W. (1991). KERA: a leadership (planning) challenge for school boards and superintendents. *Kentucky School Boards Association Journal, 10* (2), 15.

Simpson, J.F. (1991). Journal of the reform year. *Executive Educator, 13* (12), 29–31.

Chapter 9

SCHOOL-BASED MANAGEMENT AND THE COMMUNITY: NEW STRUCTURES FOR COLLABORATION

Historically, most school districts involved parents and community citizens who lived in their districts in very limited activities (Boyd, 1990). Most school districts had Parent–Teacher Associations or other general parent organizations operating at the schools in their districts, and many districts had sports or band booster groups who were supportive of the student activities of their particular focal interest. Some school districts occasionally took attitude surveys in their communities, and the boards of educations and administrators often modified activities in concert with the findings of these attitude surveys. In addition, parents and citizens were frequently asked to form citizens committees to assist in the passage of an increased operational tax or the passage of a bond issue. Finally, districts oftentimes appointed citizen advisory committees to study a specific issue and to make recommendations about the resolution of that issue to the board of education or the administration. These committees were usually appointed for a short period of time—usually for one year or less.

TRANSITIONS AND NEW ROLE FUNCTIONS DEMANDED BY SBM

Usually, the only residents of the school districts who had any serious and continuing input were those members of the community who were elected or appointed to the school districts' boards of education. However, there were a few districts in the nation who did involve many community members in meaningful and comprehensive decision making activities. One such school district, the West Bloomfield School District of Michigan, will serve as an example of such community involvement.

In the 1970s and 1980s the West Bloomfield School District, one of the

School-Based Management and the Community 165

better school districts in the nation, involved hundreds of community members in two very important decision making activities. The first activity was that of involving hundreds in a needs assessment and five-year planning structure, and the second was the creation and continuous use of communication-governance committees at every school site and at the central district level. Both of these methods of involving large numbers of school district residents are discussed below, beginning with their involvement in planning activities, which are outlined in Figure 9.1.

FIGURE 9.1

WEST BLOOMFIELD SCHOOL DISTRICT'S MODEL SYSTEMS PLAN FOR PROGRAM DEVELOPMENT

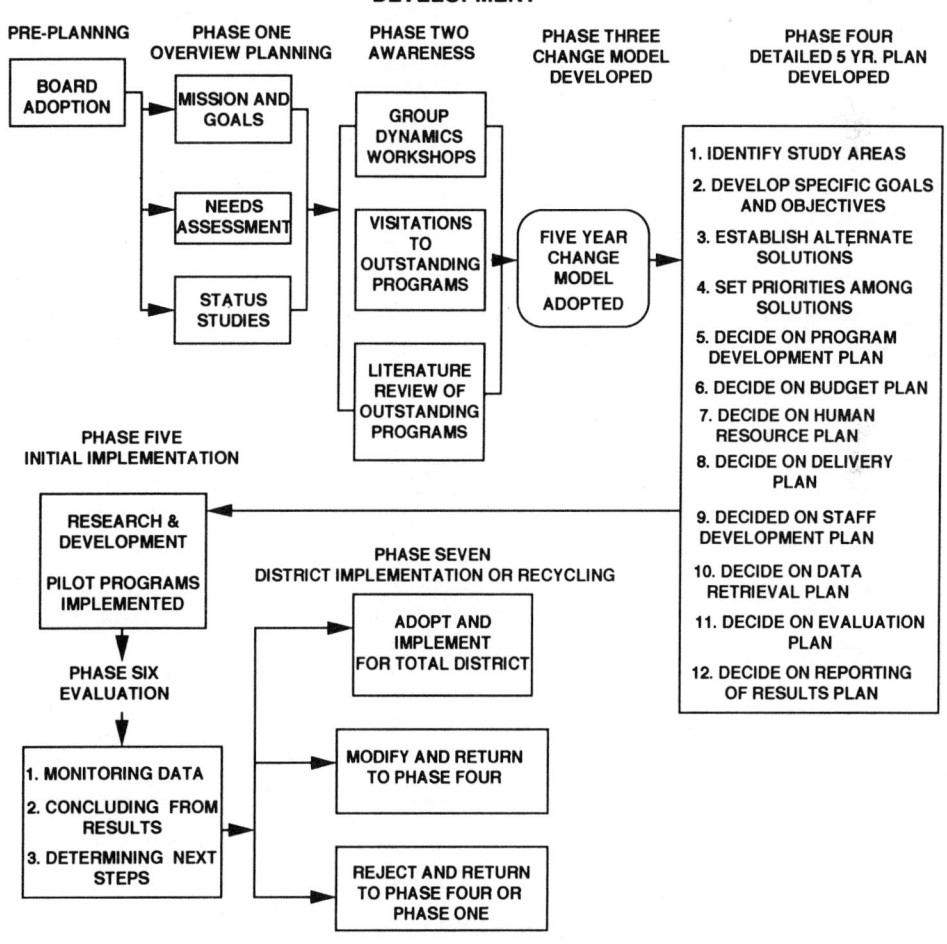

PRE-PLANNNG: BOARD ADOPTION

PHASE ONE OVERVIEW PLANNING:
- MISSION AND GOALS
- NEEDS ASSESSMENT
- STATUS STUDIES

PHASE TWO AWARENESS:
- GROUP DYNAMICS WORKSHOPS
- VISITATIONS TO OUTSTANDING PROGRAMS
- LITERATURE REVIEW OF OUTSTANDING PROGRAMS

PHASE THREE CHANGE MODEL DEVELOPED:
- FIVE YEAR CHANGE MODEL ADOPTED

PHASE FOUR DETAILED 5 YR. PLAN DEVELOPED:
1. IDENTIFY STUDY AREAS
2. DEVELOP SPECIFIC GOALS AND OBJECTIVES
3. ESTABLISH ALTERNATE SOLUTIONS
4. SET PRIORITIES AMONG SOLUTIONS
5. DECIDE ON PROGRAM DEVELOPMENT PLAN
6. DECIDE ON BUDGET PLAN
7. DECIDE ON HUMAN RESOURCE PLAN
8. DECIDE ON DELIVERY PLAN
9. DECIDED ON STAFF DEVELOPMENT PLAN
10. DECIDE ON DATA RETRIEVAL PLAN
11. DECIDE ON EVALUATION PLAN
12. DECIDE ON REPORTING OF RESULTS PLAN

PHASE FIVE INITIAL IMPLEMENTATION:
- RESEARCH & DEVELOPMENT
- PILOT PROGRAMS IMPLEMENTED

PHASE SIX EVALUATION:
1. MONITORING DATA
2. CONCLUDING FROM RESULTS
3. DETERMINING NEXT STEPS

PHASE SEVEN DISTRICT IMPLEMENTATION OR RECYCLING:
- ADOPT AND IMPLEMENT FOR TOTAL DISTRICT
- MODIFY AND RETURN TO PHASE FOUR
- REJECT AND RETURN TO PHASE FOUR OR PHASE ONE

Preplanning Phase

The superintendent and the board of education felt that the district did not possess a comprehensive needs assessment or a long-term systematic plan to study and improve the district. The superintendent was asked to develop such a plan, and this initial task was accomplished with the assistant of many employees and a few consultants. Once the initial and tentative planning model was completed, all residents of the school district were invited to a public meeting where the plan was to be explained and suggestions from the audience were to be solicited. Much advance publicity was used and the importance to the district and its students of a long-term planning effort was stressed.

The meeting was attended by approximately five hundred citizens. A few members of the audience made a few suggested modifications, and the audience was asked for a voice vote of approval or disapproval. The audience participants overwhelmingly voted approval, and encouraged the board of education and the administration to proceed.

Following this citizens meeting, the West Bloomfield Public Schools' Model Systems Plan for Program Development was officially adopted by the West Bloomfield Board of Education. At this meeting, the board directed the superintendent to proceed with the plan, and to initiate Phase One.

Phase One: Overview Planning

Phase One consisted of three activities. The activities to be accomplished during Phase One included: (1) mission and goals establishment, (2) needs assessment, and (3) status studies.

A representative group of stakeholders worked to develop a *mission statement* which was later modified and adopted. The West Bloomfield School District's Project Manager, utilizing the *Phi Delta Kappan* materials on goals, conducted workshops involving 845 parents, students, staff members, administrators, and board of education members in prioritizing the district's goals. In addition, a mailed survey was provided 424 residents who were selected on the basis of a stratified random sampling. The West Bloomfield Board of Education reviewed the results presented by all 28 respondent groups, and the board adopted a prioritized series of *goal statements* which were inserted into the board policy book.

Next, eighteen *needs validation* committees were organized. These committees varied in size from ten to twenty members. Altogether, there were 231 members involved. These included students, residents, employees, and board of education members. The majority of the committees' members were drawn, on purpose, from the residents category—132 residents in all.

The eighteen committees were organized in such a manner that each school building had a needs assessment committee, and there were check and balance committees for each major functional area that wasn't covered by the building level committees. The functional needs assessment committees possessed the same membership as the site committees; and the functional areas covered were: (1) special services, (2) vocational and career education, (3) community education, (4) instrumental music, (5) media, (6) athletics and cocurricular, (7) district instruction, (8) district personnel, (9) district building and grounds, (10) district business, and (11) district administration.

Each committee met weekly for approximately three months, and then each committee submitted a prioritized listing of needs for their areas of study. This 203-page report was presented to the West Bloomfield Board of Education.

Next, two resident members from each of the nineteen original committees were selected by their respective committees to meet weekly throughout the summer months to arrive at a district-wide set of prioritized needs. This was a difficult task, as this group had to decide if buying new books for first grade reading was of a higher priority than replacing buses, starting additional foreign language, buying new athletic equipment, buying new band instruments, and hundreds of other needs which were identified by the individual needs assessment committees. This report was delivered to the West Bloomfield Board of Education in the early fall.

Next, the superintendent and his staff took all these needs, which the final summary and prioritizing committee completed, and they completed a *status study* on each prioritized need. Some of the needs were immediately addressed by moving budget to higher priorities than those in the original budget document, some identified needs were refused because they were contrary to current policy, some needs were met by changing some rules or operating procedures, and some needs were placed on a tax referendum because the regular budget could not support their costs.

There were 250 prioritized needs, which the summary committee classified as "A" priorities from 1 to 250. Each resident received a bulletin outlining each of these needs, the current status of each need, and the planned program to meet each need. Those that required additional funding were all individually listed with a price tag for each, and the community voted some taxes to implement some of these, and did not vote to implement others.

Phase Two: Awareness

Phase Two also consisted of three activities which were: (1) group dynamics workshops for student, employees, and residents, (2) visitations to outstanding programs which appeared to have addressed one of the identified needs, and (3) a literature review. The literature review consisted of establishing a library of relevant books, journal articles, and curriculum materials that would be useful in developing action plans to meet the identified needs (a need is a discrepancy between "what is" and "what should be").

Group dynamics workshops were conducted because many of the persons who were to work on action plans were not previously empowered to make those types or decisions, and many had little or no experience working as part of a planning team. Items in the workshops stressed communications skills, planning skills, team building activities, analysis skills, presentation skills, conflict resolution skills, and consensus building skills.

Visitations to other school districts with outstanding programs were arranged for team members; and, upon their return, they filed a written report. These reports were all filed in the reference library for use by any team.

A *literature and curriculum review* collection was completed by a group of committee members and employees. These resource documents were also filed in the reference library for use by any team.

Phase Three: Change Model Development

After Phases One and Two were completed, the committees worked as a unit until they reached a consensus on a change model. This five-year model plan is detailed in Phases Four through Seven. The five-year model was intended to be renewed, with some modifications, if necessary, every five years.

Phase Four: Detailed Five-Year Plan Development

The committees agreed that the twelve questions listed in Phase Four must be completed before any action plan would be implemented. It was considered crucial that an evaluation plan be thought through prior to implementation of any action plan.

Phase Five: Initial Implementation

This phase utilized the approach of finding the lowest common denominator concept when conducting the research and development activities on a pilot basis. This concept basically implied that if an action plan could be piloted and monitored at a single classroom level, that is where it would be implemented; or if it could be implemented at a single building level, that is where it would be implemented. In any case, it would not be implemented across the entire school district or to its broadest possible application area until it was fully tested, analyzed, and deemed successful.

Phase Six: Evaluation

This phase took the data that was monitored and collected from each pilot, arrayed and analyzed the data, and drew conclusions from the results of each pilot. Next, one of three decisions was made on the basis of these conclusions.

Phase Seven: District Implementation or Recycling

After the data were analyzed and conclusions drawn, one of three decisions was made. One decision that could be made stated that the pilot was very successful, and the program should be implemented throughout the entire school district. A second decision that could be made stated that the pilot was unsuccessful and the planning group had to repeat the process starting at Phase One or Phase Four. A third decision that could be made stated that the pilot was partially successful, but that it needed additional work. Therefore, the planning group had to begin again at Phase Four.

Following the extreme success of the system's planning activities which involved all stakeholders in Phases One through Three and the district's employees in Phases Four through Seven and which had continuous progress reports to all residents of the community, the West Bloomfield Board of Education decided that it wanted to implement a permanent stakeholders' committee at each school and one for the district level. This structure is discussed below. These permanent committees were called communications-governance committees.

WEST BLOOMFIELD SCHOOL DISTRICT'S SITE-BASED COMMUNICATIONS-GOVERNANCE COMMITTEES

As current themes in local school district management research and practitioner recommendation, empowerment and school-based management are consistently present. Empowerment is praised because it allows employees, parents, and other stakeholders to be involved in decision making; and by their involvement, they gain a degree of ownership in the decisions and in the institution's vision, mission, and programs (AASA, 1990). School-based management is touted as the most effective means of school improvement; with regard to the local school district level, it is believed that the most effective decision making takes place at the level of delivery of the service—the school building level (Curley, 1988).

If one buys into the concepts of empowerment and site-based management, then the way the building's administrators operate will be greatly modified. In the area of planning to achieve a vision of what is desired in the future, the stakeholders should be involved in arriving at a desired future vision and in planning means of achieving that desired vision (Herman, 1990). In the area of operational planning, the stakeholders should be involved in the development of yearly action plans, which are designed to arrive at the desired outcomes stated in the vision statements.

With empowerment, strategic and operational planning, and school-based management as the backdrop, the discussion will be focused on a the methodology or model which the West Bloomfield School District utilized to create an environment for empowerment and site-based planning and management at the school building level. When developing a model, the following questions were addressed: (1) Why develop a communications-governance structure that empowers stakeholders at the building level? (2) What are the potential advantages and disadvantages of creating this empowerment structure? (3) What questions should be asked and answered related to the details of the operation of the empowerment structure? (4) What format shall be the best one to utilize? (5) What duties and responsibilities or charge to the empowered groups is reasonable and functional? and (6) How will the degree of success of the empowerment structure be measured?

Why Develop a Communications-Governance Structure that Empowers Stakeholders at the School Building Level?

Before a principal decides to create a communications/governance structure that empowers stakeholders, she/he must find out if the district's superintendent of schools and the board of education will allow such a structure to be developed (Watkins, 1990). If the answer from the superintendent and the board of education is a resounding "yes," then the principal must think through the reason she/he needs or wants such a structure. That is, what purpose will be served by involving stakeholders in planning and decision making at the building level? Once the principal and whomever else she/he wishes to involve in determining the purpose decide on the purpose, that statement should be placed in writing and given to all stakeholders (NASSP, 1992). An example statement of purpose for West Bloomfield High School, a school of approximately 2,000 students, might well read as follows:

Purpose of West Bloomfield High School's Communications/Governance Committees

West Bloomfield High School's Communications-Governance Committees are designed to allow a broader base of discussion and information sharing among parents, administrators, community members, students, and employees in the strategic (long-term planning with a vision) decision making and operational (short-term action planning) decision making that takes place at the building level. It is expected that this broader-based dialogue will permit and encourage the various human elements of our school's educational community to work more cooperatively and positively together, with the end result being improved quality and quantity of instructional programs as experienced by the students of West Bloomfield High School.

Once the purpose has been decided upon, it is important that the principal and those others whom she/he has involved in the initial planning, conduct a S.W.O.T. (strengths, weaknesses, opportunities, and threats) Analysis of the building level as it currently exists (Herman & Kaufman, 1991). The basic questions to be answered by this analysis are: what are the advantages and disadvantages of creating this empowerment structure? and, what exists that can assist or constrain the building level decision making and planning activities if such an empowerment structure is implemented?

What are the Potential Advantages and Disadvantages of Creating This Empowerment Structure?

Although a wide variety of strengths, weaknesses, opportunities and threats, i.e., advantages and disadvantages, will be identified and analyzed at the local school building level, only a few examples will be listed to provide a feel for this planning activity, which should precede the actual implementation of a communication/governance empowerment structure.

POTENTIAL STRENGTHS might well include: (1) Many parents and community members have expressed an interest in becoming more involved with the school. (2) Teachers have been heavily involved in planning the curriculum and monitoring student achievement, and they would easily and willingly accept an important role in broader-based planning and decision making. (3) Students have not been involved in the past, and many students could play a role in planning for a more positive school climate and an enhanced instructional delivery system. (4) Classified employees have much to offer in the planning of better support systems. (5) Community businesses and industries are anxious to enter into partnerships with schools (Education Commission of the States, 1990).

POTENTIAL WEAKNESSES might well include: (1) A reluctance on the part of some administrators and teachers to allow others, especially students and parents, to have a role in planning and decision making related to areas which have traditional been considered their private authority areas. (2) Unions may object to the involvement of others. (3) Stakeholders do not have the training necessary to conduct planning and decision-making activities in a broad-based collaborative manner. (4) Some important power groups or powerful decision makers in the community may prefer to influence the school building's operation by hidden agendas and by behind the scenes activities. (5) Many individuals will not be willing to devote the time that will be required to produce high quality, comprehensive plans (McKenzie, 1991; Nyberg, 1990).

Once the strengths, weaknesses, opportunities, and threats have been identified and analyzed, the principal and the others involved in the initial design phase should anticipate the questions that might be asked and should provide answers to those questions in order that stakeholders will be knowledgeable and comfortable when they are asked to serve on the communications-governance committees (Cohen, 1988). Some sample questions are listed below.

Questions that Need Be Addressed

How will the communications/governance model tie into budget development?

Will both ad hoc (temporary) and permanent communications/governance committees be utilized?

Will ad hoc committees be given a specific charge and a specific date of termination?

How will the membership of these communications/governance committees be chosen?

Can the building level committees present their recommendations to the board of education and the superintendent as well as to the building principal?

How will overlap and conflict between and among these committees and parent teacher organizations), booster groups, and other existing support groups be avoided?

How will the committees' membership be selected?

When, and specifically, how, is this communications/governance empowerment model to be implemented?

What means of communications among and between these committees are to be used?

What are the specific duties and responsibilities or charges of the building level communications-governance committees?

Are there other detailed questions besides those addressed above that need be decided before this structure is implemented?

Once the purpose has been decided upon, the potential strengths and weaknesses have been identified and analyzed, and a comprehensive listing of specific questions has been addressed; the school principal can design the format to be utilized.

What Format Shall Be the Best One to Utilize?

A structure similar to the one discussed below should be arrived at prior to getting stakeholders involved in the communications/governance structure at the building level.

At West Bloomfield High School, the communications-governance structure which empowers the school's stakeholders was one of a tri-level approach which included: (1) permanent stakeholder communications-governance committees, (2) ad hoc committees, which could be appointed to deal with a specific plan, topic, or problem area; this committee would operate for a finite and specified time period, and (3) permanent building-wide support groups. A description of each of these groups will clarify their charges.

PERMANENT BUILDING–WIDE SUPPORT GROUPS are groups that operate under formal by-laws. Examples of this type of group are Parent Teacher Organizations, band boosters, sports boosters, and academic boosters.

AD HOC BUILDING LEVEL GROUPS are groups which are created periodically to accomplish a highly specific purpose over a prespecified time period. At the end of the specified time period, the group will make recommendations to the building principal. If the work is not completed during the specified time period, the life of the ad hoc committee can be extended for an additional specified time period. Once the recommendations are made, the group is disbanded; the principal will act on the recommendations, and will notify the committee and all others impacted by the decision of her/his actions.

PERMANENT BUILDING LEVEL COMMUNICATIONS–GOVERNANCE COMMITTEES are comprised of representatives from each stakeholder group, and the committees operate under a specific list of duties and responsibilities that are committed to writing and are widely distributed. This committee structure is the key to innovative empowerment at the school building level, and an outline of a potential structure and listing of duties and responsibilities will be helpful at this point.

Structure, Duties and Responsibilities of Building Level Communications/ Governance Committees Used by Every School Building in the West Bloomfield School District

1. The building principal shall serve as liaison to her/his building level communications-governance committee. It shall be the principal's responsibility to call the initial yearly meeting of the group, and the principal shall arrange for a meeting place, typed minutes, and other items that, from time to time, may be needed by the committee. She/he also has the responsibility to organize the initial committee selection and appointment process.

2. The committee shall be comprised of (a) up to twenty citizens selected at random from the list of citizens who have volunteered to serve, (b) one representative from each building support group that is already in existence, (c) two students from each grade level, except at the elementary school level, (d) two representatives from each classified unionized or nonunionized group (custodians, food service workers, aides, etc.), (e) two teachers selected by the teaching staff or by the teacher's union, and (f) up to five additional members appointed by the principal if she/he feels that the representatives previously selected do not represent all important stakeholder groups.

3. The committee membership shall elect a chairperson, and this chairperson must come from sources other that of administration.

4. The committee shall meet at least once monthly during the school year.

5. The committee shall be free to discuss and make recommendations related to all needs of the building's programs and all means of improving the educational climate for students and employees; and the committee shall make recommendations to these ends.

6. Recommendations made by the committee shall be committed to writing; and if the recommendations have budget implications, they should be received by the principal prior to December 1st of the year preceding the budget being planned.

7. At least once yearly, the committee shall submit a comprehensive report to the principal, and the report shall be forwarded to the superintendent of schools and to the board of education. If requested, the committee members will make themselves available for an oral

presentation before the board of education and the superintendent of schools.

8. Yearly, in June, the committee shall present a written evaluation of the committee's activities, an evaluation of the communication/ governance committee structure, and any recommendations the committee wishes to make regarding the structure or the activities of the committee for the succeeding school year.

Once all the details have been addressed, the committee made operational, and activities have taken place over the school year, there is a crucial need to evaluate the success of the committee and its activities (Lewis, 1989). Only through such evaluative exercises will the committee strengthen itself and become an ever-increasing, positive support and empowerment structure.

How Will the Degree of Success of the Empowerment Structure Be Measured?

Although numerous criteria could be used to measure the success of the communications/governance empowerment structures, the most crucial ones utilized included the following:

Have the activities and recommendations of the communications/ governance groups been accepted, and have they had a positive impact on the school building's programs and students?

Do the various representative stakeholder groups express positive feelings towards the communications/governance structure, and do they feel that they have been empowered?

Do the members of the various groups want the structure to continue, and do they volunteer to continue their membership?

Are strategic goals and objectives identified, and are action plans developed to achieve these consensus goals and objectives? In other words, is there a collective vision and mission, and have activities been focused and designed to achieve the collective mission and vision?

A Final Comment

The principals who firmly believed that site-based management was the way to improvement, and those who also firmly believed that you can best improve the programs and opportunities for students by empowering stakeholders' groups, developed their building level communications-governance structures to the fullest potential (Decker & Decker, 1988). What little the principal may have given up of her/his positional power, the outcome produced a harvest of goodwill, understanding, and support for the principal and for the activities and plans which were designed make the school one of excellence.

Now that we have discussed how the majority of school districts have utilized parents and citizens in decision making relating to their schools and have given an example of one of the unusual early attempts to involve parents and citizens in meaningful school-related, decision-making opportunities, the discussion will move to a discussion of the current structure of SBM involvement and empowerment. The use of stakeholders and parents on SBM councils is a key to community understanding and support for the individual school buildings and for the school district (Raywid, 1990).

Once there is a realization of the traditional ways that school districts have utilized parents, citizens and staff in quasi-planning activities and once there is a realization that some districts, like the West Bloomfield example, did empower many stakeholders to make decisions, it is important to discuss the current state of empowerment. School-based management is growing by leaps and bounds across the country. It is based upon two major concepts or beliefs: (1) if a variety of stakeholders (at the very least, teachers and parents) are empowered in meaningful decision-making activities, education will be improved; and (2) if the education of children and youth is to be improved, efforts must be focused at the individual school building level (Neal, 1991).

PARENT AND NONPARENT STAKEHOLDER PARTICIPATION ON SBM SCHOOL COUNCILS AND IN DECISION MAKING

Many of the school based councils include parents and other citizens in their memberships (Lieberman & Miller, 1990). There are numerous excellent reasons for including parents and other community members in the SBM councils, and empowering them to make important decisions related to the programs and other matters that take place at the individual school site where they serve as SBM council members (Boothe &

Draud, 1990). The major advantages of involving parents and community members in the SBM councils are:

- Involvement brings understanding.
- Involvement brings ownership.
- Involvement provides information which can and will be shared with other parents and adults in the community. Thus, the basis for understanding and support for the school building efforts is greatly increased.
- Collaboration among teachers, principals, parents, and other members of the community builds a trusting relationship; and it brings the joy of sharing successes with others who have worked with them to bring about desired outcomes.
- Checks and balances are provided when the professional staff and the community members share ideas and efforts.
- Climate in the schools and in the entire district usually improves when a wide variety of stakeholders work together to improve the education offered the children and youth of the community (AASA, 1988; Education Commission of the States, 1988, 1991).

CORPORATE PARTNERSHIP OPPORTUNITIES

Although not directly related to most patterns discussed under the topic of school-based management, another important structure is taking place in many individual school buildings in this country. The opportunity to develop an education-business partnership exists in almost every school district. These education-business partnerships take on the format of an *adopt-a-school*, or as many other formats that are only limited by the imagination of those developing the partnerships. Some of the most frequent structures include:

- Adopt-a-school, which usually implies that one or more businesses choose a specific individual school in the district towards which they will focus efforts on assisting that school's students and employees. The businesses may provide equipment or supplies, they may provide speakers, and they may have representatives attend all or most of the students' activities.
- Businesses may include teachers and administrators in many of their corporate training activities.

- Businesses may allow students to visit their work places and shadow a specific employee for a day or two.
- Some businesses will employ specialized teachers in the summer to update them on the latest technologies utilized by their specific business, with the implication that this learning will be shared by the students of those teachers.
- Some businesses will sponsor award events recognizing the achievements of children and young people.

Again, the specifics are numerous and only limited by the imagination of the school building's professional staff and the sponsors. However, it is important to realize that the schools should also share with their sponsors. If they can assist with training; if they can develop recreational activities for employees of their corporate sponsors; if they can have the children recognize the contributions of the employees of their corporate sponsors; or if they, in some other way, can share with their sponsors a two-way relationship, it will strengthen the bond between the sponsors and the school building's staff.

Finally, it is in the interest of business to assist schools in improving the education of the children and youth for two very important reasons: (1) business desires better educated workers in the future to enable them to compete with foreign competition and utilize advanced technology, and, (2) leaders of business will not move their operations into areas where schools are substandard, and their management personnel will not subject their children to substandard education. Therefore, it is clear that education-business partnerships make good sense for the schools and for corporate America (King & Swanson, 1990).

COMMON NATIONAL PATTERNS AND RECOMMENDATIONS FOR IMPLEMENTATION

Lindelow and Heynderickx (1989) described school-based management as often allying itself with the community involvement movement. They note that "the first step in forming such a council occurs when teachers, parents, and community groups voice their desire for involvement. The actual development of the council is determined by the support and commitment of the superintendent, the school board, and the school principals. Each council's structure is unique, responding to the philosophy and needs of a particular district. Procedures for selecting council members and defining their authority are specified in policies written at the very start of the process" (p. 133). The formation of an advisory committee of some sort to facilitate SBM implementation was recommended by NASSP in 1989. Variation does extend across many council structures; some are composed of teachers elected schoolwide (or by grade level or department); some councils are made up of representatives from pre-existing committees, both school and community (David, 1989). The decision making authority of the principal in conjunction with the councils varies; some decisions are retained, others are dealt with by council consensus. Similar recommendations for council formation were provided by Access (1990):

- Councils should be self-selected or elected by a majority of constituency members. While some teams have been appointed by principals or by a combination of organizations such as faculty councils, PTO's, or administrators, those that are selected by the membership of the constituencies represented have more legitimacy.
- Councils should be a microcosm of the school community: teachers, support staff, the principal, parents, residents, and students. There should also be a cross-section of grades, races, sex, and cultures (p. 7).

Certain commonalities of SBM school councils do exist; most meet on a regular basis, are involved in overall planning and in budgetary preparation, serve in at least an advisory capacity on other matters, are representative of various stakeholder or constituency groups, have certain power limitations, have clear chairperson designation, and employ ground rules for process (Neal, 1991).

RECOMMENDATIONS AND IMPLICATIONS FOR TRAINING OF COMMUNITY MEMBERS INVOLVED IN SBM ACTIVITIES

To be successful, school-based management requires substantial investments in training, particularly in human relations skills that will facilitate shared decision making. Since SBM is an inclusionary process, the sharing of information and communication among the various participants, including parents and community leaders, is critical (Lewis, 1989). The building of trust and rapport, of creating skill and confidence in others, dealing with change, and managing the work are process tasks for councils. The need for collaborative capacities has been documented in other chapters; McKenzie (1991) detailed these skill areas as consisting of group problem solving, awareness of group behaviors, negotiation and consensus building, planning, and a sense of the responsibilities of representation.

The educational content and action areas which school councils may be charged to address or to impact in some decision-making capacity are also areas of training need. If councils are to be active in the three described SBM areas of budget development and expenditure, personnel activities, and curricular development (described in Chapter 1), then both the practitioners and lay council members will require some professional preparation (Crowson, 1992). This is borne out further in Chapter 10. As an example of such content and process training, Hess (1991) describes the Chicago Local School Councils' (covered in more detail in Chapter Six) experiences in training in budgets, educational theory pertinent to their attendance centers particular needs, including the development of a school improvement plan, and the principal's performance. Chicago has tried to provide thirty hours of annual training, and has offered training in a common SBM curriculum for aspiring Council members.

Limited resources has caused the common experience of most school councils to conclude that the preparation is inadequate, and that much more staff development is needed in both group process skills, in strategic and operational planning, and in the particular areas of school decision making are the local council's purview.

SUMMARY

A historical note about the traditional uninvolvement of parents and community members in meaningful school input was followed by the description of a model systems plan for program development, as an example of broad-based community involvement in comprehensive decision-making activities. This model included a needs assessment and a long-term planning model. A similar description of the development of model site-based governance committees was provided with empowerment, strategic and operational planning, and SBM as the backdrop. Issues which were addressed in this section included: the justification for the development of a communications-governance structure that empowers stakeholders at the building level; the potential advantages and disadvantages of creating this empowerment structure; the questions which should be asked and answered related to the details of the operation of the empowerment structure; the format best utilized; the reasonableness of the duties and responsibilities of the empowered groups; and how to measure the success of the empowerment structure.

The push for empowerment and the current structure of parent and community involvement on SBM councils was explored. The major advantages of this participation were listed, and a connection made to corporate partnership opportunities for schools. Common national patterns of recommendation for implementation reveal a variety of council structure and decision-making purview. There is some consensus on the need for broad-based representation and on council function and procedure. Agreement also exists on the need for substantial investments in training, particularly in human relations skills that will facilitate shared decision making, including such collaborative capacities as group problem solving, awareness of group behaviors, negotiation and consensus building, planning, and a sense of the responsibilities of representation.

The educational content and action areas which school councils operate upon, such as budget development and expenditure, personnel activities, and curricular development require some professional preparation. The common experience of most school councils in training has been the inadequacy of preparation, due to lack of temporal and financial resources.

EXERCISES

1. Describe any existing community involvement structures in your district. How broad-based are they?

2. Assess the readiness of your district for a comprehensive governance committee structure, such as the one described in the chapter. How could the models described be made to work?

3. Consider the sample questions posed about the communications governance committee, in light of your district's needs. Which format would be the best one to utilize?

4. Evaluate the impact in your district of the formation of local school decision-making councils.

5. Which decisional areas and types of training would fit your typical district council?

REFERENCES

AASA. *A new look at empowerment.* (1990). (AASA Stock Number 021-00278). Washington, DC: American Association of School Administrators, pp. 1–3.

ACCESS – Clearinghouse for Information about Public Schools (1990). *School based improvement and effective schools: A perfect match for bottom-up reform.* Columbia, MD: Clearinghouse for Information about Public Schools, a service of the National Committee for Citizens in Education, p. 7.

Boothe, J. & Draud, J. (1990). Making site-based management work. *Kentucky School Boards Association Journal,* 9 (3), 9–10.

Boyd, W.L. (1990). Balancing control and autonomy in school reform: The politics of perestroika. In J. Murphy (Ed.), *The educational reform movement of the 1980's* (p. 92). Berkeley, CA: McCutchan Publishing Corporation.

Cohen, M. (1988). Restructuring the education system: Agenda for the 1990's. In *Results in Education,* Washington, D.C.: National Governors' Association Center for Policy Research, pp. 16–17.

Crowson, R.L. (1992). *School-community relations, under reform.* Berkeley, CA: McCutchan Publishing Corporation, pp. 218–221.

Curley, J. (1988). Site-based management flourishes. *The School Administrator,* 5 (45), 31–32.

David, J.L. (1989). Synthesis of research on school-based management. *Educational Leadership,* 46 (8), 45–53.

Decker, L.E. & Decker, V.A. (1988). *Home/school/community involvement.* Arlington, VA: American Association of School Administrators, pp. xi–xvii.

Education Commission of the States. (1990). *Education agenda 1990.* Denver, CO: Education Commission of the States, pp. 4–5.

Education Commission of the States. (1991). *Exploring policy options to restructure education.* Denver, CO: Education Commission of the States, p. 35.

Herman, J.J. (1990). Strategic planning: Reasons for failed attempts. *Educational Planning,* 8 (9), 36–40.

Herman, J.J. and Kaufman, R. (1991). Making the mega plan. *The American School Board Journal,* 178, (5), 24–25, 41.

Hess, G.A., Jr. (1991). *School restructuring, Chicago style.* Newbury Park, CA: Corwin Press, Inc., p. 175.

King, R.A. & Swanson, A.D. (1990). Resources for restructured schools: Partnerships, foundations, and volunteerism. *Planning & Changing,* 21 (2), 94–107.

Lewis, A. (1989). *Restructuring America's schools.* Washington, D.C.: American Association of School Administrators, pp. 226, 237.

Lewis, J., Jr. (1989). *Implementing school-based management... by empowering teachers.* Westbury, NY: J.L. Wilkerson Publishing Company, p. 266.

Lieberman, A. and Miller, L. (1990). Restructuring schools: What matters and what works. *Phi Delta Kappan,* 71 (10), 759–764.

Lindelow, J. and J. Heynederickx. (1989). School-based management. In S.C. Smith & P.K. Piele (Eds.), *School leadership: Handbook for excellence* (2nd ed.) (pp. 132–133). Eugene, OR: ERIC Clearinghouse on Educational Management.

McKenzie, J.A. (1991). *Site-based management: A practical guide for practitioners.* Flemington, NJ: Correct Change Publishers, p. 49.

NASSP. (1989). School site management. National Association of Secondary School Principals' *The Practitioner,* 16 (2), 1–6.

NASSP. (1992). *A leader's guide to school restructuring: A special report of the NASSP Commission on Restructuring.* Reston, VA: National Association of Secondary School Principals. pp. 32–33.

Neal, R.G. (1991). *School based management: A detailed guide for successful implementation.* Bloomington, IN: National Educational Service, p. 82–89.

Nyberg, D.A. (1990). Power, empowerment, and educational authority. In S.L. Jacobson and J.A. Conway (Eds.) *Educational leadership in an age of reform* (p. 59). New York: Longman.

Raywid, M.A. (1990). Rethinking school governance. In R.F. Elmore and Associates, *Restructuring schools—the next generation of educational reform* (pp. 164–166), San Francisco, CA: Jossey-Bass Publishers.

Watkins, P. (1990). Agenda, power, and text: The formulation of policy in school councils. *Education Policy, 5* (4), 315–331.

Chapter 10

SCHOOL-BASED MANAGEMENT AND STATE DEPARTMENTS OF EDUCATION AND LEGISLATURES: LIBERATING THE INDIVIDUAL SCHOOL THROUGH MANDATE

The education reform movement of the 1980s instigated a wave of reforms, many of them originating at the state level. Twenty-three states have increased high school graduation since 1980, nearly every state has strengthened teacher certification requirements, forty-nine states have instituted some form of student assessment, and forty-seven states have underwritten new curriculum guides. State policy makers have begun to look for additional avenues to spur achievement, and efforts are beginning to focus on strengthening schools as organizations. A shift from regulation to incentives and mobilization of "institutional capacity" is beginning to occur in many states; strategies to empower are replacing program mandates (Education Commission of the States, 1989). Recommended policy options for restructuring at a state level were also the focus of the Education Commission of the States in 1991; regarding leadership policies, the Commission proposal proposed that "The state ensure that business leaders, teachers, principals, parents, state and local school board members, state department of education officials and others participate in creating a shared vision and becoming advocates for the future of education" (p. 22). Further state policy recommendations in the document are concerned with establishing a waiver system and with parent and community involvement. Regarding inclusion of stakeholders, the Commission recommends that states endorse shared decision making for districts and schools. Lewis (1988) also reported on restructuring state control, and quoted Michael Cohen's (a National Governors Association policy expert) suggested steps for state leadership. The states should support restructuring by:

- Articulating a vision of restructured schools.
- Encouraging local experimentation with various school structures.

- Reducing unnecessary administrative and regulatory barriers to experimentation with promising approaches.
- Providing ongoing implementation support and technical assistance to schools and districts trying new approaches.
- Linking rewards and sanctions for schools to their performance.
- Researching and disseminating results to other schools (p. 124).

This chapter briefly considers school-based management as a restructuring strategy at the state level, followed by a description of the two landmark SBM efforts in the states of Texas and Kentucky. A case study of five local school councils in Kentucky provides a closer view of shared decision making. The chapter closes with a perspective on the two restructuring efforts.

SCHOOL-BASED MANAGEMENT: STATE RESTRUCTURING STRATEGY

The history of school-based management, particularly its early implementation, reflects shared decision-making innovation and SBM impetus which frequently originated at the state level, through incentives programs, capacity building, or system changing. Many states are still mandating restructuring and change through traditional approaches (Crowson, 1992), but a number of them, over the past twenty years, have implemented some type of reform or restructuring activity. Some states which have had some element of state-supported, shared decision making and school-based management include Florida, Ohio, New York, Arkansas, California, Maine, and Massachusetts. More information may be found in the Appendix, which reports on the fifty state departments' of education current involvement in school-based management.

In 1991, Lally reported on the trend of state departments turning towards helping rather than regulating, and on the reform efforts to "stand the typical education hierarchy on its head. They want to take the bureaucracies arranged so neatly and intricately above each school building and turn them upside down, putting individual schools at the top of the chain of command. Whether it is named school-based management or restructuring or decentralization, the impulse to turn decisions over to schools challenges basic assumptions about those hierarchies" (p. 8).

Most of those state level school-based management projects have been reflected in scattered implementation and in individual district initiative. Efforts to avoid prescriptives and to maintain broad-brush reform guidelines have been the norm. Two states, however, have recently legislated sweeping SBM requirements, requiring statewide participation in decentralization and shared decision making.

TEXAS AND KENTUCKY: STATEWIDE SBM LABORATORIES

Restructuring for Diversity: The Texas Model

In following the national reform movement and societal concern for educational quality, Texas has experienced almost a decade of major change in the field. Beginning in 1979 with statewide student minimum mastery assessments, legislatively-initiated changes included the passage of two significant bills; the Educational Opportunity Act (House Bill 72) and the adoption of a statewide curriculum for grades K–12 (House Bill 75). Not only was the content of the instructional program specifically defined, but virtually every operational aspect of the educational process was affected (Herman, 1989). This mass of detailed legislative mandates imposed constraints which eventually served, at times, to rigidly inhibit innovative instructional strategies. There were some individual district initiatives during the 1980s aimed at meeting the needs of the increasingly diverse, majority minority school population. There is now a second Texas wave of reform focused on *decreasing* the role of the state; the new outlook at the state level is to "clear the path for campus-based initiatives aimed at improving outcomes for all students" (Texas Education Agency, 1992, p. 1–2).

In June of 1990 the Texas State Senate passed Senate Bill 1, which provided for the establishment of district and campus committees, gave principals primary authority for campus staff appointments after consultation with faculty, tied principal appraisal to student attainment of performance objectives, and allowed for waivers for inhibitions in law or state rules. In May of 1991 the State House of Representatives passed House Bill 2885, requiring "site based decision making," which directed the campus committees created in the Senate Bill to undertake responsibility for improving student outcomes through goal setting, curriculum, budgeting, staffing patterns, and school organization. A State Advisory Committee on Site-Based Decision Making was established in September of 1991 as a collaborative team (representing teachers, board members, business leaders, principals, central office administrators, superintendents, and education service centers); the group has analyzed the provisions of the law and reached consensus on advising the commissioner on how to address the requirements. A resource guide was developed to assist districts in developing their required plans for site-based decision making. The intent of the law, the Advisory Committee has stressed, is that "each district must develop its own plan within the context of the law and local policy and local condition" (Texas Education Agency, 1992, p. 1–5).

Excerpts of the Texas Senate and House Bills are presented here:

Senate Bill 1
(June, 1990)

21.7532 Campus Performance Objectives

(a) For each school year, the principal of each school campus, with the assistance of parents, community residents, and the professional staff of the school.... shall establish academic and other performance objectives of the campus for each academic excellence indicator adopted under Section 21.7531 of this code.... The objectives must be approved by the district's board of trustees.

(b) In this section, "parent" means a person who is a parent of or person standing in parental relation to a student enrolled at a school.... and who is not an employee of the school or the school district.... "community resident" means a person 18 years of age or older residing in the attendance area of a school.... but this does not include a person who is a parent of a student enrolled in that school or a person who is an employee of the school or the school district.

21.930 District-Level Decision Process

(a) The board of trustees of each school district shall adopt a policy to involve the professional staff of the district in establishing and reviewing the district's educational goals, objectives, and major district-wide classroom instructional programs.

(b) The board shall establish a procedure under which meetings are held regularly with representative professional staff and the board or board designee.

(c) The board shall adopt a procedure.... for the professional staff within the district to nominate and elect the representatives who will meet with the board or board designee as required under the provisions of this section.... Two-thirds of the elected representatives must be classroom teachers. The remaining representatives shall be campus-based staff.

(d) This section does not prohibit the board from conducting meetings with teachers or groups of teachers other than the meetings described by this section.

(e) Nothing in this section shall be construed as creating a new cause of action or as requiring collective bargaining.

House Bill 2885
(May, 1991)

TEC §21.931

(a) Each school district shall develop and implement a plan for site-based decision making not later than September 1, 1992. Each district shall submit its plan to the commissioner of education for approval.
(b) Each district's plan:
  (1) shall establish school committees;
  (2) may expand on the process established by the district for the establishment of campus performance objectives; and
  (3) shall outline the role of the school committees regarding decision making related to goal setting, curriculum, budgeting, staffing patterns, and school organization.
(c) A school committee established under this section shall include community representatives. The community representatives may include business representatives.
(d) The commissioner may not approve a plan that the commissioner determines contains one or more provisions that may be construed as limiting or affecting the power of the board of trustees of the school district to govern and manage the district or as limiting the responsibilities of the trustees.
(e) The commissioner shall identify or make available to school districts various models of implementing site-based decision making under this section not later than January 1, 1992. . . . The commissioner shall arrange for training in site-based decision making through one or more sources for school board trustees, superintendents, principals, teachers, parents, and other members of school committees.
(f) Nothing in this section may be construed as creating a new cause of action or as requiring collective bargaining.

(Senate Bill 351)
(April, 1991)

TEC §11.273: Waivers and Exemptions

(a) Except as specifically prohibited under subsection (e) of this section, a school campus or district may apply to the *commissioner of education* for a waiver of a requirement or prohibition imposed by law or rule that the campus or district determines inhibits student achievement.
(b) An application under this section must include a written plan developed by the campus principal or district superintendent, as appropriate, and faculty of the campus or district that states the achievement objectives of the campus or district and the inhibition imposed on those objectives by the requirement or prohibition and shall be approved by the district's board of trustees.
(c) The *commissioner* may grant a waiver under this section for a period not to

exceed three years. A prohibition on conduct that constitutes a criminal offense may not be waived.
(d) A school campus or district for which a requirement or prohibition is waived under this section for a period of three years may receive an exemption from that requirement or prohibition at the end of that period if the campus or district has fulfilled the achievement objectives submitted to the *commissioner*.... The exemption remains in effect until the *commissioner* determines that achievement levels of the campus or district have declined.
(e) A school campus or district may not receive an exemption or waiver under this section from requirements imposed by federal law or rule, including requirements for special education or bilingual education programs.... A school campus or district may not receive an exemption or waiver under this section from a requirement or prohibition imposed by state law or rule relating to:
   (1) curriculum essential elements, excluding teacher methodology used by a teacher and the time spent by a teacher or a student on a particular task or subject.
   (2) restrictions on extracurricular activities
   (3) health and safety
   (4) competitive bidding
   (5) elementary class size limits
   (6) minimum graduation requirements
   (7) removal of a disruptive student from the classroom
   (8) suspension or expulsion of a student
   (9) at risk programs
   (10) prekindergarten programs
   (11) educational employee and educational support employee rights and benefits.... or
   (12) special education or bilingual education programs
(f) A school district or campus that receives a waiver under this section for textbook selection may select for purchase a textbook not on a state-adopted multiple list....
(g) The *commissioner* in considering exemptions or waivers shall provide as much regulatory relief as is practical and reasonable to campuses or districts that are considered high performing (Texas Education Agency, 1992)

Kentucky Perestroika

The Kentucky Education Reform Act of 1990 was the outcome of a process which began after the Kentucky Supreme Court ruled the state's system of school governance and finance unconstitutional in June of 1989. A landmark school reform package was then created in the Kentucky General Assembly, mandating school-based management, abolishing the state department of education, and instituting a system of rewards and sanctions intended to hold schools accountable. As the situation developed in Frankfort and elsewhere in the state, media comparisons with the Soviet political upheaval (*perestroika*) were inevitable. Possibly the most distinctive and visible part of the reform package is the requirement for every district to implement School-based Decision Making (SBDM) by July 1, 1996. As a Kentucky Education Reform Act (KERA) mandate potentially affecting 1,300 schools, the SBDM format of operation requires the formation of a local school council, with elected parent and teacher representation and with the principal serving as chairperson. The council is charged with the decision making for a substantial range of school operational matters, and with the development of policies to support those areas. The sections of the Kentucky law (also presented in Chapter Eight) pertaining to school-based management are presented here, as an explication for the preceding discussion and as a reference for the case study to follow.

Kentucky Law: KRS Chapter 160, Sections 14 and 15

Section 14: School-Based Decision Making.

1. By January 1, 1991, the school board shall adopt a policy for implementing the school-based decision making approach, and policies related to KRS 160.340 must be amended to further implement this approach related to professional development activities (sections 2 & 3 of HB 940).
2. Each participating school shall form a school council composed of 2 parents, 3 teachers, and the principal or administrator. More can be added, but the proportion must remain the same. Parents cannot be related to any school employee.
   a. Teachers shall be "elected" for 1 year terms by a majority of teachers.
   b. Parents shall be "selected" by the members of the PTO of the school; or, if none exists, by the largest organization of parents formed for this purpose.
   c. The principal or head teacher shall chair the council.

The Council's and Principals' Responsibilities Include:
(1) Set school policy to provide an environment to enhance students' achievement and meet the goals of Sections 2 and 3 of this act. The principal shall be the primary administrator and instructional leader

of the school; and, with the assistance of the total school staff, shall administer the policies established by the school council and school board.

(2) All staff "may" be participants. The staff shall divide into committees according to their areas of interest. A majority of each committee's members shall "elect" a chair to serve a one-year term. Each committee shall submit its recommendations to the school council for consideration.

(3) The council and each committee shall determine the agenda and frequency of meetings. The meetings shall be open to the public with the exceptions provided in KRS 61.810.

(4) Within the funds available from the school board, the council "shall" determine the number of persons to be employed in each job classification at the school, and can make personnel decisions on vacancies. It cannot recommend transfer or dismissals.

(5) The council "shall" determine which instructional materials and student support services shall be provided in the school.

(6) From a list of applicants recommended by the superintendent, the principal "shall" select personnel to fill vacancies, after consultation with the school council.

(7) To fill a principal vacancy, the school council "shall" select from among those persons recommended by the superintendent, and the superintendent "shall" provide additional applicants upon request.

(8) The council shall adopt a policy to be implemented by the principal in these additional areas:

(a) Determination of curriculum, including needs assessment, curriculum development, alignment with state standards, technology utilization, and program appraisal within the local school board's policy.

(b) Assignment of "all" instructional and non-instructional staff time.

(c) Assignment of students to classes and programs.

(d) Determine the schedule of the school day and week subject to the beginning and ending times and school calendar set by the school board.

(e) Determine the use of school space during the school day.

(f) Plan and resolve issues regarding instructional practices.

(g) Select and implement discipline and classroom management techniques; including the roles of students, parents, teachers, counselors and principals.

(h) Select extracurricular programs and determination of policies relating to student participation based on academic and attendance requirements, program evaluation and supervision.

3. The Local Board Policy on School-Based Decision Making "shall" also address:

　a. School budget and administration (discretionary funds; activity and other school funds; funds for maintenance, supplies and equipment; and accounting and auditing).

　b. Assessment of individual student progress, including testing and reporting of student progress to students, parents, the school district, the community and the state.

　c. School improvement plans, including the form and function of strategic planning and its relationship to district planning.

　d. Professional development plans developed pursuant to Sections 12 and 13 of this act.

　e. Parent, citizen and community participation including the relationship of the council with other groups.

　f. Cooperation and collaboration within the district and with other districts, public agencies and private agencies.

　g. Requirements for waiver of district policies.

　h. Requirements for record keeping by the school council.

　i. A process for appealing a decision made by a school council.

　j. In addition, the school board "may" grant to the school council any other authority permitted by law.

4. The school board "shall" make liability insurance available to all members of the school council when performing duties as school council members.

5. After the effective date of this act, any school in which two-thirds (2/3) of the faculty vote to implement school-based decision making may do so.

6. By June 30, 1991, each school board shall submit to the Chief State School Officer, the name of at least one (1) school which has decided to implement school-based management. If no school so votes, the school board "shall" designate one (1) school to implement it.

All schools shall implement school-based management by July 1, 1996. However, by a majority vote of the faculty, a school performing above its threshold level requirement, as determined by the Department of Education, may apply to the State Board for exemption from this requirement.

7. The Department of Education shall develop sample guidelines to assist local boards in the development of their policies, and it shall provide professional development activities to assist schools in implementing school-based decision making.

8. A school that chooses to have a different school-based model than the one outlined, can request an exemption by describing the model, submitting it through the board of education to the Chief State School Officer and the State Board for approval.

There has been and continues to be much observation and opinion written about the KERA and on the function of the SBDM local school councils. In addition to briefly considering this state legislation in Chapter 8 and in this chapter, the authors also chose to focus on the early impact of SBDM in an actual Kentucky district.

EARLY IMPLEMENTATION OF SCHOOL-BASED DECISION MAKING: CASE STUDY OF A KENTUCKY SCHOOL DISTRICT

In the late fall of 1991 the authors conducted on-site interviews in a school district in Kentucky in which several schools had recently opted to implement school-based decision making (SBDM). With the cooperation of the superintendent, five school sites were selected for the study, and interviews arranged with the SBDM site council members of each building. The interview sessions were audiotaped for later transcription and analysis of common themes and response patterns. An interview protocol was designed to probe the council members' perceptions of SBDM function and initial impact on the school, and to ascertain their perception of their preparedness for council service. (Note—the Kentucky term of SBDM and the authors' term of SBM used to designate site councils are intended here to mean the same groups.) Additionally, a school-based management questionnaire, framed largely around the language of the 1990 KERA law and designed in three formats for parents, teachers, and principals, was completed by each of the interviewees. Each school site council consisted of the same configuration of members; one principal, three teachers, and two parents, as required by the law.

Description of Case Study Schools

The high school in the study has an enrollment of almost 1400 students in grades 9–12, a teaching staff of approximately 80, and a classified staff of approximately 20. The racial mix of African-American and Caucasian (no other minorities were reported) is 13 percent and 87 percent, respectively. Twenty-one percent of the student population is participating in the Free and Reduced Lunch Program.

Two elementary schools in the study had a K–8 grade level span:

K–8 elementary school #1 has an enrollment of approximately 230 students, a teaching staff of approximately 20, and a classified staff of approximately 12. The racial profile is 100 percent Caucasian. Thirty percent of the student population is participating in the Free and Reduced Lunch Program.

K–8 elementary school #2 has an enrollment of approximately 190 students, a teaching staff of approximately 10, and a classified staff of approximately 8. The racial profile is 100 percent Caucasian. More than 40 percent of the student population is participating in the Free and Reduced Lunch Program.

The K–6 elementary school has an enrollment of approximately 150 students, a teaching staff of approximately 15, and a classified staff of approximately 10. The racial profile is 98 percent Caucasian; less than 2 percent of the population is African-American (no other minorities were reported). Approximately 25 percent of the student population is participating in the Free and Reduced Lunch Program.

The primary grades center has an enrollment of approximately 230 students, a teaching staff of approximately 10, and a classified staff of approximately 12. The racial profile is 80 percent Caucasian; and 20 percent African-American (no other minorities were reported). Approximately 36 percent of the student population is participating in the Free and Reduced Lunch Program.

School-Based Management Interview Responses

The interview questions are provided here, with a school-by-school summary of the responses of the council members. The duration of most of the interviews was approximately one to two hours, and, except for one interview which was conducted at the county's school administration building, all interviews were conducted at the individual schools, in the agreed-upon location of the regular site council meetings.

SBM Site Interview Questions and Responses

1. Were you given any training to assist you when the SBM Council began?

High School: The Council indicated that they had had twelve hours of locally-provided training (provided for all of the County teachers), as well as training provided through other sources, such as the Kentucky Education Association.

K-8 elementary school #1: The Council indicated that they had received an evening and one-half day training, and still had more to undergo.

K-8 elementary school #2: The Council indicated that they had received the twelve hours of locally-provided training; the principal had been trained by the superintendent.

K-6 elementary school: The Council had received the district training.

Primary grades center: The Council had received the district training.

If yes, what types of training did you receive to prepare your for your role as a member of the SBM council?

High School: The members described policy review, all-staff orientation training on the details of the KERA, local training (with materials) to prepare for the role, and a parental member awareness session.

K-8 elementary school #1: Members indicated that the content addressed the processes necessary to have in place to begin as a Council, such as the development of a mission statement.

K-8 elementary school #2: Members had received training in policy and goal formation, curriculum, different kinds of instructional planning, budget, monitoring of student achievement, and in a number of the KERA laws. They were given an assistance contact number for the state Office of Accountability. The principal is a charter member of a statewide steering committee of SBDM principals, and a support network of the same has formed within the County. Peer training assistance had been provided in meeting with Council members from other Kentucky schools who had a longer history of SBDM.

K-6 elementary school: The Council indicated that the training had addressed the basic SBDM functions.

Primary grades center: Members indicated that they had received the basic orientation, and had been made aware of other available training, but felt that their team members were so compatible that none was necessary at the time.

2. Are you currently receiving any training that will assist you in performing well in your SBM Council's activities?

High School: The respondents felt that it was available upon request, and that they were experiencing self-training as they meet collaboratively. Their training needs were policy writing, attaining a common council vocabulary, and preparation for handling difficult decisions yet to come. They felt that it might be the job of the chair or principal to provide council training.

K-8 elementary school #1: The members were undergoing some specific program training with the district consultant.

K-8 elementary school #2: Some update and further training was planned with the district consultant.

K-6 elementary school: The member indicated that they had requested additional training.

Primary grades center: The members had experienced some further training.

   If yes, what types of training are you receiving?

High School: No specific types are being received; there is, rather, a sense of technical help available upon request.

K-8 elementary school #1: Council members described a human resources format; communications skills, group skills, and decision making.

K-8 elementary school #2: Members described no current training; only past and upcoming training.

K-6 elementary school: Members described no current training; only past and upcoming training. They had requested further training during the fall.

Primary grades center: The members had undergone some specific group process training.

3. Do you feel you need to receive additional training in order to perform your SBM Council's activities well?

High School: The members again described the "trailblazing" experience of being one of the first operating councils as carrying built-in training of its own, but acknowledged that future decisional situations might demand further training.

K-8 elementary school #1: Parent members felt that they needed more training than the teachers, simply due to the unfamiliar setting, and to their newness in programmatic issues.

K-8 elementary school #2: Members felt that it would be helpful, but expressed more concern for uncertainty at the state level, particularly in connection with the Office of Accountability. Some Council situations have arisen which seem to require statutory resolution. They recommend codifying the ongoing KERA interpretations being made at the state level into some statewide dissemination form. Like the other K–8 school, they expressed concern for accountability minus fiscal support. Offers for further training have been made at the state level, and more local training is planned, particularly in the areas of Effective Schools and school improvement.

K-6 elementary school: The Council suggested further training.

Primary grades center: The Council indicated that they did not anticipate the need for any further group process, on-site training; their size, cohesion, and common curriculum assisted the consensus process.

If yes, what types of training do you recommend you receive?

High School: Members felt it was too early to determine the needs, but speculated upon later needs, which might include training in specialized program areas, such as curriculum and guidance, and acknowledged that future councils would have an easier job, since they would not have to write as much policy, for example. They noted that the continual interpretation and refinement of KERA might require some training; and that future councils would have the advantage of a broader existing network of fellow councils to call upon for assistance. At this early implementation stage, all councils were neophytes.

K-8 elementary school #1: The council subcommittee process and how it functions was a training concern.

K-8 elementary school #2: They recommend codifying the ongoing KERA interpretations being made at the state level into some statewide dissemination form. Like the other K–8 school, they expressed concern for accountability minus fiscal support. Offers for further training have been made at the state level, and more local training is planned, particularly in the areas of Effective Schools and school improvement.

K-6 elementary school: The Council suggested budget and finance as possibilities, and, possibly, curriculum. They recommended training in accountability, especially at the state level. Next year will be easier, with terms defined and Councils established. It is easier to reach consensus with a smaller school; consolidation may affect this, and require further training.

Primary grades center: None were recommended.

4. What types of decisions have you made thus far as an SBM council?

High School: None had been made by this council, as yet; they were still in initial formation stages.

K-8 elementary school #1: They had established a budgetary subcommittee, some basic Council agenda-forming procedures, and were working on local policies.

K-8 elementary school #2: The members have worked on parent nominations, hired teachers over the summer, created a split class, changed the schedule, made class assignments, prepared a budget, and considered increasing the ungraded format into grades 4 and 5.

K-6 elementary school: The Council had handled hiring of a new principal, some student supervision problems, and a decision to exceed class size caps.

Primary grades center: The Council had handled a decision not to exceed class size caps, somewhat in resistance to central office pressure.

Why did you make each of the decisions you mentioned above?

High School: Not applicable.

K-8 elementary school #1: Most of the policies had been left as they were, but some clausal changes were occurring. The other decisions were purely functional and initiative in nature.

K-8 elementary school #2: The decisions reflected Council consensus for strategies to improve the instructional program, particularly in the split class formation. They had worked slowly to become familiar with procedures.

K-6 elementary school: The Council decision reflected teacher input regarding what was best for students; they put a time limit on the cap size decision. Selection of the new principal was an outcome reflecting Council parental and teacher preference for a positive, motivated, highly-involved, hands-on leader, who felt comfortable with SBDM.

Primary grades center: The staff did not support going over the class size cap, feeling it was best for student needs that the limit stand.

5. Do you feel your SBM Council's efforts have strong support from the board of education and the superintendent of schools?

High School: The Council felt support.

K-8 elementary school #1: The Council felt that it was hard to tell; the Board seemed to be for SBDM.

K-8 elementary school #2: They felt general support, but it was tempered by a teacher reassignment situation, which had involved some negotiations with the Central Office personnel.

K-6 elementary school: The Council felt support, particularly from the former superintendent.

Primary grades center: The Council was uncertain of how the Board and superintendent perceived them. One of them had been told that they were supportive.

Why did you answer as you did above?

High School: The Council felt it had seen nothing but support, cooperation, and encouragement from them, and, also, from the Council Member principal.

K-8 elementary school #1: Support had been provided in getting started. They felt that they needed to keep district and state policy in mind.

K-8 elementary school #2: The interpretations of the KERA, especially in the initial stages of implementation, may require some extra facilitation for all levels, and some subsequent training, as well.

K-6 elementary school: The former superintendent's support for the principal selection process had been especially strong.

Primary grades center: The Council felt that everyone in the County had had difficulty with the change brought by SBDM. They noted that there is a generous Board SBDM policy in place; more so than in other systems.

6. *What successes do you feel your SBM council has had?*

High School: The members felt that they had come together as a Council in a positive way.

K-8 elementary school #1: The Council described a sense of pride at having implemented SBDM. It may be too soon to tell about further successes.

K-8 elementary school #2: The Council described how they had handled the split class/reassignment situation, including their appeal to the state department for a clarification.

K–6 elementary school: Selection of the new principal was a real source of pride and of strongly felt, visible empowerment for the Council.

Primary grades center: Though they had had but few meetings, they were proud of their unanimity and ability to come to consensus despite differences.

Why do you feel the above were successful?

High School: The members felt that they had observed their own developmental process, and had done all the initial things necessary to be a success.

K–8 elementary school #1: There was pride in having been able to elect a Council and members on first ballot. The training experience was also perceived as a success.

K–8 elementary school #2: They felt that they had negotiated a difficult situation quite ably, and had received support from the state department.

K–6 elementary school: The prestige of taking such a key personnel action as the hiring of a principal had an apparent galvanizing effect on the Council. They spoke of the general effects of SBDM; the efficacy of funneling problems through the Council members; the enhancement of the team effect and the sense of being asked, instead of told, what to do; and the accolades of neighboring schools.

Primary grades center: They talked through problems, and considered what was best for all the school's students.

7. What failures or problems do you feel you have had as a SBM Council?

High School: The Council felt it had experienced scant opportunity to fail as yet; they anticipated having to deal with problems or stumbling blocks, but did not anticipate outright failure.

K–8 elementary school #1: There has not been very much at-large parental participation.

K–8 elementary school #2: The reassignment/split class situation is still problematic since the Central Office interpreted it as a transfer, which is an area not in the control of the Council.

K–6 elementary school: The Council perceived no failures; they had simply gone forward with tasks, aided by their best professional knowledge, and felt that they had done well, given the initial stages and need for more training. They felt help was at hand through the state department, if needed.

Primary grades center: The Council perceived no failures.

Why do you feel the above failed or became problems?

High School: Not applicable.

K-8 elementary school #1: Some members felt that community members may not realize that they could come to Council meetings and could have input.

K-8 elementary school #2: The members felt that there is an overlap of their jurisdiction with that of others, and that such finely-grained distinctions will impede personnel matters. They have been empowered to hire, but not to realign teacher assignments within their programs.

K-6 elementary school: Not applicable.

Primary grades center: Not applicable.

8. What do you feel are the strengths of this current SBM approach?

High School: The parent members praised the opportunity for interested parents to become involved—with more say and control—in schools, in contrast to the estrangement so many parents now feel towards their public schools. While the principal was previously perceived as having been quite democratic, the feeling among the staff is that now all teachers will have input. All praised the local empowerment effect, noting that it is difficult for a school board to make blanket policy for each school. Now each Council can address that necessary uniqueness.

K-8 elementary school #1: Members described beginning the Council process as a very positive experience, especially sharing in decision making and responsibility, and anticipate more involvement to come. Members have gone into the experience with an attitude of doing what it takes to get the job done correctly. They feel able to assess what is best for their school, rather than someone from elsewhere in the County.

K-8 elementary school #2: The Council feels that the system has changed from unilateral decision making to a collaborative format, which may be more defensible (to the public, for instance) when there is disagreement over decisions made.

K-6 elementary school: Teachers had previously felt "drained of motivation"; now, they feel pride in newly-conferred control. They applaud the customization effect of SBDM, and welcome the extra funds provided for Council instructional expenditure. The hand-picked new leader was a "breath of fresh air," and was cooperating with and maximizing the effect of the Council.

Primary grades center: Parent members felt that they had a stronger voice than in the past. Teachers feel the same, adding that while they may not get exactly the Council decision they want, at least there is participation. The team approach provides more breadth of input and insight.

9. What do you feel are the weaknesses of this SBM approach?

High School: The members expressed concern for appropriate procedure if there were to be substantial disagreement and a voting tie on an important issue; they were not sure if this contingency was covered in the locally developed SBM policies. The SBDM law is very general and affords many interpretative opportunities. Money will play an important part in the school's determination of its own destiny, and only the minimum support has been forthcoming from the district and the state, for council informational support and for instructional expenditure. Budgets are already overstretched. The members felt that the state department will have to redefine direction if all of the Council accountability described in the law stays intact and there are no resources to support the Councils. They recognized that the state department was also experiencing the initial difficulties and learning process uncertainties of the KERA implementation; their personnel are on call and available, however.

K-8 elementary school #1: Lack of training and lack of community-wide publicity concerning the Council's activities. It is felt that the public does not know how much authority they actually have via their representation on the council.

K-8 elementary school #2: They cited real and anticipated inconsistencies within the law; the fine points of interpretation; for example, despite the strong theme of avoidance of nepotism in the KERA, there are no such requirements for Council membership.

K-6 elementary school: It is difficult to convene the Council, working around teacher and parent schedules; decision making delays ensue. The school is fortunate, members felt, in that its size and physical plant allow for rapid dissemination of Council information and an equally rapid opportunity for staff consensus. This must be problematic in larger schools. The members would like to see other Kentucky school Councils in action.

Primary grades center: There is limited time to do the tasks. Also, the teacher aides—very involved and valued members of this staff—cannot be represented on the Council. They described the Texas SBM law as too loose and the Kentucky one as too rigid. Parent at-large participation is limited.

10. What do you suggest be done to improve this current SBM approach?

High School: The members said that it was difficult at this early stage to predict, but felt that it would be important to monitor Council activities and group process as they progressed through the year.

K–8 elementary school #1: Members expressed that they needed further general training in SBDM, and that such training should be publicized, to draw in their community. Specific needs are not known yet.

K–8 elementary school #2: The Council agreed that time and experience will assist the process. It does seem like "passing the buck" as to who is responsible for decision making. Some newsletter or communication put out by the Office of Educational Accountability outlining ongoing interpretations of the law would be helpful.

K–6 elementary school: There is a sense of euphoria now, which may not persist. Usually, the teachers and parents elected to Councils are, predictably, busy and highly-involved people, with conflicting schedules. The public does not seem to comprehend the decision-making purview of the Council, nor do they see the public access opportunity. Public information committees should be set up to showcase the Council's functions and activities.

Primary grades center: Members would be interested in seeing other SBDM models and implementations. Inclusion of teacher aides on Councils and state or district resource support for meeting time (frequently scheduled at extremely early or late points of the day) devoted to Council service were recommended. They would not actually want all personnel selection responsibility; they feel that the initial screening should be done at the central level.

11. How long have you been operating as an SBM Council?

High School: This Council officially began on the day of the interview.

K-8 elementary school #1: They had a first meeting in October, but had made the decision to form an SBDM Council when school opened.

K-8 elementary school #2: The Council had been in effect almost a year.

K-6 elementary school: The Council had been in effect for six months.

Primary grades center: The Council had been in effect for three months.

12. How does your SBM Council usually arrive at decisions?

High School: Not applicable.

K-8 elementary school #1: Discussion usually results in everyone trying to find a collective solution. They have been working on policies. Sometimes they go back into official session after a work session and endorse their previous proposals as Council decisions.

K-8 elementary school #2: The Council comes to consensus.

K-6 elementary school: Members thrash over details, and come to a unanimous decision, (at least, so far). Their team's distinctive bonding and openness have precluded any real disagreements; the parent members have gained new insights into the workings of schools.

Primary grades center: The Council comes to consensus.

13. On a scale of one (1) to ten (10), with ten being the best score, what score would you give your SBM operation at this point in time?

High School: Council members felt they scored a 10; there were good feelings about the assembled team, and about the entry level activities (training, selection of members) which had preceded the formation of the Council.

K-8 elementary school #1: The members felt that they scored somewhere between 5 and 7, in light of their policy and goals/objectives development. They could better assess, they indicated, at the end of the year.

K-8 elementary school #2: Ten was their score, they agreed, at this time.

K-6 elementary school: The members felt that they scored 15 on the scale of 10, in a burst of clearly visible pride.

Primary grades center: The members felt that they scored 11 on the scale of 10; or, at least, no less than 9.

14. Are there any other major points or additional information or opinions you care to share before we end this interview?

High School: The Council felt optimistic that it would be a good year working together, since none of the members were strangers to each other, having served together on other projects and committees over the years. They considered the SBM concept to be solid, applauding the close-to-the-customer aspect of it. There was some pride in having been the first County high school to implement a Council; anticipation of leadership modeling and precedent-setting was discernible. They felt the particular burden of being one of the first Councils, and were especially sensitive, due to the size of the staff and the parent group, of adequately representing such large numbers of constituents. There was parental anticipation of the opportunity to make positive growth changes.

K-8 elementary school #1: Members described the feeling of not realizing how involved the process was; it is a learning experience, and they do not wish to rush the developmental aspect of it.

K-8 elementary school #2: There was some apprehension among these Council members since they were anticipating an election of new parent members; the complexion of the team will, of course, change as a result.

K-6 elementary school: Members described a great sense of self-pride in their distinctive rapport and accomplishments, especially in light of the fact that they had felt somewhat unprepared for the decisions they made.

Primary grades center: They expressed a funding concern over the halving of the SBDM per-student funds, when applied to kindergarten students, since there is only a half-day program for them. It creates an inadequate supply base.

15. Do you feel that you are a valued member of your school's SBM Council?

High School: The parent members expressed that, even without the vehicle of a Council, that they always felt welcome in the schools and that they were positive places for parents; not enough parents go into schools to avail themselves of participatory opportunities. In light of that good climate, however, they were glad to sit as members on a policy-making Council.

K-8 elementary school #1: They feel support from faculty, particularly at the primary building; teachers trust them with input. Communication is strong. All would have to feel valued Council members, or they would not be there; they intended to do the best possible job. The principal pointed out that he (and others across the state) was the only nonelected member; consideration of value may be moot.

K-8 elementary school #2: There was general agreement that they felt valued.

K-6 elementary school: There was general agreement that they felt valued.

Primary grades center: There was general agreement that they felt valued.

Common Interview Response Patterns

- Entry-level and start-up training had been provided for the Councils; there were emerging and anticipated needs for further training in such areas as budget development, curriculum, and group process.
- Observation of and networking with more experienced Councils would help.
- Further SBDM implementation details should be disseminated by the state department of education; Councils did perceive the state department as a viable source of SBDM assistance.
- Time to meet and adequate funds to manage are scarce.
- Council actions in personnel and in instructional program may run counter to or overlap central office and local board policy.
- Parents felt exceptionally positive about the SBDM process.
- Members felt pride in their initiative as a newly-formed Council and in their common outlook, goals, and skills for consensus.
- There was unanimous appreciation of the participatory and empowering aspects of SBDM, and an appreciation of the advantages offered by a team approach.
- Council members displayed a sense of the responsibilities of constituent representation, a pervasive attitude of goodwill, and a clear focus on school improvement.

School-Based Management Questionnaire

In addition to the Council interviews, the authors had each respondent complete the following questionnaire, with the intent of probing more specifically into the Councils' implementation details of the School-Based Decision Making part of the Kentucky Education Reform Act, and with the intent to provide a private as well as group opportunity to respond to some of the issues addressed in the site interview instrument. There were separate informational introductions on each instrument to distinguish it as a response from a principal, teacher, or parent; the internal questions were identical. The questionnaire is reproduced here, with a narrative reporting and a summary of the responses of the three types of Council members.

SCHOOL-BASED MANAGEMENT QUESTIONNAIRE

The Kentucky Education Reform Act of 1990 provides for much more important decision making power to be provided to the school level. It is our purpose to discover how much authority has been delegated, how well the process is working, and what you see as the strengths and weaknesses of the process. Please answer the following questions. Feel free to add additional sheets if you wish.

1. Do you feel that school-based management has strengthened your decision making power as a principal, teacher, or parent? (check one) _____ YES NO _____

Response: All but one indicated "yes"; the only negative response was quantified by the information that the respondent had felt decision-making latitude already existed prior to SBDM implementation.

2. Do you feel that school-based management has made you more accountable for the results received by your school? (check one) _____ YES NO _____

Response: All but three indicated "yes"; the three negative/"not applicable" respondents were parents.

3. Are you pleased with the changes that school-based management has brought to your school? (check one) _____ YES NO _____

Response: All but two indicated "yes"; the two "not applicable" respondents were parents.

Why did you answer the above as you did?

Response: Members felt that that control had been returned to the school, and that teachers were more positive and were sensing a difference in climate; parents felt involved and empowered. There were concerns about the time demanded by decision making. Some respondents saw little difference as yet; many commented upon the early stage of the Council process and the absence of experience.

4. Has your SBM School Council established policies in accordance with the goals of the Kentucky Reform Act of 1990? (check one) _____ YES NO _____

Response: Twelve members reported "yes"; five reported "no"; two noted that such establishment was in process.

If yes, which policies has your school's SBM Council adopted? (please list)

Response: Members reported policy adoption in the eight curricular and instructional operational areas (refer to the Kentucky law outlined at the beginning of the chapter), provisions for policy revision, and indicated an awareness of district level SBDM policy development.

5. Do you advertise your SBM Council's meetings? (check one) _____ YES NO _____

Response: All members but one answered "yes"; one parent member was unsure.

Do you have visitors or observers at your SBM Council's meetings? (check one) _____ YES NO _____

Response: This was split approximately half and half between "yes" and "no"; some members indicated that it was not applicable.

If yes, what is the average number in attendance? (list number) _____

Response: Numbers mentioned were one or two visitors/observers.

What is the largest number of visitors or observers to ever attend one of the SBM Council's meetings? (list number) _____

Response: The largest numbers were between 45–50; the least were between 2 and 5.

6. Has your SBM Council appointed subcommittees consisting of people who do not serve on the Council? (check one) _____ YES NO _____

Response: Six indicated "yes"; twelve indicated "no"; the negative responses were accompanied by explanation that such appointments were planned or in progress.

If yes, for what purposes were the subcommittees appointed? (please list)

Response: Members indicated subcommittees addressing finance/budget, discipline/guidance, technology, and policy review; some subcommittees were in the process of being formed.

NOTE: THE FOLLOWING RELATE DIRECTLY TO THE AUTHORITY DELEGATED TO THE SBDM COUNCILS BY THE KENTUCKY REFORM ACT OF 1990.

7. Has the SBM Council, within available funds, determined the number of persons to be employed in each classification at your school? (check one) _____ YES NO _____

Response: All responses were negative.

If yes, what categories of employees were involved? (please list)

Response: The "no's" were accompanied by explanations that this had been determined before the Councils met; many of the Councils' actual dates of initial formation precluded their participation in such decision making. It is a responsibility yet to come.

8. Has the SBM Council made decisions on which candidates to hire to fill vacancies at your school? (check one) _____ YES NO _____

Response: This was split approximately half and half between "yes" and "no."

If yes, what categories of employees were involved? (please list)

Response: The members named principal, teacher, library aide, and Chapter I aide. Several indicated that vacancies had not yet occurred.

9. Has the SBM Council determined the instructional materials to be used by the teachers and students? (check one) _____ YES NO _____

Response: All members but one answered "no."

   If yes, what instructional materials were involved? (please list)

Response: A few members mentioned basic teaching supplies. Other members indicated that this was in budgetary progress at this time.

10. Has the SBM Council decided which student support services (guidance, etc.) should be provided in your school? (check one) _____ YES NO _____

Response: All members but one answered "no."

   If yes, which student support services were involved? (please list)

Response: Responses mentioned guidance, student activities, and adolescent day care.

11. If your school's principal leaves, do you believe that the SBM Council should have the authority to choose the new principal? (check one) _____ total authority; _____ shared with superintendent and board; _____ no authority.

Response: Thirteen members wanted total authority; ten wanted to share the authority with the superintendent and board. The "yes" and "no" votes were split almost evenly within each of the three types of respondent categories.

12. Has the SBM Council determined the curriculum to be offered in your school? (check one) _____ YES NO _____

Response: All members but one answered "no."

   If yes, which parts of the curriculum? (please list)

The "yes" vote indicated anticipation of involvement in adoption of a reading curriculum.

13. Has the SBM Council determined the computer and other technological resources to be provided in your school? (check one) _____ YES NO _____

Response: All members answered "no" or "not applicable."

   If yes, which resources? (please list)

Response: No responses were provided.

14. Has the SBM Council decided on the assignment of where the teachers and other school employees spend their time during the day? (check one) _____ YES NO _____

Response: All but two members indicated "no."

   If yes, please list the specifics below.

Response: Comment was included which indicated that some Councils had given this authority to the principal, while retaining the right of Council revision.

15. Has the SBM Council decided on the schedule of time to be allocated to different subjects or activities during the school day and school week? (check one) _____ YES NO _____

Response: All but two members indicated "no."

If yes, what specific decisions has the SBM Council made? (please list)

Response: Comment was included which indicated that some Councils had given this authority to the principal, while retaining the right of Council revision. A comment also addressed the difficulty of implementing any substantial deviation from existing schedules because of shared district transportation and common bus scheduling problems.

16. Has the SBM Council decided on how the school space should be used during the school day? (check one) _____ YES NO _____

Response: Five members answered "yes"; twelve members answered "no."

If yes, what decisions were made? (please list)

Response: Members described the assigning of a special education teacher to a classroom, and noted that, while many of these decisions were left to the principal, some were in process at this time.

17. Has the SBM Council made decisions related to the instructional practices at the school? (check one) _____ YES NO _____

Response: Three members answered "yes"; fourteen answered "no."

If yes, please list those decisions below.

Response: The commentary described a Council decision to exceed class size caps. Further comments indicated that a subcommittee for this area was being formed, and that many of these decisions were at present left to the principal.

18. Has the SBM Council selected the discipline and classroom management techniques to be used in the school? (check one) _____ YES NO _____

Response: Four members answered "yes"; thirteen members answered "no."

If yes, please list those decisions below.

Response: Detention techniques had been determined by one Council; other commentary described selection of a subcommittee and the leaving of this matter to the principal, at present.

19. Has the SBM Council decided the roles of students, parents, teachers, counselors and the principal in the areas of discipline and classroom management? (check one) _____ YES NO _____

Response: All responses were negative or "not applicable."

If yes, please list your decisions below.

Response: Members indicated that no actual policies had been yet developed, and that the County policies were being followed. They anticipated local school revisions as the year progressed.

20. Has the SBM Council decided which extra curricular (athletics, band, clubs, etc.) are to be offered by the school? (check one) _____ YES NO _____

Response: All responses were negative or "not applicable."

If yes, please list your decision below.

Response: Members indicated that no actual policies had been yet developed, and that the County policies were being followed. They anticipated local school revisions as the year progressed.

21. Has the SBM Council asked the school board to exempt their school from any district policies? (check one) _____ YES NO _____

Response: All responses were negative or "not applicable." Members indicated that they felt the new status of the Councils precluded this; one respondent indicated uncertainty as to whether the state would approve exemptions.

If yes, please list the specific policies involved.

Response: No responses were provided.

22. What do you personally feel are the strengths of the current school-based management approach in your school district and in your school?

Response: Members described: enhanced communication and cooperation with and among staff; teacher ownership; a "whole-school" focus; parent and teacher input and local involvement; shared decision making; diversity of representation in Council structure; and improved focus on school improvement and student needs. Also mentioned were pride, enthusiasm, utilization of myriad talents, and empowerment through handling personnel and budgetary matters.

23. What do you personally feel are the weaknesses of the current school-based management approach in your school district and in your school?

Response: Members mentioned: newness of process; lack of time to meet; need for more training; scarcity of funds for budgetary function; only partial involvement and awareness of some staff and community; sense of Board still retaining governance; and a statewide need for classified personnel representation on Councils. Some members indicated that they were unsure at this time of any weaknesses.

24. What suggestions would you offer to improve the current school-based management approach in your school district and in your school?

Response: Members recommended: more release time and money; provision of sample policies and procedures and the opportunity to network or observe other Councils; more training, conveniently scheduled; earlier Council inception; clarification of policy particulars and of Council authority; and publicity for the Councils' functions and activities.

Common SBDM Council Questionnaire Responses

- A general pattern of support and positive attitude prevailed.
- Some Councils had adopted policies and appointed subcommittees; others had not.
- While meetings were advertised, except for an initial meeting to elect parent representatives, public attendance was scant.

The response patterns directly related to provisions of the Kentucky law indicated that:

- In the Council decision-making areas of: numbers of persons employed; personnel selection; determination of instructional materials and student support services; principal selection; determination of curricular offerings; determination of technological resources; determination of instructional time; scheduling and space; instructional practices; discipline management; extracurricular activities; and exemption from district policies—
  - Most of these areas had been left undisturbed by the Councils, for the present; or entrusted to the principal
  - Some decision-making activities were in progress at the time of the inquiry
  - Some constraints, such as time, money, and existing policy may impede Council activity in these areas

With regard to the responses regarding SBDM strengths, weaknesses, and Council recommendations:

- There was virtual unanimity in the perceived benefits of SBDM
- Members cited lack of: time, money, policy, and procedural specificity, and Council visibility
- Members recommended further training, peer networking and provision of more resources

Combined Conclusions from Interviews and Questionnaires

With regard to the early stage status of the Councils at the time of the inquiry:

- Group cohesion dynamics were beginning to develop, as members grappled with issues and process, simultaneously.
- There was a significant awareness of this, and a common agreement about the limitations of the Council's impact during their first year.

Other conclusions were that:

- Time to meet and resources to support Council function are needed.
- Further training is needed, in group process and in particular content areas of Council responsibility.
- There is a "Kentucky Effect"; a need to network with sister Councils; and a need for policy and procedural specificity and commonality of KERA interpretation.
- Councils members are, essentially, enthused about serving; optimistic for the long-term benefits of SBDM, and take great professional and community pride in having taken such a major step towards the improvement of their school.

In January of 1992 a repeat of the questionnaire process was completed, with the same participants. There were reiterations of the same themes, and no new response patterns emerged. The councils did report that they were much more involved in activities, and were progressing with the ongoing actions described in their original responses.

All of the councils responses and reactions are borne out, many times over, in historical and current literature on school-based management and shared decision making. Not every respondent could be said to be fluent in awareness of SBM content and research. Nevertheless, the five Kentucky SBDM Councils in this study spoke of their experience in the terminology of that existing knowledge base, and thus provide the field a further affirmation of effective SBM implementation recommendations.

CONCLUSION

The Texas legislation requiring the development and implementation of a site-based, decision-making plan carried a date of September 1, 1992, as the official beginning of the law taking effect. There will undoubtedly be a period of initial implementation efforts and adjustments, as there was in Kentucky. Certainly the impact of the KERA is beginning to take definite shape; as of this writing, there are no discernible Texas outcomes regarding the adoption of a state level site-based decision making model. The Kentucky and Texas models have similarities in statutory provision and in legislative intent. The KERA seems more prescriptive, particularly in the local school council design and in the designation of those councils' areas of responsibility. There is more latitude in the Texas legislation in the area of council formation and areas of responsibility. It is interesting to note that this legislation also directly addresses the SBM legal and compliance issues raised in Chapter 6, that it seems to seek to preserve the absence of collective bargaining (which was considered in Chapter 4), and that it directly speaks to the school board-school council relationship. That relationship in the Kentucky model is handled more indirectly through a requirement for aligned policies at the two levels. There has been some confusion about the intended relationship, focusing on a seeming lack of clarity regarding the Kentucky school councils' actual authority (Van Meter, 1991). Both states do require that the site councils support, or at least not undermine, the state curriculum.

Much national focus has been placed on Kentucky since the inception of the KERA in 1990; Texas should soon share that spotlight, at least in the arena of school-based management and shared decision making. As of this writing, Kentucky is already experiencing some change and reaction from the field. Unions in Kentucky's Boone and Johnson counties have filed legal challenges against the state law requiring every school to create a site-based decision-making council by 1996; the unions contend that their school boards lack the authority under the law to approve or review the council-developed site improvement plans (AASA, 1992). Additionally, Kentucky Governor Brereton Jones recently indicated that parts of the KERA may be subject to a budget crunch which has hit the state; he proposed to maintain, at least, the essential elements of the reform act (Harp, 1992).

Both states seem to have made an effort to reconcile the seeming contradiction of mandating flexibility as they implemented the two decentralized models. Kentucky has attempted to change the focus of accountability, moving from a production model to a professional model (Lally, 1991). Finally, both states' intentions may very well be expressed by the Texas Education Agency:

> While it may appear paradoxical that the state dictate local decision making mechanisms, this legislation represents a major philosophical turning point at the state level. It is the message that it is the business of local communities and their respective school systems to determine how educational programs will be structured—and that the state's role is to establish the standards for performance, determine district accountability with respect to state standards, and coordinate technical support to assist local districts in their efforts to improve student performance. Equally clear is the message that local school districts must also decentralize decision making (p. 103).

SUMMARY

A brief perspective on the scope of state department of education and legislative national level reform preceded a description of the variety and range of state department restructuring strategies, with a common emphasis on assistance, rather than regulation, of local districts. Despite recent national efforts to avoid prescriptives, the states of Texas and Kentucky have mandated SBM within larger reform packages, and have become, essentially, national laboratories for its implementation.

The 1991 Texas requirement for SBM, more recent than that of Kentucky, was preceded by a mass of major legislatively-initiated change during the 1980s. There seems to be a reverse of this trend with the passage of site-based decision making, aimed at facilitating the improvement of student outcomes. A collaborative state level advisory team and resources to support SBM facilitation have been established. Excerpts of the Texas law were provided.

The Kentucky Education Reform Act evolved as a 1990 landmark school reform package which mandated, among other restructuring changes, school-based decision making (SBDM), implemented via a phased-in process. Excerpts of the Kentucky law were also reported, and provided a reference for the chapter's major component—a case study of a Kentucky school district's implementation of SBDM. Descriptions of the schools and their local SBM councils preceded a detailed reporting of each Council's experience with the early stages of shared decision making. Results of both council member questionnaires and on-site interviews were reported and summarized. Combined response patterns included: the development of group cohesion dynamics; the awareness of this of the limitations of the council's impact during their first year; the sense that time to meet, resources to support Council function, and further training were needed; the sense of a need to network with sister councils; and the need for policy and procedural specificity and commonality of the law's interpretation. Council's members were enthused about serving, optimistic for the long-term benefits of SBDM, and took great professional and community pride in having undertaken such a major step towards the improvement of their school. These responses and reactions are borne out, many times over, in historical and current literature on school-based management and shared decision making.

Both the Kentucky and Texas models have similarities in statutory provision and in legislative intent. The KERA seems more prescriptive, particularly in the local school council design and in the designation of those councils' areas of responsibility. There is more latitude in the Texas legislation in the area of council formation and areas of responsibility. Some change and reaction from the field to these mandates is occurring, mostly in Kentucky. Legal challenges and revenue shortfalls are impacting the KERA. Both states have attempted to reconcile the seeming contradiction of mandating flexibility as they implemented these two decentralized models, which represent a major philosophical turning point at the state level.

EXERCISES

1. Estimate the level of educational quality prescriptives and regulations required by your state department of education; is it substantial, or more laissez-faire in nature?
2. Which of these regulations or areas of compliance would be most at odds with a statewide SBM implementation model?
3. What would be the nature of those state waivers necessary to facilitate SBM?
4. Consider both the Texas and Kentucky shared decision-making models; how adequate or applicable would they be for your state?
5. With regard to the experience of the local school councils in the case study, analyze the likely responses in your district under the same conditions and SBM implementation process. Would there be substantial similarity or difference?
6. Given the nature of Kentucky's more established SBM record, what would you predict concerning the early impact and outcome of the Texas SBM implementation?

REFERENCES

AASA (1992). Where do you draw the line in shared decision making? *The School Administrator, 1* (49), 8–15.

Crowson, R.L. (1992). *School-community relations, under reform.* Berkeley, CA: McCutchan Publishing Corporation, pp. 131–132.

Education Commission of the States (1989). *Policy guide: A state policy maker's guide to public school choice.* Denver, CO: Education Commission of the States, p. 1.

Education Commission of the States (1991). *Exploring policy options to restructure education.* Denver, CO: Education Commission of the States, pp. 22, 28, 36, 42.

Harp, L. (1992). Ky. reforms may buckle under budget crunch, Jones says. *Education Week,* January 22, 1992, 15.

Harrington-Lueker, D. (1990). Kentucky starts from scratch. *American School Board Journal, 177* (9), 17–21.

Herman, J.L. (1989). Instructional leadership skills and competencies of public school superintendents. *Dissertation Abstracts International, 50,* 1503-A. (DA8920723) p. 3.

Lally, K. (1991). Changing of the old guard: States turn toward helping rather than regulating. *The School Administrator, 3* (48), 8–12.

Lewis, A. (1989). *Restructuring America's schools.* Washington, DC: American Association of School Administrators, p. 124.

Miller, M.H., Noland, K., & Schaaf, J. (1990). *A guide to the Kentucky Education Reform Act.* Frankfort, KY: Legislative Research Commission.

Texas Education Agency, Meno, L.R., Commissioner of Education, & the State Advisory Committee on Site-Based Decision Making. (1992). *Resource guide on site-based decision making and district and campus planning.* Austin, TX: Texas Education Agency, pp. 1-2–1-5, VI 2–VI-9.

Van Meter, E.J. (1991). The Kentucky mandate: School-based decision making. *NASSP Bulletin, 75* (532), 52–63.

Chapter 11

SCHOOL-BASED MANAGEMENT AND SCHOOL REFORM: RESTRUCTURING FOR COLLABORATION

The decade of reform which began in the early 1980s was an era of heightening federal, state, and local focus on the plight of education, and is evidenced by the numerous state and federal reports and legislative actions occurring over that time frame. As early as 1975, this concern began to be felt in national level reform:

> Since 1975, 37 states have developed school or district planning programs; 47 states have established new curriculum development or technical assistance initiatives; 15 have created state-level effective schools programs; 44 have state-run staff development programs for teachers and 31 have such programs for administrators; 29 states have developed new incentive programs for teachers; 7 require new field experiences for teachers; and 16 have required supervised internships for beginning teachers. (Herman, 1989)

This chapter presents a collection of views and a historical perspective of school-based management as a forerunner, early strategy, and, ultimately, critical component of the school reform and restructuring movements. Its catalytic role in early reform is acknowledged, and the strand of its presence in the 1980s series of commission reports and task force outcomes is traced. SBM's emergence as a dynamic tool of restructuring and as a companion and underlying innovation to Effective Schools implementation efforts and school improvement initiatives is outlined. Finally, the federal role in school-based management as part of school restructuring is examined.

THE DECADE OF REFORM: SPRINGBOARD FOR SCHOOL-BASED MANAGEMENT

Education was one of the top concerns of governors and corporate officers as described in the 1983 report of the Task Force on Education for Economic Growth; the same year *A Nation at Risk: The Imperative for*

Educational Reform warned that the "educational foundations of our society are presently being eroded by a rising tide of mediocrity that threatens our very future as a nation and a people" (Herman, 1989, p. 5). Both this Task Force of the Education Commission of the States and the National Commission of Excellence in Education of 1983 emphasized the national need for educational leaders to implement proposed changes.

By the end of 1983, the Task Force of the Education Commission of the States reported that "Hardly a month has passed without the release of a major report by a prestigious group of citizens concerned about the nature of American education" (Herman, 1989, p. 2). Passow (1988) indicates that by May of 1984, the United States Department of Education had commented that the enormity of school reform concern had the promise of renewal via the multiplicity and diversity of initiatives that were underway.

Since that time, various reports have continued to criticize the educational system and demand reform (Moorman & Egermeier, 1992). Summarizing the survey of the 1984 Education Commission of the States, *A Nation Responds,* Passow noted that the sweep of the reform movement could be reduced to two themes; more academic rigor, and higher performance standards for teachers. Passow also reported that the Policy Analysis for California Education of 1986 asserted that if "the hopes of educational reform and improvement" were to occur, the action had to shift from the state to the local level—to the "persons who actually manage and deliver educational services to students" (p. 3). He reported from the 1986 National Governors' Association *A Time for Results* that the emphasis was on the need for excellence that springs from the local level, commenting that, "Governors don't create excellent schools; communities—local school leaders, teachers, parents, and citizens—do" (p. 4).

The 1986 Carnegie Forum on Education and the Economy report, *A Nation Prepared,* called for a restructuring of the professional environment and of the nature of the teaching force; revision of the recruitment, education, and induction of teachers; changing salaries and career opportunities to reflect market realities; relating incentives to schoolwide performance; and the provision of the technology, services, and staff required for teacher productivity. Some reviewers see the report as a blueprint for the "second wave of reform." This reform and the national demand for educational productivity have addressed not only the content of the educational process, but also the structure and management of these systems (Herman, 1989). Ornstein (1991) reported that during the period from 1983 to 1990 the states created more education policies and regulations than during the preceding twenty years. On a national scale, more than 1,000 state regulations affecting some dimension of school reform were created during that time.

In May of 1988, *Newsweek* assessed the state of school reform:

> All 50 states have adapted some form of reforms, some starting before 1983. More than a dozen have completely overhauled their school systems. Roughly 40 states have raised high-school graduation requirements; in 19, students must pass a test to receive diplomas. Forty-six have mandated competency tests for new teachers; 23 have created alternative routes to certification. Teacher salaries have increased, on average, more than twice the rate of inflation, to $28,031 this year. Six states are now legally empowered to "take over" educationally deficient schools.... a new appreciation of the importance of collaboration is forming, and this is contributing to recognition of a broadened range of efficacy and responsibility for the schools and to new levels of sustained governmental, business, and citizen participation (Chance, 1988, p. 2).

SCHOOL-BASED MANAGEMENT AS A STRUCTURAL AND MANAGERIAL TOOL OF REFORM

A discernible strand of calls for school-based management and a consensus of SBM recommendations can be found in the myriad reports and task force outcomes of the decade of school reform.

The National Governors Association described policy making in terms of empowering leadership at the school level (Lewis, 1988). SBM is built on two basic beliefs, according to *School-Based Management* (1988), the joint task force statement of the American Association of School Administrators, the National Association of Elementary School Principals, and the National Association of Secondary School Principals (see Chapter 1). These beliefs are that:

> Those most closely affected by decisions ought to play a significant role in making those decisions.
> Educational reform efforts will be most effective and long-lasting when carried out by people who feel a sense of ownership and responsibility for the process (p. 6).

Project Education Reform created a network of districts selected by their governors believed most capable of carrying out the reforms outlined by the National Governors' Association report *Time for Results*. In collaboration with the U.S. Department of Education (which provided technical assistance and consultation), the governors focused on exempting districts from inhibiting regulations. The governors' report suggested:

- redesigning schools to create greater teacher decision making
- providing for school-based management — permitting schools to make decisions and holding them accountable for outcomes

The 1988 report on this Project Education Reform, from the participating district superintendents, included suggestions to expedite the SBM change process:

- deregulation of laws and standards for successful districts
- increase in principal decision making on budget, curriculum, and personnel (Lewis, 143–150)

A publication of the Education Commission of the States, *The Next Wave*, is a synopsis of recent education reform reports, summarizing the outcomes achieved when almost every state raised standards and implemented other commission-recommended improvements. Reform reports which address the issue of school-based management include:

- The 1985 California Commission Report *Who Will Teach Our Children?*, recommends the involvement of teachers in decision making.
- The 1986 *Tomorrow's Teachers: A Report of the Holmes Group,* which recommends changing the structure of schools by developing models for new divisions of authority among teachers and administrators.
- The 1986 Carnegie Task Force on Teaching as a Profession *A Nation Prepared: Teachers for the 21st Century,* which recommends restructuring schools to provide a professional environment for teachers to decide how to meet goals; and suggests restructuring the teaching force to introduce "lead teachers" to help redesign the schools.
- The 1986 Education Commission of the States' *What Next? More Leverage for Teachers* suggests that current policies must decentralize responsibly, neither too specifically nor too piecemeal. Things such as giving teachers control over time and materials are more important than money.
- The 1986 National Governors' Association *Time for Results: The Governors' 1991 Report on Education* recommends allowing a real teacher voice in decisions, and the provision of incentives and technical assistance to districts to promote school-site management (Green, 1987).

Summary of Common Reform Report Points

- Other things—attitudes, climate, relationships, community support—are as important as money
- Real reform is local, because the act of learning is ultimately an individual act (Green, 1987).

In *Restructuring America's Schools* (Lewis, 1988), it was noted that the 1988 Carnegie report on inner city schools, *An Imperiled Generation—Saving the Urban Schools,* included the priorities of:

- building an effective governance arrangement, where schools "are viewed as units to be inspired.... educational leadership must be school based."
- renewal programs that affect structure and curriculum and the capabilities of educators within a school to improve them.

The 1988 Center for Policy Research in Education summarized urban clusters of changes in *Improving Inner-City Schools: Current Directions in Urban District Reform:*

- provide school autonomy and flexibility in designing and implementing improvement
- build capacity at local school sites (Lewis, 1988)

SBM ROLE IN THE RESTRUCTURING OF EDUCATION

In the educational reform literature of the 1980s, many references, direct and indirect, were made to school-based management; as the decade wore on, it became more of a separate and distinctly described innovation. There are many references (Hanson, 1991) to the "waves" of reform; problematic descriptions and program advisory thrusts that changed over the years. Hanson has described the crop of mid-1980s reports as a *bottom-up* approach to reform, stressing that teachers have been assigned a societally difficult task without sufficient authority to accomplish it. The second wave of reform reports focused on restructuring which should empower, rather than manage, teachers; an effort to enhance teachers' professional status by providing them with more autonomy, training, trust, and collegial opportunity.

During the late 1980s and early 1990s the focus of reform literature and professional assessment of its impact changed from the reporting of recommendations and calls for change and restructuring to a more summary and analytic view of the trends within the reform movement. As an established change component, school-based management then became a constant theme in restructuring frameworks during the latter part of the decade. In 1986, Raywid (1990) notes that the excellence movement moved away from reform and towards restructuring, resulting in two changes: "fundamental and pervasive alterations in the way we organize and institutionalize education and alterations in the way in which public schools are governed and held accountable to the public" (p. 142). She also notes that, while different restructuring proposals have not been totally in agreement, that two broad strategies have emerged for setting desired restructuring changes in motion: *school site management* and *choice*.

Sheingold (1991) provides definitions for the term restructuring; the central theme underlying many restructuring efforts is that the system itself must be reorganized from top to bottom, and a structure created in which authority and responsibility are aligned—"in which those who are charged with getting the job done, namely the schools and teachers, have the authority and the support they need to do it" (p. 21). This means that schools must be accountable for outcomes, rather than for adherence to guidelines and regulations. Likewise, in 1990, Lieberman and Miller described school-based management, participatory decision making, and teacher leadership as effective concepts supporting two of the building blocks of restructuring—the rethinking of the structure of the school and the focus on a professionally supportive work environment.

Sergiovanni and Moore (1989) affirmed that what school reform needs is "a long-term commitment to the hard business of inquiry and educational reconstruction where the agenda for reform resides—in schools.... True reform must go where the action is" (pp. 108–109). They also note that reformers know that restructuring is most likely to succeed if they focus on the individual school for reform within the broader context in which that school functions.

Some unresolved issues raised by the reform reports and recommendations centered around the impact of school-based management on the current safeguards and instructional quality *insurance policies* which exist at the state level. Many of the recent reform studies call for more confidence in teachers, principals, schools, and districts, but recommend that states be ready to intervene when efforts often miss the mark. Over the long run, fundamental restructuring, a change matrix, is required, altering the relationship between the system and the state as authority is delegated downward to the districts and the schools. One aspect of such a restructured system includes flexible, team-centered, adaptable, and decentralized decision structures present at each school, with management autonomy delegated to people at the building level and with substantive teacher involvement in academic planning (Green, 1988).

As Ornstein (1991) pointed out, "State reform, then, must be played out in the classrooms and schools of America, and state-initiated reforms must conform—or at least be modified—to local politics, processes, and perceptions" (p. 50). He cites a recent California study of 10 school districts identified with a number of successful reform strategies, which showed that school sites—including the teachers and administrators—are "crucial for implementation of school reform" (p. 51). New York State has a Comprehensive School Improvement Planning process, which includes site-based collaboration and planning among its five principles of reform. His list of 20 *Principles for Improving Schools,* included in the article, is a mix of Effective Schools research and school improvement recommendations, and has a subtext of school-based management components in the descriptions of teamwork, professional enhancement and empowerment, and community involvement.

The ASCD *Update* (1991) reported that the Business Roundtable, a coalition of approximately 200 corporations, is sponsoring a nine-point plan for restructuring the U.S. education system. Their public policy agenda outlines the essential components of a successful education system; one of these is that school-based staff must have a major role in making instructional decisions. In 1990 the National Governors' Association task force on education issued a report, "Educating America: State Strategies for Achieving the National Education Goals"; it has three broad categories, one of which is restructuring the K–12 system. The report urges states to decentralize school management and governance (Olson, 1990a). In the same issue, it was pointed out that in 1988 the Education Commission of the States and the Coalition of Essential Schools created a collaborative effort, the *Re: Learning* project. Several states were initial members, and others were asked to become networking sites charged with redesigning their systems. Washington's Governor Booth, chairman of the ECS, indicated that teachers, parents, and students should be the center of the learning community—part of rethinking public education from the ground up (Olson, 1990b).

The increase of employee ownership in the private sector has been a cornerstone of recent attempts to raise productivity, Toch (1991) noted in an article considering the school choice implications. Proponents of school restructuring and reform have supported giving teachers and principals a greater stake in the day-to-day management of their schools through shared decision making and site-based management.

AFT President, Al Shanker (1990), in an article considering restructuring and incentives, described the reform decade's remedies as an "avalanche of regulations" (p. 347), and contrasted it with the trend of deregulation in the private sector. He noted the reorganization of the Chicago schools (see Chapter 6) and the resulting creation of 542 highly-parentally empowered individual local school councils. He proposes a competitive system of monetary incentive-driven, voluntary, nationwide school improvement initiatives. To make this work, however, Shanker realizes that participating schools must have the leeway to develop novel approaches; to be exempted from regulations that would inhibit schools from pursuing effective change (except for such obvious exceptions as regulation of health, safety, and civil rights), even from those regulations affecting union contracts. Shanker does note that school boards would have to release full budgetary control to these schools.

The Education Commission of the States' *Education Agenda* (1990) mentions the launching of many promising state initiatives; support for site-based management and proposals to increase parental involvement were among them. In their vision for the future of American education they include: a welcoming of heterogeneity in structures, schools, and curricula; and an affirmation of the shared responsibilities of all stakeholders in the educational enterprise. One of the strategic directions and priorities for action includes the promotion of system change. This systemic change can be accomplished by several actions; the 1990 *Agenda* includes the showcasing of alternative strategies, approaches, or models; the delineation of shared responsibilities, and the promotion of new coalitions of stakeholders to create solutions for change.

Arthur Andersen's "Think Tank" in 1990 produced a report, "A New System of Education: World-Class and Customer-Focused," which contains recommendations for improved educational productivity through fundamental changes. They noted that, just as important as a commitment to excellence, is the need to decentralize decision making to the local school level, and to involve teachers more in the development of strategies to improve student learning. Effective change management strategies and support systems for such organizational transformation must also be developed if fundamental changes are to occur. The current system requires restructuring through sound management techniques; particularly, the successful business innovation of a more flexible work environment, geared to greater teacher empowerment and decision making.

Maeroff (1992) notes in an article on the parallel paths of the English and American school systems as they pursue reform, that there is now a British program of "local management of schools," which applies to every English publicly-operated school; the creation of "one big Chicago" (p. 355) with regard to governance. Each of Britain's schools has a governing body and receives funds from the local educational authorities (divisions equivalent to U.S. local school districts) which are used to support locally determined expenditure and staffing.

Additionally, publicly operated schools may "opt out" to become "grant-maintained" (p. 355); they are then wholly supported by a direct grant from the national government. By way of contrast, however, curriculum control in Britain is beginning to accrue to the central government, despite the opposition of teachers as they voice arguments for professional authority, one of which is that curricular responsiveness is best handled by those in closest contact with the consumer.

The pending national curriculum and accompanying national testing system have popular British support, however, outside the profession. It is worth noting that teachers there have traditionally chosen from a wide range of nationally standardized tests those which they feel are appropriate and have used them flexibly, both in timing of administration and in purpose.

Additionally, a commercial attitude is developing as schools employ marketing techniques to promote their emerging distinctively different programs. A private school scenario, similar to that which could occur in school choice if newly-empowered schools begin to sell their particular curriculum and unique features, is emerging. The national grant-maintained status of the new breakaway English schools has also evolved into the necessity for some of these emancipated institutions to seek other sources of income, such as supplemental grants, to augment their budgets.

Pipho (1991) reported that the Iowa State Education Association reviewed the state of reform in Iowa and addressed building level reform issues having the greatest potential for transforming schools. One leverage point identified by the teachers was decentralization of decision making. The Iowa report recommends that state, local, and federal governments work on programs to facilitate this as systemic change. They also strongly recommended time: for planning comprehensive school change through shared decision making; for professional growth to support such change; and for discretion over the use of such time.

CONNECTIONS WITH EFFECTIVE SCHOOLS RESEARCH AND SCHOOL IMPROVEMENT

David (1989) noted that school-based management is being implemented today to bring about substantial change in educational practice, and to empower school staff to create conditions for school improvement. The delegation of authority is a critical distinction between school-based management and school improvement; SBM is broader in scope in that it impacts how authority and responsibility are shared between a district and its schools. David points out two pitfalls identifiable in the literature on SBM and in the publications on school improvement and organizational change—the substitution of "surface" participation for genuine authority, and the need for leadership and support to accompany delegation of authority. Research on successful school improvement and organizational change has common strands that merge with themes found in successful examples of district delegation of authority; district support for experimentation and for site leadership; and opportunities for staff development for teachers and principals. With reference to the Effective Schools studies, the implementation of SBM amplifies the need for principal leadership—one of the Effective Schools correlates. David notes that the degree to and the process by which school authority is shared is largely in the hands of the principal. Districts with a history of successful decentralization have a like history of instructional leadership. The NASSP Practitioner (1989) defined several SBM potential implementation areas which were clearly Effective Schools-related: instructional delivery and support; school climate; facility cleanliness and security; and parent and community involvement. It stressed SBM principal leadership, the involvement of students, staff, and parents in exploring alternatives for effective instruction via a customized curriculum, and the enhancement of climate and a safe and orderly environment as a result of broad-based involvement—all clearly related to Effective Schools characteristics.

In 1988 Conley, Schmidle, and Shedd commented that the literature on Effective Schools suggests that the close cooperation in such schools is achieved through participatory efforts; participation in these schools is associated with enhanced group and organizational effectiveness.

Cohen in 1988 drafted a paper for the National Governors' Association which considered a restructuring agenda for the 1990s, noting that improvement of school productivity and student learning demands substantial restructuring, based on what is known from Effective Schools research. The approach he proposes, of schools forming and adjusting their own improvement structures and processes as needed, has implications for decisions being made "close to the action by teachers and principals at the school site level" (p. 12). Localized decisions about instructional organization require that decisions involving staffing, inservice, and curriculum decision and development not only be delegated downward, but that resources devoted to these areas be allocated to the school site.

The National Committee for Citizens in Education, who in 1978 held the first national symposium on SBM, reports that a significant degree of autonomy at the local school level is essential for school improvement, noting that the school site council was the keystone and critical mechanism for SBM-facilitated, effective school improvement. Chubb of the Brookings Institute commented that more control a school had over aspects which affect performance, the more likely it was to exhibit those qualities related to school effectiveness. Democratic decision making, a team managerial style, collegial cooperative relations between staff and administration, and autonomy from outside interference were some of the characteristics possessed by effective schools. (ACCESS, 1990).

Levine, in 1991, reviewed some guidelines which emerged from systematic districtwide efforts to enhance the effectiveness of groups of schools. Referring to the monograph *Unusually Effective Schools: A Review and Analysis of Research and Practice,* he described guidelines derived from these significant improvement projects. Two of these were directly related to SBM: that effective school projects must avoid dependence on paper-driven bureaucratic process and mandated components; and that the success of an effective schools program depends on a "judicious mixture of autonomy for participating faculties and control from the central office, a kind of 'directed autonomy'" (p. 392). In the same journal, Taylor and Levine point out that in the absence of a comprehensive improvement process addressing restructuring at the district level as well as at the school level, school-site management as a solo implementation will cause confusion and frustration. The research on Effective Schools can provide a framework and direction for SBM; in the setting of mission and in the determining of curricular initiatives. They describe SBM as developing coincidentally with the Effective Schools model for school improvement; and report that SBM implementation often accompanies Effective Schools projects, as evidenced by the development of site councils and training for collaboration provided at these schools. During the 1980s SBM and Effective Schools research began to "coalesce in the pragmatic plans of many educators interested in improving schools for all children" (p. 395).

FEDERAL INITIATIVES AND SCHOOL-BASED MANAGEMENT

In April of 1991, President Bush unveiled a major domestic initiative: *America 2000: An Education Strategy,* with the intent of improving troubled elementary and secondary schools.

AMERICA 2000 STRATEGY PRESIDENT BUSH'S FOUR-THEME BLUEPRINT FOR BETTER EDUCATION

For Today's Students:
- Develop national exams for English, math, science, history, geography
- Urge colleges to use exam results when admitting students; employers, when hiring
- Urge differential pay for teachers, based on competence, subjects taught
- Encourage schools to issue "report cards"—comparisons of states and the 110,000 public schools

For Tomorrow's Students:
- Urge business to fund nonprofit group to research and develop nontraditional approaches to education
- Urge communities to develop plans for alternative schools, with limited federal funding

"A Nation of Students":
- Improve adult literacy
- Ask business and labor to establish job-related skill standards

Communities for Learning:
- Urge parents to be involved in children's education
- Urge communities to set educational goals

Bush indicated that he would ask Congress for $690 million, mostly for $1,000,000 seed grants to open a prototype "New American School" in each of the 535 congressional districts, plus two others for each state, by

1996. He has enlisted business leaders to raise at least $150,000 million to underwrite the costs of designing the new schools, which he said should "break the mold" and throw out the rule book for existing schools. The most entrepreneurial component of *America 2000* is the creation of the 535 million-dollar federal grants slated for the start-up costs of those brand-new, experimental, "break-the-mold" schools.

Doyle (1991) describes the type of schools likely to be created as a result of *America 2000* as similar to Sizer's Coalition of Essential Schools, Levin's Accelerated Schools, Comer's School Development Program, and RJR Nabisco's Next Century Schools. The RJR Nabisco project is intended to provide "venture capital" (p. 188) for the nation's public schools—via a three-year grant cycle; amounts of up to $250,000 are intended to "stimulate bold reforms in American public elementary and secondary education" (p. 188). The objective of Next Century Schools is to improve academic performance by investing in education " 'entrepreneurs' who will design and administer their own programs"(p. 188).

U.S. Deputy Secretary of Education David Kearns (1991) spoke to *America 2000's* national goals, noting that for the recommended school change to take place, legislative change must facilitate local communities' efforts. Chapter I deregulation was suggested as an example of something that local schools could do more efficiently, if cut loose. Sewall (1991) notes that *America 2000* explicitly forges a bond with the National Governors Association—as an outgrowth of the NGA's set of educational objectives developed in the fall of 1989, followed by the creation of six national goals (preschool readiness, high school completion, citizenship, science and math achievement, adult literacy, and drug/violence-free schools), which evolved as a preamble for Bush's plan. Among the provisions is increased flexibility in carrying out regulations.

One role which the federal government has successfully undertaken for over a century is that of catalyst for redesign and restructuring. However, in an article by Howe (1991), the problems posed by the 535 New American Schools plan include being required to both accept *America 2000's* new academic world standards in five core subjects and to accept the use of the plan's achievement tests, even though the proposed charter for those 535 innovative schools guarantees freedom from "all constraints" (p. 197). *America 2000* affirms that curricula should remain under local control—hence, school-based control—but the academic core and testing stipulations appear to be contrary to the mold-breaking tenor of the proposal.

A similar concern was raised by Clinchy (1991) in considering that the implementation of parental school choice must be combined with a true marketplace diversity of approaches to education. Teachers and principals must be able to choose the kind of schooling they wish to provide, operating through the school-level autonomy necessary to make that marketplace diversity possible—to create, as the *America 2000* New American Schools proposal purports, "one-of-a-kind high-performance schools" (p. 212). However, if a nationally-mandated curriculum and accompanying national testing actually emerges, as currently recommended by President Bush's Advisory Committee on Educational Policy, then the rhetoric about "'revolutionary' reform, about the research and development of 'bold new ideas,' about cutting the red tape of federal and state regulations, about the 'new generation of American schools,' and about giving the people in individual schools the authority to create and put into practice their own vision of what the school will be and how it will operate," is a "massive internal contradiction" (p. 213). Clichy's concern for this contradiction is further expressed in the probability that, despite anticipated federal and advisory committee rhetoric about the guaranteed freedom of the newly-established, mold-breaking schools to meet those mandated goals and testing standards in their own unique and innovative ways, there will be (as all experienced educators could predict) an accompanying body of regulations governing the *how* of instruction as well as the *what.*

The concept of school choice is fast becoming a companion issue to school-based management, as well as a common and predictable political refrain of the 1990s, from schoolhouse to statehouse to White House. In 1990 Raywid briefly considered these restructuring strategies, describing them as sharing the key elements of: presuppositions of sufficient autonomy to permit meaningful decision making; the involvement of teachers in decisions currently closed to classroom staff; and the built-in promise of teacher and parent empowerment. She distinguishes them, however, as different strategies with regard to assumptions about change, decisions involving improvement, and sequence and priorities. SBM involves and empowers teachers and parents (frequently through peer representation) via broad policy decision on budget making, personnel, and curriculum; is a long-term change; usually leaves schools accountable to central administrators; assumes school transformation as a possibility; is relatively new is distinct practice; and aims at some level of school consensus. Choice is a more profound change; it is a sharply etched and immediately-felt restructuring innovation; aims at individual teacher or collaborative program redesign; makes true customers out of parents and vests them with accountability power; and has a definable implementation track record in several states. As a growing political watchword, choice will remain a controversial and visible educational issue; its natural affinity with SBM will likewise remain an issue.

SUMMARY

Early in the decade of educational reform, the foundation for a strong trend towards school-based management and shared decision making was being laid. While the initial reports and recommendations were focused on a substantial increase in regulation and a raising of achievement standards, by mid-decade the calls for SBM, usually embedded in teacher empowerment language, were more distinct. As the reform thrust evolved into the more broadly conceptualized restructuring effort, the recommendations for an SBM-type process as a viable and essential component of systemic change became almost unanimous in the literature and state and national reports of the latter part of the decade. The consensus on SBM as a deregulating process and as an empowering strategy was substantial.

School-based management as a constant theme in the restructuring frameworks of the latter part of the decade became the obvious vehicle to achieve two significant goals; the rethinking of the structure of the school site and the focus on professionalization. Unresolved reform issues center around the uncertain outcomes of SBM's school autonomy, but the consistent and growing chorus of task force reports call for decentralization. In these, comparisons of SBM with private sector deregulation have been constant, as have the proposed initiatives for a heterogeneity of structures and the promotion of new stakeholder coalitions. Examples of SBM in Chicago and Great Britain were given.

The logical connections with Effective Schools research, school improvement, and school choice give SBM a certain utility and flexibility of function within the larger frameworks of reform and restructuring. Recent federal initiatives and SBM were compared.

EXERCISES

1. Of all the national reports which emerged during the 1980s, which do you feel had the most impact, and why?

2. What do you feel are the most important outcomes of the decade of reform? Which are most likely to endure in the field of education?

3. What response could be made to the critics who fear the loss of regulatory safeguards in schools?

4. Which elements of *America 2000* could be facilitated by the implementation of SBM?

5. Is SBM a natural companion or prerequisite for school choice? Why?

REFERENCES

A new system of education: World-class and customer-focused. (1990). Arthur Anderson & Co., Societe Cooperative, pp. 1–4, 6–7.

ACCESS—Clearinghouse for Information about Public Schools (1990). *School based improvement and effective schools: A perfect match for bottom-up reform.* Columbia, MD: Clearinghouse for Information about Public Schools, a service of the National Committee for Citizens in Education, pp. 11–15.

ASCD. (1991) Restructuring the education system: A view from business. *Association for Supervision and Curriculum Development Update, 33* (5), 4.

Carnegie Forum on Education and the Economy (1986). *A nation prepared: Teachers for the 21st century.* New York. Carnegie Forum on Education and the Economy, pp. 57–59.

Chance, W. (1988). Changing the terms of discourse. In *School reform in 10 states.* Denver, CO: Education Commission of the States, pp. 2, 6–11.

Clinchy, E. (1991). America 2000—Reform, revolution, or just more smoke and mirrors? *Phi Delta Kappan, 73* (3), 210–218.

Cohen, M. (1988). Restructuring the education system: Agenda for the 1990's. In *Results in Education,* Washington, D.C.: National Governors' Association Center for Policy Research, pp. 12–13.

Conley, S.C., Schmidle, T., & Shedd, J.B. (1988). Teacher participation in the management of school systems. *Teachers College Record, 90,* (2), 259–280.

David, J.L. (1989). Synthesis of research on school-based management. *Educational Leadership, 46* (8), 45–53.

Doyle, D.P. (1991). America 2000. *Phi Delta Kappan, 73* (3), 185–191.

Education Commission of the States (1990). *Education Agenda 1990.* Education Commission of the States, Denver, CO: pp. 8, 11.

Green, J. (1987). *The next wave: A synopsis of recent education reform reports.* Denver, CO: Education Commission of the States, pp. 1–10.

Hanson, E.M. (1991). *Educational administration and organizational behavior.* Boston: Allyn and Bacon, pp. 352-353.

Herman, J.L. (1989). Instructional leadership skills and competencies of public school superintendents. *Dissertation Abstracts International, 50,* 1503-A. (DA8920723) pp. 1-2.

Howe, H., II. (1991). America 2000 — A bumpy ride on four trains. *Phi Delta Kappan, 73* (3), 192-203.

Kearns, D. (1991). Kearns offers course quality for schools. American Association of School Administrators' *Leadership News, 90,* 1, 5.

Levine, D.U. (1991). Creating effective schools: Findings and implications from research and practice. *Phi Delta Kappan, 72* (5), 389-393.

Lewis, A. (1989). *Restructuring America's schools.* Washington, DC: American Association of School Administrators, pp. 143-150, 152-153.

Lieberman, A. & Miller, L. (1990). Restructuring schools: what matters and what works. *Phi Delta Kappan, 71* (10), 759-764.

Maeroff, G. (1992). Focusing on urban education in Britain. *Phi Delta Kappan, 73* (5), 355-358.

Moorman, H. & Egermeier, J. (1992). Educational restructuring: generative metaphor and new vision. In J.J. Lane & E.G. Epps (Eds.) *Restructuring the schools: Problems and prospects* (pp. 25-29). Berkeley, CA: McCutchan Publishing Corporation.

NASSP. (1989). School site management. National Association of Secondary School Principals' *The Practitioner, 16* (2), 1-6.

National Commission on Excellence in Education. (1983). *A nation at risk: The imperative for educational reform.* Washington, DC, U.S. Government Printing Office. National Endowment for the Humanities, p. 5.

NewsLeader. (1991). Essential components of a successful education system; the Business Roundtable Education Public Policy Agenda. National Association of Secondary School Principals' *NewsLeader, 38* (6), 1.

Olson, L. (1990a). Conferees reiterate need for fundamental reforms. *Education Week,* August 1, 1990, p. 6.

Olson, L. (1990b). N.G.A. lists strategies for achieving national goals. *Education Week,* August 1, 1990, p. 7.

Ornstein, A.C. (1991). Reforming American schools: the role of the states. *National Association of Secondary School Principals Bulletin, 75* (537), 46-55.

Passow, H.A. (1988). Whither (or wither?) school reform? *Educational Administrative Quarterly, 24,* (3), 246-256.

Pipho, C. (1991). Teachers, testing, and time. *Phi Delta Kappan, 73* (3), 182-183.

Raywid, M.A. (1990). Contrasting strategies for restructuring schools: Site-based management and choice. *Equity and Choice, 7* (2), 26-28.

Raywid, M.A. (1990). The evolving effort to improve schools: Pseudo-reform, incremental reform, and restructuring. *Phi Delta Kappan, 72* (2), 139-143.

School-Based Management (1988). (AASA Stock Number 0221-00209), Washington, D.C.: American Association of School Administrators, National Association of

Elementary School Principals, and National Association of Secondary School Principals.

Sergiovanni, T.J., & Moore, J.H. (1989). *Schooling for tomorrow.* Boston: Allyn and Bacon, pp. 108–109.

Sewall, G.T. (1991). America 2000—An appraisal. *Phi Delta Kappan, 73* (3), 204–209.

Shanker, A. (1990). The end of the traditional model of schooling—and a proposal for using incentives to restructure our public schools. *Phi Delta Kappan, 71* (5), 345–357.

Sheingold, K. (1991). Restructuring for learning with technology: The potential for synergy. *Phi Delta Kappan, 73* (1), 17–27.

Taylor, B.O. & Levine, D.U. (1991). Effective schools projects and school-based management. *Phi Delta Kappan, 72* (5), 394–397.

Toch, T. (1991). Public schools of choice. *American School Board Journal, 178* (7), 18–21.

Chapter 12

SCHOOL-BASED MANAGEMENT AND THE FUTURE

Chapter 12 will address five major areas. First, the preceding eleven chapters of the book will be summarized, and SBM trends of the eleven chapters of the book will be discussed within the context of the total education reform movement. Third, the pertinent leadership trends that are required within the structure and processes of school-based management will be highlighted. Fourth, a summary of state and national implementations and the future implications of these trends will be discussed. Finally, the implications for the training and recruitment of individuals who will be comfortable with and work well within a school-based management structure will be emphasized.

SUMMARY OF CHAPTERS ONE THROUGH ELEVEN

Chapter 1 traced the origins of SBM as historical practice and connected it to productive business patterns of decentralization and employee empowerment. The rationales for SBM were outlined, drawn from current literature. Common themes reflected were leadership, social impact, and productive organizational dynamics. A range of definition for SBM followed; three common definitional elements were presented. The key components of school-based management, related to the literature, include strategic planning, a decision-making model, representational groups, annual plans and performance reports, and waivers from regulation. A number of the early and more recent SBM district implementations were described, and their common experiences and patterns of activities were outlined. Themes included freedom from restraint, broad-based involvement, budget and personnel decision-making authority, a focus on the principal, improved public relations, and a blend of accountability and authority. Later trends included local council formation and empowerment, an extension of training content, and an increase in SBM involvement in curriculum.

Chapter 2 was dedicated to school district culture and the impact of school-based management on the culture which exists prior to the implementation of SBM. School district culture was defined as the beliefs and values held, the standard processes and activities utilized, and the traditions maintained by the students and employees of the school district and by the community members who live within the geographical bounds of the school district. The major changes that are taking place in the United States and the world which impact the schools were reviewed. Next, Chapter 2 discussed some means of assisting in the very difficult task of changing school culture. Stress was placed on the fact that this process is a long-term effort; it is not a quick fix. School climate assessments with intervening action programs designed to improve the climate were mentioned as techniques which will assist in changing the school culture in a positive direction. Chapter 2 ended with a discussion of the strategic and operational planning skills that are required to implement and maintain a successful SBM structure.

Chapter 3 established the connection between teacher empowerment and contemporary corporate managerial theory, and presented definitions and rationales for school-based management. Common points included the professionalization effect; the enhancement of the learning process as empowered practitioners make collaborative decisions in a collegial environment, and the heightened effectiveness of delivery point empowerment. The background of teacher empowerment heavily impacts the existing educational structure; this was described as somewhat changed by SBM and by earlier innovations, but labor-management divisiveness persists. Support and facilitation for empowerment were presented as raising questions about the division of responsibility and authority, and about the developmental and cultural change facilitation required by empowerment, as well as the more practical and critical elements of released collaboration time and training resources. The discernible state and national trends of teacher empowerment; and an accumulating body of research, practice, and teacher preparation which reflects shifts in district structure, the redefinition of professionalism, and new differentiations of teacher function, concluded the chapter.

Chapter 4 discussed the changes that came about in the collective bargaining rights of public employees; much of that original bargaining between boards of education and teacher unions became adversarial in nature. Exceptions were described as appearing in the 1960s and 1970s, such as QWL (Quality of Work Life) programs and Quality Circles, which dealt with collaborative decision making between employees and management. Another described positive trend, Win/Win Negotiations, also came about during those decades. It was described as a collaborative problem-solving method between management and teacher unions to reach a master contract agreement in an environment of trust, cooperation and mutual benefits. The potential strengths of teachers' unions as supporters of school-based management were outlined, and the potential power and decision-making conflicts between traditional union power and the power delegated to SBM committees were also outlined. Next, Chapter 4 discussed peer coaching as a means of professional development for school-based management committee members, and ended with a discussion of the requirement to make adjustments and develop new accountability structures. In those school districts which possess both school-based management councils and employee unions, adjustments in both empowerment structures and in accountability were described as needing to be made by the prime players within the school districts' official structures.

Chapter 5 focused on school-based management as it blurred the lines between dimensions and domains of principalship and teachers and other professionals. Principal role and function were investigated; with an emphasis on the profound change SBM would demand of traditional school leaders as key players in decentralization and restructuring. Personal power and empowerment characterize principal relationships with other professionals in a school-based management environment; those linkages were described as strongly impacted by the perceptions and attitudes of the school leader. Teacher empowerment was the pivotal issue, with consideration given to the developmental stages which accompany involving teachers in decision making. The view of the school leader as a teacher of teachers rather than a manager of process was recommended. Strategies to successfully implement school-based management were included. Implications for training in SBM were reflective of the role changes described; skills in goal setting, strategic and operational planning, and group process were recommended.

Chapter 6 was concerned with the unique and highly impacted role and function of the central office in the context of school-based management. A historical perspective began the chapter, outlining the centralization trend of the last half of the century, and the current restructuring decentralization emphasis. A section on new SBM roles and organizational patterns of central office personnel summarized the continuing theme of current research and thought about the site support function and resident-expert status of central office personnel. The inherent problems and solutions to the dispersal of central power were examined; policy waivers, determination of decision-making boundaries, and the redrawing and articulation of overlapping areas of responsibility. Examples of the transitions demanded by SBM were illustrated by the experience of three large school systems. The redistribution of authority and the amount of power dispersed were considered in the Dade County, Florida, Los Angeles, and Chicago school systems. Such items as personnel selection and budgetary discretion were investigated in these systems and in two international school systems: Great Britain and Spain. Implications and recommendations for the function and changing role of the central office were provided through a focus on three key areas of district level responsibility: budget development, personnel management, and curricular and instructional management. There is a consensus within the literature and a strong field rationale to decentralize all three areas; this must be balanced against legal, financial, compliance, and optimum resource use practicalities. A final note reflected upon the future of the central office function in a school-based management environment.

Chapter 7 discussed the changes in the roles to be played by the superintendent of schools in school districts which implement school-based management. It began by tracing the changes in the historical roles of the superintendents of schools; and it suggested how successful SBM transitions could be made. The changing superintendency leadership demands were indicated by a reported series of recommendations made by various professional groups in the 1980s and early 1990s. A comprehensive checklist of questions to be answered by any decision makers who are considering school-based management was presented. A discussion of the implications for realignment of interactions with the traditional school decision makers was shared, since school-based management has two major directional decision-making changes; it empowers teachers and other nontraditional decision makers; and it takes decision-making power from the central level and focuses it at the individual school site level. The implications of SBM on the superintendent's interactions with the board and central office personnel were elaborated upon, describing possible areas of conflict. Common national and state patterns of SBM implementation were described, focusing on the new expectations of the superintendent in a decentralized setting. Implications for training included the need for group decision-making models and processes, collaborative strategies, team development, and employee empowerment.

Chapter 8 focused on the topic of the school board and the alterations required in the traditional governance structures and policies for districts implementing school-based management. Portions of the Kentucky Education Reform Act relating to school-based management were summarized to indicate the actions required of all school boards. The chapter next presented a checklist of possible SBM decision-making areas, including those to be made at the central level, the school building level, or by a combination of both. The areas included staffing and related personnel services; staff development and training; instructional programs; purchasing of equipment and supplies; governance policies; transportation services; cocurricular and athletic activities; guidance and counseling; custodial, food, and maintenance services; budgeting and accounting; and collective bargaining provisions. Chapter 8 ended with a presentation of common national and state patterns of SBM implementation, both mandated and voluntary examples. These major thrusts of most SBM implementation areas were policy-related and require board procedural alignments and facilitations. The approval and support of the board was described as an essential component of successful school-based management implementation.

Chapter 9 focused on new structures for collaboration with community members that are created in school districts implementing school based management structures and processes. The traditional means of involvement were described, and the fact made that the only community members who traditionally have had decision making opportunities were school board members. An example of involvement of many community members, from the West Bloomfield School District of Michigan, was provided as a possible model. The involvement of hundreds of the district's citizens in the completion of a needs assessment and strategic planning model and the creation of communications/governance committees, comprised of many citizens, at each of its school buildings were detailed. Next, the chapter discussed the roles of parents and other citizens in the various SBM councils and the opportunities for community involvement when there are school-business partnerships. Chapter 9 concluded with a discussion of common national and site patterns of implementation, revealing a variety of council structure and decision-making purview. There was some consensus on the need for broad-based representation and on council function and procedure, and strong agreement on the need for substantial investments in training, particularly in human relations skills that will facilitate shared decision making.

Chapter 10 provided a brief perspective on the scope of state department of education and legislative national level reform, and described the new variety and range of state department restructuring strategies, with a common emphasis on assistance, rather than regulation, of local districts. Two states provided a focus for SBM implementation investigation; Texas and Kentucky have mandated SBM within larger reform packages, and have become, essentially, national laboratories for its implementation. Excerpts of both state statutes were provided. The chapter's major component was a case study of a Kentucky school district's implementation of SBM. Descriptions of the schools and their local SBM councils preceded a detailed reporting of each Council's experience with the early stages of shared decision making. Results of both council member questionnaires and on-site interviews were reported and summarized. Combined response patterns included: the development of group cohesion dynamics; the awareness of this of the limitations of the council's impact during their first year; the sense that time to meet, resources to support council function, and further training were needed; the sense of a need to network with sister councils; and the need for policy and procedural specificity and commonality of the law's interpretation. Councils' members were reported as enthused about serving; optimistic for the long-term benefits of SBDM, and taking great professional and community pride in having undertaken such a major step towards the improvement of their school. Both the Kentucky and Texas models have similarities in statutory provision and in legislative intent, though the KERA seems more prescriptive. Some change and reaction from the field to these mandates is occurring. Both states were presented as having attempted to reconcile the seeming contradiction of mandating flexibility as they implemented these two decentralized models.

Chapter 11 linked SBM with the larger context of school reform and restructuring, laying the foundation for a strong trend towards school-based management and shared decision making. While the initial reports and recommendations described were focused on a substantial increase in regulation and a raising of achievement standards, the calls for SBM, usually embedded in teacher empowerment language, became more distinct. Recommendations for an SBM-type process as a viable and essential component of systemic change became almost unanimous in the described literature and state and national reports of the latter part of the decade. The consensus on SBM as a deregulating process and as an empowering strategy was noted as substantial. School-based management as a constant theme in these restructuring frameworks was presented as becoming the vehicle to achieve both rethinking of the structure of the school site and the focus on professionalization. While reported unresolved reform issues centered around the uncertain outcomes of SBM's school autonomy, the consistent and growing chorus of task force reports called for decentralization. Examples of SBM in Chicago and Great Britain were given. Recent federal initiatives and SBM were compared, and connections made with Effective Schools research, school improvement, and school choice.

COMBINED TRENDS WITHIN THE CONTEXT OF THE EDUCATION REFORM AND RESTRUCTURING MOVEMENT

If the critics of America's school districts; which include legislators, teachers' union officials, corporate leaders, researchers, and many people who work within education, are correct when they state that our schools must be drastically reformed if we, as a nation, are to compete successfully with other nations in this environment of technological and knowledge explosions; there is much work to be done. If this view is correct, modifications in the current structures and processes of our schools are not going to be sufficient to achieve this improvement goal. Rather, drastic surgery and massive changes in our rebuilt structures and processes have to be developed.

The trends toward (1) empowerment of teachers, parents, and others, (2) emphasis of decision making and accountability at the school site level, (3) the expectation that the school building principal will truly be an instructional leader and a collaborative decision maker, and (4) the reduction in the traditional decision-making power of union leaders, boards of education, and central administrators; all combine as restructuring imperatives within school-based management, and all are essential elements of the process. In the reform language and collective thrust of the previous decade, there are recommendations and substantial practice accumulating in each of these trends. The cumulative effect is one of profound and systemic change in education (Herman & Herman, 1991). A similar and more expanded view of this transformation was shared by Hill, Bonan, and Warner in 1992 in reporting on a study analysis of the experience of school systems currently leading the way in school based management reform. They concluded that:

1. Although school-based management focuses on individual schools; in fact, it is a reform of the entire school system. Real change demands that the expectations and controls of a centralized system be eliminated. Unless the commitment to long-term decentralization is made, issues will continue to be settled by policy pronouncements, and hedged compliance will replace the sense of enfranchisement that should prevail.

2. School-based management will lead to real changes at the school level only if it is the system's basic reform strategy, not just one among several reform projects. It must be seen as the central strategy, and must be communicated to the public as such. The informal and out-of-channel communications that operate in every district when minor issues need resolving will change; parents and community members, as well as district employees, must learn to work through the school councils.

3. Site-managed schools are likely to evolve over time and to develop distinctive characteristics, goals, and operating styles. Principals and teachers, newly empowered, will begin to develop specific and well-defined missions, climates, and methods of instruction. Despite the need for some uniformity of high quality, variety will eventually prevail and schools will become less and less alike.

4. A system of distinctive decentralized schools requires a rethinking of accountability. School staff members—principals and teachers—will become accountable as professionals. The price of this freedom is a new set of obligations; to take responsibility for one's performance as an individual and for the performance of the school as a whole. It also creates the obligation to consult with and anticipate the reactions of diverse constituencies, such as parents, special interest groups, review and accreditation groups, and state and local education agencies.

Together, all of these trends combine to clearly indicate that it will not be business as usual in our schools, and that significant and dramatic changes are to be made. Since change is the key ingredient in the hoped-for improvement of our schools, it is crucial that we understand the change process. Some of the elements in getting a critical mass of employees, students, and community members to support dramatic changes involve the following:

- An individual leader or a group of stakeholders must conceptualize a vision of what the schools are to look like at some future point in time.
- A critical mass of stakeholders who are going to be called upon to be involved in envisioning what the schools are to look like in the future, must be made aware of the new vision and of the changes that will be required to achieve that vision; and they should be given an opportunity to provide feedback.
- Whenever possible, this feedback should be used to make necessary or desired changes in the original vision.
- Activities must be decided upon and activated to implement the required changes, and people have to be motivated to act in the directions of the desired changes.
- A system must be inaugurated and maintained to collect data, to provide support for those implementing the change, and to provide the necessary skill training for those implementers who do not possess the necessary skills.
- Finally, a system of recognition of individuals and groups who contribute to the desired change direction should be maintained, and celebrations should be held whenever a milestone is reached.

EDUCATIONAL LEADERSHIP TRENDS AND SBM

Accustomed to a centralized context, many principals and teachers have come to focus on tasks that are discrete, bounded, and noncontroversial. If school-based management is to work, they must come to take more initiative and responsibility to serve their students (Hill, Bonan, & Warner, 1992). As described in Chapters 3 and 5, there are teacher and principal empowerment trends relating to this situation. There is a need to strengthen the intellectual foundation of teachers, and to create a climate for their learning connectedness and developing sense of collegiality. Principals, as key players in the SBM game, must develop corresponding capacities for collaboration and for facilitation of school improvement, and must develop curricular and instructional fluency.

Leadership trends that must be developed, for the present leaders who do not possess them and for those aspiring to leadership positions, include three major thrusts. These thrusts are: (1) the ability to envision and to get others to envision the "what should be" future state for the schools, (2) the ability to empower others in meaningful decision making, and (3) the ability to be a strategic and operational planner or, at the very least, to coordinate strategic and operational plans (Herman, 1989). In essence, the leader must combine all these skills, possessing the ability to motivate and good human relations, in order to be a true leader. It is clear, then, that the educational leaders of the future must be *change agents.* This is a view supported by the Southern Regional Education Board (formed in the late 1940s by the fifteen southern state legislatures to advance education in the region); the intent of their leadership training program is to create those change agents (Crews, 1990). Similarly, Hall and Hord (1987), in considering three bodies of literature, leadership, change, and principal role, conclude that the principal is indeed the best situated leader in the school for making school improvements.

Barth (1990) expands this view of leadership to support his vision of improving schools from within; a community of leaders is needed, built through efforts of coalition building and collegial relationships, particularly between principals and teachers. Leaders must be able to set general directions and create environments and structures that enable each individual in the school community to discover their own skills and talents, and, in so doing, to enable students to discover theirs. The leadership requirements for successful school-based management require, in actuality, a multidimensional model, in which the school site personnel and stakeholders—principal, teachers, and parents—operate synergistically as they lead their schools, supported by the symbolic leadership of the superintendent and the resource-providing and capacity-building leadership of the central office personnel. The creation of broadly-based policy, and the establishment of standards, and the provision of ongoing implementation support and technical assistance are the respective leadership roles of the school board and the state department of education. The radical transformation of school governance through school-based management will require multiple leadership roles and interactions, as a brand new system of operating schools is implemented.

IMPLICATIONS FOR PROFESSIONAL PREPARATION AND TRAINING

It is quite clear that the educational leaders who are to implement school-based management must be recruited with a careful eye towards the skills, knowledges, and attitudes mentioned throughout this volume as requirements for the successful implementation of school-based management. Also, it is clear that university training must inculcate the future educational leaders in these skills, knowledges and attitudes through both academic courses and field-based experiences. Review of the literature and of publications focused on school-based management and leadership has shown that some training and preparation program will need to be focused exclusively on administrators, but a substantial portion might be more appropriately provided to administrator/teacher teams. Training should, indeed, reflect the work of the school and include problem-centered materials. A broad and continuing training program for all members of the school community, including school board members and central office staff, should reflect the program integration required by the interdependency of the individuals in a school-based environment (Mojkowski, 1991).

SUMMARY OF STATE AND NATIONAL SBM IMPLEMENTATION PATTERNS AND FUTURE IMPLICATIONS

There is a clear consensus for a gradual and waiver-supported SBM implementation model, multiple stakeholder involvement, transfer to the local site of a substantial amount of budgetary and personnel resource determination, extensive training in such areas as collaboration and group decision making, provision of resources to support that training and time for professional interaction, and the use of multiple measures of accountability. As more and more districts begin to employ an SBM model, newer patterns are emerging: the involvement of curriculum as an area of SBM activity, the emergence of the significant interaction between principals and teachers, the enhancement of public relations and community support, the alteration of the central office function, and the growing significance of the accountability dimension. The impetus for SBM implementation has usually come from the ranks of superintendents and school boards; however, there are patterns of state-supported initiatives or mandates (frequently in combination with other restructuring efforts).

Schlechty (1990) considered the task of this restructuring in light of his vision of schools for the future. As candidates for change, he recommends that participatory leadership should be the mode of operation, and that all schools and departments should be assessed in terms of their capacity for and commitment to shared decision making. He also recommends a restructuring of the central office so that its personnel are responsive to building level initiatives and are able to serve as a collection and monitoring point for the assessment of results, as catalysts for innovation, and as facilitators of an exchange of information about improvement and advances. Thirdly, he recommends a thorough review of policies, procedures, rules, and regulations, with a view to changing constraints and with the intent to provide training for teachers and principals as they assume the responsibilities related to these constraints.

The authors believe that, with respect to school-based management, future implications include the following:

- A much more open system of communications and decision making at the school building and school district levels.
- The empowering of many citizens and employees who have been disfranchised in the past.
- A confusion, hopefully of a temporary nature, about who is accountable for the decisions that have been made.
- Emphasis on outcomes rather than on resources and processes, and an especial emphasis on student learning outcomes.
- An absolute requirement for strategic and operational planning and strategic and operational management.
- An emphasis towards data collection and evaluation of objectives.
- A continuing need for the training of employees and other stakeholders.
- The development of team building groups who work collaboratively to solve problems and to make changes.
- The realization that change is ever present, and that changes that are instigated must be measured for their effectiveness and efficiency.

CONCLUSION

This book has viewed the different components, dimension, and impacts of school-based management as the centerpiece of school restructuring and as a continual presence and critical element in school reform. The prognosis is uncertain, as it should be, with all structural changes of this nature. SBM implies substantial systemic change; alteration of governance in such a stratified and historic institution as public education is essentially profound cultural change, as are all of the current reform and restructuring proposals. Cultural shifts and the transformation of people-serving structures are essentially evolutionary and incremental in nature (Schiller & Freed, 1992). Those school districts that have successfully decentralized, David (1989) notes, have done so over a period of five to ten years.

Several factors will constrain the success of widespread implementation of school-based management; the sustained time frame required is a significant one. Historically, popular innovations in education have demanded more short-term appeal. Also, it is possible that the decentralization models presented in the book are suitable only for large or medium-size districts; *de facto* decentralization of some type frequently exists in small districts due to the limited numbers of personnel; empowering individuals in such situations may simply be an attempt to make informal practice formal. Additionally, there are concerns that a downsizing approach to education may become unnecessarily prescriptive and intrusive. Boyd (1990) quotes Ellen Goodman as asking, "How can you manage flexibility? Is that a contradiction in terms? Businesses want plans and controls. The new workers want options and individual treatment." Is it possible to have both?

Peters and Waterman (1982) have observed that this tension is resolved by excellent companies as they possess simultaneous loose-tight properties; they are, in reality, both centralized and decentralized, and distinguished by the co-existence of firm central direction and maximum individual autonomy. Boyd (1990) reflects on these diverging thrusts, seeing them as simultaneous imperatives for organizational improvement. That balanced combination of autonomy and control is the particular hallmark of school-based management. What is largely undetermined and controversial, as yet, are the details of that balanced combination. Nevertheless, it is the authors' firm conviction that school-based management offers an ideal vehicle for the true improvement of teaching and student learning, and for the effective educational environment needed for the next century.

SUMMARY

The chapter summarized the preceding eleven chapters, then traced the SBM reform trends of those chapters within the context of school reform. These included: empowerment of teachers, parents and others; emphasis on decision making and accountability at the school site level; the expectation that the school building principal will be an instructional leader and a collaborative decision maker; and that the reduction in the traditional decision-making power roles combine as restructuring imperatives within school-based management. In the reform language and collective thrust of the previous decade, there are recommendations and substantial practice accumulating in each of these trends, reflecting altered accountability structures and the creation of unique delivery systems. Change, as catalyst and systemic process impact, underlies all of these trends.

Three major thrusts characterize SBM leadership trends: the ability to envision and to get others to envision the "what should be" future state for the schools; the ability to empower others in meaningful decision making; and the ability to be a strategic and operational planner. This view is supported in the literature and research and reflects the need for leaders to set general directions and to create optimum environments and structures for learning. The leadership requirements for successful school-based management require, in actuality, a multidimensional model, in which the school site personnel and stakeholders operate synergistically as they lead their schools. The radical transformation of school governance through school-based management will require multiple leadership roles and interactions, as a brand new system of operating schools is implemented.

Future and current educational leaders who are to implement school-based management must acquire the skills, knowledges, and attitudes mentioned throughout this volume. Review of the literature and of publications focused on school-based management and leadership has shown that some training and preparation programs will need to be focused exclusively on administrators, but a substantial portion might be more appropriately provided to administrators/teachers working in teams. A broad and continuing training program for all members of the school community should reflect the program integration required by the interdependency of the individuals in a school-based environment.

There is a clear state and national consensus for a gradual and waiver-supported SBM implementation model, multiple stakeholder involvement, transfer to the local site of a substantial amount of budgetary and personnel resource determination, extensive training in such areas as collaboration and group decision making, provision of resources to support that training and time for professional interaction, and the use of multiple measures of accountability. Newer patterns are beginning to emerge: the involvement of curriculum as an area of SBM activity, the emergence of the significant interaction between principals and teachers, the enhancement of public relations and community support, the alteration of the central office function, and the growing significance of the accountability dimension.

Future implications for SBM include the following: a much more open system of school communications and decision making; the empowering of many citizens and employees who have been disfranchised in the past; a temporary confusion about who is accountable for decisions that have been made; emphasis on outcomes rather than on resources and processes; an absolute requirement for strategic and operational planning and strategic and operational management; an emphasis towards data collection and evaluation of objectives; a continuing need for the training of employees and other stakeholders; the development of team building groups who work collaboratively; and the realization that change is ever present, but that changes that are instigated must be measured for their effectiveness and efficiency.

SBM implies substantial systemic change; alteration of governance in such a stratified and historic institution as public education is essentially profound cultural change, and is therefore essentially evolutionary and incremental in nature. Factors which will constrain the success of widespread implementation of school-based management include this required sustained time frame; also, it is possible that the decentralization models presented in the book are suitable only for large or medium-size districts; *de facto* decentralization of some type frequently already exists in small districts. Additionally, there are concerns that a downsizing approach to education may become unnecessarily prescriptive and intrusive. The coexistence of firm central direction and maximum individual autonomy is questionable; yet that balanced combination of autonomy and control is the particular hallmark of school-based management, which offers an ideal vehicle for this and the next century's improvement of teaching and student learning.

EXERCISES

1. Which of the described combined SBM reform trends do you feel will be the most enduring, and why?
2. Which of the elements required to support dramatic systemic change do you think are the most achievable in your district?
3. Compare the quality of your professional preparation with that

described as needed for SBM leadership. What elements are already present, and which ones would need further training?

4. Reflect and estimate the possibility, in your district, and on a national scale, of achieving that balance of autonomy and control which is the hallmark of school-based management.

REFERENCES

Barth, R. (1990). *Improving schools from within.* San Francisco, CA: Jossey Bass, Publishers, p. 145.

Boyd, W.L. (1990). Balancing control and autonomy in school reform: The politics of perestroika. In J. Murphy (Ed.), *The educational reform movement of the 1980's* (pp. 88–89, 94). Berkeley, CA: McCutchan Publishing Corporation.

Crews, (1990, December 9). *To change schools, leaders have to head for the deep water.* The Birmingham News, p. 3D.

David, J.L. (1989). Synthesis of research on school-based management. *Educational Leadership, 46* (8), 45–53.

Hall, G.E. & Hord, S.M. (1987). *Change in schools: Facilitating the process.* Albany, NY: State University of New York Press, p. 51.

Herman, J.J. (1989). Strategic planner: one of the changing leadership roles of the principal. *The Clearing House, 63* (2), 56–58.

Herman, J.J. & J.L. (1991). *The positive development of human resources and school district organizations.* Lancaster, PA: Technomic Publishing Company, pp. 245–246.

Hill, P.T., Bonan, J.J., & Warner, K. (1992). Uplifting education. *National School Board Journal, 179* (3), 21–25.

Mojkowski, C. (1991). *Developing leaders for restructuring schools: New habits of mind and heart.* Washington, NJ: National LEADership Network Study Group on Restructuring Schools, p. 49.

Peters, T.J. & Waterman, R.H. (1982). *In search of excellence: Lessons from America's best-run companies.* New York: Warner Books, p. 15.

Schiller, R.E. & Freed, C.W. (1992). Who will be at the leadership helm in the 1990's? *The School Administrator, 49* (3), 46–47.

Schlechty, P.C. (1990). *Schools for the twenty-first century.* San Francisco, CA: Jossey Bass, Publishers, p. 145–146.

APPENDIX

State-by-State Implementation of School-Based Management State Department of Education Questionnaire

A questionnaire was sent in December of 1991 to the fifty state departments of education to inquire about the presence of school-based management implementation, and to determine the nature of that implementation, based on existing SBM research and literature. The responses varied widely, just as the do the types and range of SBM implementation in the field:

- Forty-four states have permitted or mandated some type of school-based management; in most cases, the projects were permitted. The only statewide mandates for SBM are in Kentucky and Texas (described in Chapter 10).
- This SBM implementation, for the most part did encompass the areas established by common practice and research: decentralized budget-making authority, decentralized personnel decision making, decentralized curricular decision making, and school-based councils.
- State-provided SBM training has occurred in thirty-two states, in the common practice and research areas of communication, budget, decision making, and policy making. There was slightly less training provided in budget than in the other areas.
- Thirty-seven states reported some voluntary school-based management implementations in individual schools or districts.
- This implementation did encompass the areas established by common practice and research: decentralized budget-making authority, decentralized personnel decision making, decentralized curricular decision making, and school-based councils. There were more unknown areas here since this information was not always available to the state departments. Most of the schools and districts which did implement SBM seemed to do so in all of the areas.
- Thirty-two states reported that some training had been provided (mostly at the local level) for those schools and districts voluntarily implementing school-based management. This training did encompass the areas established by common practice and research: communication, budget, decision making, and policy making, and planning. Less was known about the training provided for these voluntary implementations, though most of the schools and districts which did implement SBM seemed to do so in all of the areas.
- Further information provided by some of the state departments revealed school-based management's linkages with other restructuring projects or initiatives. It was frequently described as part of state or district level efforts in strategic planning, in

school improvement, in Effective Schools processes or projects, and in grant initiatives. Some states included statutory information which revealed a slight pattern of legislative initiative or invitation to implement SBM.

• With regard to the response patterns on the questionnaire, blanks are left where the respondents provided no mark; this frequently occurred because of the absence of information on SBM activity in the state. States marked with an asterisk represent special cases. The state departments of Michigan and Missouri described an absence of specific information, but both indicated that the level of individual school district autonomy in their states would facilitate SBM implementation. Michigan did describe a statutory requirement for school improvement, and noted that state aid is available for restructuring; such efforts have been quite common. Montana indicated that some of its 535 districts practice SBM, but it has not become a state issue. Washington's state department implemented SBM pilot projects in 1986, but both that legislation and funding have expired.

State-by-State Implementation of School-Based Management
State Department of Education Questionnaire

Question 1: Has the state department of education mandated or permitted voluntary pilot projects in school-based management or school-based decision making?

Question 2: Does this implementation include decentralized budget making authority, decentralized personnel decision making, decentralized curricular decision making, or school-based councils? (Response choices on both questions was: Yes/No).

State	SDE Approved Projects	Decentral. Budget Decisions	Decentral. Personnel Decisions	Decentral. Curriculum Decisions	SBM Councils
Alabama	Yes			Yes	Yes
Alaska	Yes	No	No	No	No
Arizona	Yes	No	No	No	Yes
Arkansas	Yes	No	No	Yes	Yes
California	Yes	Yes	No	Yes	Yes
Colorado	Yes	Yes	Yes	Yes	Yes
Connecticut	Yes				
Delaware	Yes	No	No	Yes	Yes
Florida	Yes	Yes	Yes	Yes	Yes
Georgia	Yes	Yes	Yes	Yes	Yes
Hawaii	Yes	Yes	Yes	Yes	Yes
Idaho	Yes	Yes	Yes	Yes	Yes
Illinois	Yes	Yes	Yes	Yes	Yes
Indiana	Yes				Yes
Iowa	Yes	Yes	Yes	Yes	Yes
Kansas	Yes		Yes	Yes	Yes
Kentucky	Yes	Yes	Yes	Yes	Yes
Louisiana	Yes	Yes	Yes	Yes	Yes
Maine	Yes	Yes	Yes	Yes	Yes
Maryland	Yes	Yes	No	No	Yes

State	SDE Approved Projects	Decentral. Budget Decisions	Decentral. Personnel Decisions	Decentral. Curriculum Decisions	SBM Councils
Massachusetts	Yes	Yes	Yes	Yes	Yes
Michigan	*				
Minnesota	Yes	Yes	Yes	Yes	Yes
Mississippi	No				
Missouri	*				
Montana	*				
Nebraska	Yes	Yes	Yes	Yes	Yes
Nevada	Yes	No	Yes	Yes	Yes
New Hampshire	Yes	No	No	Yes	Yes
New Jersey	Yes	No	No	No	Yes
New Mexico	Yes	Yes	Yes	Yes	Yes
New York	Yes	Yes	No	Yes	Yes
N. Carolina	Yes	Yes	Yes	No	Yes
N. Dakota	Yes	No	No	No	No
Ohio	Yes	No	No	Yes	Yes
Oklahoma	Yes	Yes	Yes	Yes	Yes
Oregon	Yes	Yes	Yes	Yes	Yes
Pennsylvania	Yes		Yes	Yes	Yes
Rhode Island	Yes	Yes	Yes	Yes	Yes
S. Carolina	Yes	?	?	Yes	Yes
S. Dakota	No				
Tennessee	Yes	Yes	Yes	Yes	Yes
Texas	Yes	Yes	Yes	Yes	Yes
Utah	Yes	Yes	Yes	Yes	Yes
Vermont	Yes	No	No	Yes	No
Virginia	Yes	Yes	Yes	Yes	Yes
Washington	*				
W. Virginia	Yes	Part	Part	Yes	Yes
Wisconsin	Yes	No	No	No	No
Wyoming	Yes	Yes	Yes	Yes	Yes

State-by-State Implementation of School-Based Management 257

Question 3: Have any participants in this school-based management process been provided with training for its implementation? Has this training been provided in the areas of communication, budget, decision making, or policy making. (Response choices were: Yes/No).

State	Training Provided	Communication	Budget	Decision Making	Policy Making	Planning
Alabama	Yes	Yes		Yes	Yes	Yes
Alaska	No	No	No	No	No	No
Arizona	?					
Arkansas	Yes	Yes	Yes	Yes	Yes	Yes
California	Yes	Yes	Yes	Yes	Yes	Yes
Colorado		Yes	No	Yes	Yes	Yes
Connecticut						
Delaware	Yes	Yes	No	Yes	Yes	Yes
Florida	Yes	Yes	Yes	Yes	Yes	Yes
Georgia	Yes					Yes
Hawaii	Yes	Yes		Yes		Yes
Idaho						
Illinois	Yes	Yes	Yes	Yes	Yes	Yes
Indiana	Yes	Yes		Yes	Yes	Yes
Iowa	No	Yes	Yes	Yes	Yes	Yes
Kansas	Yes	Yes		Yes		Yes
Kentucky	Yes	Yes	Yes	Yes	Yes	Yes
Louisiana	No					
Maine	Yes	Yes	No	Yes	Yes	Yes
Maryland	Yes	Yes	Yes	Yes	No	Yes
Massachusetts	Yes	Yes	Yes	Yes	Yes	Yes
Michigan	*					
Minnesota		Yes	Yes	Yes	Yes	Yes
Mississippi						
Missouri	*					
Montana	*					
Nebraska	Yes	Yes	Yes	Yes	Yes	Yes

State	Training Provided	Communication	Budget	Decision Making	Policy Making	Planning
Nevada	Yes	Yes	No	Yes	Yes	Yes
New Hampshire	Yes	Yes	Yes	Yes	Yes	Yes
New Jersey	Yes	Yes	Yes	Yes	Yes	Yes
New Mexico	Yes	Yes	?	Yes	Yes	Yes
New York	?					
N. Carolina	Yes	Yes	No	Yes	No	Yes
N. Dakota	No					
Ohio	Yes	Yes	No	Yes	Yes	Yes
Oklahoma	Yes	Yes	Yes	Yes	Yes	Yes
Oregon	Yes	No	No	No	No	No
Pennsylvania	Yes	Yes		Yes	Yes	Yes
Rhode Island	Yes	Yes		Yes		Yes
S. Carolina			•			
S. Dakota						
Tennessee	Yes	Yes	Yes	Yes	Yes	Yes
Texas	Yes	Yes	Yes	Yes	Yes	Yes
Utah	Yes	Yes	Yes	Yes	?	Yes
Vermont	Yes	Yes	No	Yes	Yes	Yes
Virginia	Yes	Yes		Yes		Yes
Washington	*					
W. Virginia	Yes	Yes	No	Yes	No	Yes
Wisconsin	No					
Wyoming	Yes	Yes	Yes	Yes	Yes	Yes

Question 4: Does your state have any individual schools or districts which have voluntarily (independent of state department of education impetus) implemented school based management or school based decision making? Does this implementation include decentralized budget making authority, decentralized personnel decision making, decentralized curricular decision making, or school-based councils? (Response choices were: Yes/No/Not known)

State-by-State Implementation of School-Based Management

State	Voluntary SBM Projects	Decentral. Budget Decisions	Decentral. Personnel Decisions	Decentral. Curriculum Decisions	SBM Councils
Alabama	Yes	?	?	?	?
Alaska	Yes	Yes	Yes	Yes	Yes
Arizona	?				
Arkansas	Yes	No	No	Yes	Yes
California	Yes	Yes	Yes	Yes	Yes
Colorado	Yes	Yes	Yes	Yes	Yes
Connecticut	Yes	?	?	?	?
Delaware	Yes	?	?	Yes	Yes
Florida	Yes	Yes	Yes	Yes	Yes
Georgia	Yes				
Hawaii	No				
Idaho	?	?	?	?	?
Illinois	?				
Indiana	Yes	?	?	?	?
Iowa	Yes	Yes	Yes	Yes	Yes
Kansas	Yes	Yes	Yes	Yes	Yes
Kentucky	Yes	Yes	Yes	Yes	Yes
Louisiana	Yes				
Maine	Yes	?	?	Yes	?
Maryland	Yes	?	?	?	?
Massachusetts	Yes	Yes	Yes	?	Yes
Michigan	*				
Minnesota	Yes				
Mississippi	Yes	?	?	?	?
Missouri	*				
Montana	Yes	?	?	?	?
Nebraska	Yes	Yes	Yes	Yes	Yes
Nevada	?				
New Hampshire	Yes				

260   *School-Based Management: Current Thinking and Practice*

State	Voluntary SBM Projects	Decentral. Budget Decisions	Decentral. Personnel Decisions	Decentral. Curriculum Decisions	SBM Councils
New Jersey	Yes	Yes	Yes	Yes	Yes
New Mexico	Yes	Yes	Yes	Yes	Yes
New York	?				
N. Carolina	No				
N. Dakota	?				
Ohio	Yes	No	No	Yes	Yes
Oklahoma	Yes	Yes	Yes	Yes	Yes
Oregon	Yes	?	?	?	?
Pennsylvania	Yes				
Rhode Island	Yes	Yes	Yes	Yes	Yes
S. Carolina	Yes	?	?	?	?
S. Dakota	?				
Tennessee	Yes	Yes	Yes	Yes	Yes
Texas	Yes	Yes	Yes	Yes	Yes
Utah	Yes	?	?	?	Yes
Vermont	Yes	Yes	Yes	Yes	Yes
Virginia	Yes	?	?	Yes	Yes
Washington	Yes	?	?	?	?
W. Virginia	?	?	?	?	?
Wisconsin	Yes	?	?	?	?
Wyoming	Yes	Yes	Yes	Yes	Yes

Question 5. Have any participants in this school based management process been provided with training for its implementation? Has this training been provided in the areas of communication, budget, decision making, policy making, or planning? (Response choices were: Yes/No/Not Known).

State	Training Provided	Communication	Budget	Decision Making	Policy Making	Planning
Alabama	No					
Alaska	?					
Arizona	?					

State-by-State Implementation of School-Based Management

State	Training Provided	Communication	Budget	Decision Making	Policy Making	Planning
Arkansas	Yes	Yes	No	Yes	No	No
California	Yes	Yes	Yes	Yes	Yes	Yes
Colorado		?	?	?	?	?
Connecticut	?	?	?	?	?	?
Delaware	Yes	Yes	?	Yes	Yes	Yes
Florida	Yes	Yes	Yes	Yes	Yes	Yes
Georgia	Yes					Yes
Hawaii	?					
Idaho	?	?	?	?	?	?
Illinois	?					
Indiana	Yes	?	?	?	?	?
Iowa	Yes	Yes	Yes	Yes	Yes	Yes
Kansas	Yes	Yes	Yes	Yes	Yes	Yes
Kentucky	Yes	Yes	Yes	Yes	Yes	Yes
Louisiana	Yes	Yes	?	Yes	?	Yes
Maine	?					
Maryland	?	?	?	?	?	?
Massachusetts		Yes	Yes	Yes	Yes	Yes
Michigan	*					
Minnesota	Yes	Yes	Yes	Yes	Yes	Yes
Mississippi	?					
Missouri	*					
Montana	?	?	?	?	?	?
Nebraska	Yes	Yes	Yes	Yes	Yes	Yes
Nevada	?					
New Hampshire						
New Jersey	Yes	Yes	Yes	Yes	Yes	Yes
New Mexico		Yes	No	Yes	Yes	Yes
New York	?					
N. Carolina	No					

State	Training Provided	Communication	Budget	Decision Making	Policy Making	Planning
N. Dakota	?					
Ohio	Yes	Yes	No	Yes	Yes	Yes
Oklahoma	Yes	Yes	Yes	Yes	Yes	Yes
Oregon	?					
Pennsylvania	Yes					
Rhode Island	Yes	Yes	?	Yes	?	Yes
S. Carolina	Yes	?	?	Yes	?	Yes
S. Dakota	?					
Tennessee	Yes	Yes	No	Yes	Yes	Yes
Texas	Yes	Yes	Yes	Yes	Yes	Yes
Utah	?	?	?	?	?	?
Vermont	?	?	?	?	?	?
Virginia	?					
Washington	?	?	?	?	?	?
W. Virginia	?	?	?	?	?	?
Wisconsin	?	?	?	?	?	?
Wyoming	Yes	Yes	Yes	Yes	Yes	Yes

GLOSSARY

Accountability — the requirement to answer for the results of professional effort, usually expressed and measured as student achievement and outcomes and institutional effectiveness.

Action Plan — is an operational plan which clearly and comprehensively answers the questions of Why? What? How? When? Who? and Where? as these questions apply to a specific set of tasks and procedures designed to achieve an objective.

Alternate Futuring — is the process of deciding a variety of possible futures for an organization. Each alternate, then, can be analyzed for its probability and for its desirability.

Collective Bargaining — is the legally required process wherein both the school district's board of education's negotiation team and the exclusive representatives of a union's negotiation team meet, confer, and bargain in good faith for the purpose of executing a written master contractual agreement which incorporates all of the agreements reached during the bargaining process.

Decentralization — dispersion or distribution of educational functions and authority from a central power level to regional or local school authorities.

Deconcentration — involves the transfer of tasks and work load to other units, but there is no real authority redistributed.

Delegation — involves the actual transfer of decision making authority to a lower level in the hierarchy; this must, however, be executed within a firm policy framework.

Devolution — involves the shifting of authority to an autonomous unit which may then act independently; once devolution occurs, the authority is not retrievable.

Effective Schools Research — cluster of characteristics correlated to school effectiveness, usually described as: instructional leadership; clear and focused mission; an emphasis on instruction; safe and orderly school climate; monitoring and measuring of achievement; time devoted to learning; and parent and community support.

Empowerment — a fundamental transfer of authority, usually to teachers or other professionals within a school system; the process of allowing employees to make decisions related to assigned work tasks, involving them in the creation of ways to maintain a productive and satisfying work environment, and involving them in day-to-day problem solving and decision making.

External Scanning — is the activity of collecting and monitoring data from the external environment in which the organization (school district or university) exists for the purpose of identifying trends over time which can be utilized to assist in planning strategies for the future.

Governance — authoritative direction or control within a school district or within a state or regional educational structure.

Internal Scanning — is the activity of collecting and monitoring data from within the internal environment of the organization (school district or university) for the purpose of identifying trends over time which assist in planning strategies for the future.

Local School Councils — representatively appointed or elected groups or teams of school stakeholders, frequently charged with substantial decision-making responsibility or substantial advisory capacities.

Loose Coupling — the notion that the structural elements of a school system are only minimally connected, and that only a strong stimulus or impact in one part of the system is felt in another.

Macro Level Planning — is strategic planning that begins with beliefs about the total organization as its goal.

Magnet Schools — institutions which develop unique learning environments, usually through curricular or programmatic specialization, intended to attract students of common educational interests but diverse socioeconomic backgrounds.

Management — is the collective body of individuals who are employed to oversee and to operate the day-to-day affairs of a school district within the policies and directives of a board of education.

Master Contract — is the document bargained and agreed to by both sides in the negotiations process.

Mega Level Planning — is planning that begins with beliefs about society as its goal.

Micro Level Planning — is strategic planning that begins with beliefs about a subgroup within the total organization.

Needs — discrepancies between "what is" and "what could be" or "what should be," in strategic planning.

Negotiation — is the active and formal give and take between members of a union's negotiation team and a management's negotiation team which ultimately ends in a master contract which governs the provisions, activities, and accommodations agreed to by both union and management.

Participation — means that subordinates have more input into the decision.

Peer Coaching — a process wherein one or more individuals, usually teachers, assist one or more other individuals to acquire skills, knowledge, or effective behaviors.

Preferred Futuring — is the process of selecting the most desired future from the group of alternate futures that have been developed. This preferred future becomes the cornerstone for the organization's vision.

Professionalization — the enlargement of teacher discretion in making decisions, both in the immediate workplace and in the larger context of school and system.

Quality Circles — generally, are groups of six to eight employees who identify problems within their work place; develop potential solutions to each problem; present their proposed solution to management and, if management approves, the circle implements its solution.

Quality of Work Life — is the degree to which such factors as trust, caring, recognition, interesting work, and opportunities for input exist in the employees' work place and are indicated by satisfaction, low absenteeism, and high motivation. The qualitative level can be assessed, and strategic plans can be developed to improve or maintain the qualitative level that is desired within the future vision of the organization.

Restructuring — concept which encompasses the need to rethink educational mission in view of changing conditions and imperatives; to exchange traditional forms of schooling and professional practice for new pedagogical and organizational structures.

Scenario — is a written narrative describing a future. This technique can be helpful if a variety of experts are asked to develop a future scenario for the organization, those consensus elements are identified and redistributed to the experts for additional comments, and this process continued until a consensus scenario is agreed upon.

School-Based Decision Making (SBDM) — a model for school improvement that allows for building level shared decision making; the vehicle through which research on what constitutes effective schools will be implemented (Kentucky Education Reform Act term).

School-Based Management (SBM) — A structure and process which allows greater decision-making power related to the areas of instruction, budget, policies, rules and regulations, staffing, and all matters of governance; and a process which involves a variety of stakeholders in the decisions related to the local individual school building.

School Climate — unique set of internal characteristics which affects the lives of those in a school; the tone or atmosphere.

School District Culture — the beliefs and values held, the standard processes and activities utilized, and the traditions maintained by the students and employees of the school district and by the community members who live within the geographical bounds of the school district.

School Improvement — refers to any systematic effort to improve the conditions of or the effects of schooling.

Shared Decision Making (SDM) — a collaborative decision-making process which involves multiple individuals representing different assignments within the individual school or different areas of the school district.

Stakeholders — are the local community residents, including parents, students, or other persons who have an interest or stake in what takes place in the school district.

Strategic Planning — long-term planning to achieve a future vision of "what could be" or "what should be".

SWOT Analysis — is a process utilized by strategic planners to identify, collect, monitor, analyze, and synthesize data about the strengths, weaknesses, opportunities, and threats that exist in the internal environment of the organization and that exist in the external environment with which the organization interacts. These data are useful in planning strategies and tactics which capitalize on strengths and opportunities, and minimize or overcome weaknesses and threats in a manner that maximizes the possibility of achieving the organization's vision.

Systemic Change — the transformation of a social system through integration and mutual reinforcement.

Trend Extrapolation — is the process of using monitored data over a period of years to identify trends; and, then, using these trends to predict future directions that should be considered when developing the strategic plan for the organization.

Union — is the official recognized bargaining unit which has the authority to collectively bargain a master contractual agreement with the management of a school district, and which has the authority and responsibility to represent all union employees on a day-to-day basis.

Vision — is a clear mental picture or written statement of what the strategic planners expect or desire their organization to look like and deliver at some point of time in the future. It is the description of the planners' determination of "what should be" or "what can be" at some future date.

Waiver — release or exemption from some external regulation or requirement, usually imposed by the school district or state department of education.

Win/Win — is a term that indicates that a positive and collaborative relationship exists between management and labor which is highly beneficial to both parties.

INDEX

A

A Nation at Risk, 6, 219
A Nation Prepared, 56, 220, 222
accountability, 9–11, 17–19, 45–48, 50, 55, 61, 71, 75–77, 81–82, 87, 89, 91–93, 101, 105, 110, 125–126, 160, 198, 203, 215, 224, 232–233, 237, 239, 242–243, 246–249
accounting, 144, 159, 193, 240
accreditation, 107, 243
achievement, 14, 16, 31, 51, 87, 89, 102, 125–126, 129, 143, 147–148, 153, 172, 179, 189, 191, 196, 231, 233
action plans, 31, 34, 39, 40, 64, 126, 168–169, 176
action programs, 26, 32, 35, 38, 41, 238
adversarial union/management relations, 61, 68–69, 71–72, 78, 238
allocation of personnel, 130
allocation of resources, 46, 103, 127
alternative vision, 39
America 2000, 230–232
American Association of School Administrators, 7, 9, 29, 55, 57, 97, 124, 125, 138, 221
American Federation of Teachers, 62, 74, 77, 226
analysis skills, 168
Annual Gallup Poll of Public Attitudes Towards Schools, 57–58
assignment of employees, 108
assistant principals, 84, 90, 115, 149
athletic director, 115
attitude surveys, 33, 164
authority, 4, 9, 11, 16, 18–19, 32, 47, 52, 55–56, 58, 78, 81–83, 85–89, 93, 98, 101, 103, 105, 108, 111, 134, 145, 147, 152, 155, 158, 161, 172, 179, 180, 187, 203, 208, 210–212, 215, 222–224, 227–228, 232, 237–239
autonomy, 3, 6–7, 9–11, 13–15, 18–19, 45–46, 50, 58, 77, 85, 91, 137, 148, 223, 225, 229, 232–233, 242, 248, 250

B

beliefs, 13, 26, 38–41, 237
bidding, 155, 190
board of education, 3, 9, 13, 28, 49, 57, 63–66, 68–76, 107, 109, 115–116, 118, 121, 129–130, 132–134, 136, 139, 142–162, 164, 166–167, 171, 173, 175, 179, 185, 187–189, 192, 200, 202, 215, 238, 240, 242, 245, 256
bond issues, 63, 164
budget, 9–19, 32, 47–49, 54–55, 57, 67, 69, 82, 84, 86, 92, 98, 101–104, 106–112, 126–127, 130–131, 133, 142–144, 154–155, 159–160, 167, 173, 175, 180–182, 187, 189, 193, 196, 198, 199, 207, 209, 210, 212, 215, 222, 226, 232, 237, 239, 240, 246, 249
bureaucracy, 5, 9–10, 46, 48, 54, 58, 85, 96, 100, 102–103, 229
business, 4–8, 10, 12, 19, 44, 102–103, 170, 172, 178, 185, 188, 221, 226, 230, 231, 237, 241, 248

C

career ladder, 13, 125
categorical programs, 127
Center for Policy Research in Education, 223
central office, 7, 9, 12–15, 17, 53, 57, 71–72, 75–76, 81, 86, 91, 96–112, 116, 131, 133, 134, 137, 139, 158, 161, 165, 188,

central office (*continued*)
199–201, 204, 207, 239–240, 245–247, 249

centralization, 3, 5, 6, 14, 103, 110–111, 239, 243, 248

certification, 221

Chicago, 17, 57, 102–103, 105, 111–112, 120, 181, 226–227, 233, 239, 242

Chicago School Reform Act, 17, 102–103

civil rights, 103, 226

class size, 190, 199, 211

classified personnel, 12, 101, 172, 195, 212

climate, 25–42, 68, 70, 107, 125–126, 135, 148, 172, 175, 178, 206, 208, 223, 228, 238, 243–244

closed systems, 8, 132

co-curricular activities, 159, 167, 240

Coalition of Essential Schools, 225, 231

collaboration, 6, 12, 17, 45–46, 48–49, 51, 52, 58, 61, 63, 68, 69, 70, 71, 72, 74, 77–78, 83, 85–86, 88–89, 91–93, 103, 107–110, 126, 128, 132, 136–137, 139, 148, 160, 161, 172, 178, 180, 182, 193, 202, 216, 221, 225, 230, 233, 238, 240–242, 244, 246, 248, 249, 250

collective bargaining, 4, 12–13, 16, 115, 118, 126–127, 135, 138, 159, 188–189, 214, 238, 240

collegiality, 3, 48–49, 51–52, 54–55, 57–58, 78, 84–85, 87–88, 223, 229, 238, 244–245

committees, 4, 14, 15, 34, 65, 67, 73, 77, 106–107, 147–148, 155, 164, 165, 166, 167, 169, 173–176, 180, 187, 189, 192, 199, 206, 209, 211, 213, 239, 241

community, 7, 9, 11–12, 14–16, 19, 26, 30–31, 33, 38, 46, 48, 70, 72, 77, 81, 87, 89, 92, 97–98, 100, 102, 110, 126, 128–130, 132, 144, 146, 148, 151, 153, 185, 188, 193, 202–204, 212, 214–216, 220, 223, 225, 228, 230–231, 238, 241, 243, 245–246, 249

competencies, 125, 136–137, 138

compliance, 214

conflict resolution, 72, 168

consensus, 8, 11, 15, 18, 19, 38, 82, 89, 92, 100, 105, 106, 111, 112, 147, 148, 164–182, 188, 199, 201, 203, 205, 207, 221, 232, 233, 240, 241, 242, 246, 249

consultant, 199, 107, 110, 166, 197

control, 6, 10, 16, 19, 46, 48, 56, 84, 87, 96, 138–139, 202, 222, 229, 231, 248, 250

corporate and managerial theory, 5–6, 8, 26, 28, 44, 93, 178, 179, 219, 242

corporations, 63, 182, 225

councils, 4, 10–13, 16–18, 19, 50, 55, 57, 61, 65–67, 71, 73, 77, 84, 89, 91–92, 101–105, 108, 133–134, 142–145, 147–153, 155–156, 158, 177, 179, 181–182, 186, 191–214, 216–217, 226, 230, 239, 241, 243

counselors, 144, 193, 211

culture, 4, 8, 11, 26–27, 51, 58, 68, 69, 71, 78, 82, 85–86, 88, 93, 132, 158, 180, 237, 247, 250

curriculum, 4, 9–19, 32, 45, 48–57, 62, 66, 82, 84, 86–87, 89–90, 93, 96, 99, 101–102, 104–105, 109–112, 115, 125–126, 144, 147, 168, 172, 181–182, 185, 187, 189–190, 192, 196, 198, 207–208, 210, 213, 215, 219, 222–223, 226–229, 231–232, 237, 240, 244, 246, 249

D

data collection and analysis, 36, 38, 42, 127, 247

decentralization, 3, 5, 9, 10, 11, 14, 16, 18–19, 44, 56, 74, 85, 90, 92, 96, 98, 103, 105–110, 111–112, 186–187, 215, 217, 222, 224, 226, 227–228, 233, 237, 239–240, 242–243, 248, 250

Department of Education, 150, 220, 221

deregulation, 13, 46, 222, 226, 231, 233, 242

desegregation, 4, 12–13, 127

discipline, 14, 16, 47, 102, 144, 192, 209, 211, 213

downsizing, 5, 248, 250

E

Education Commission of the States, 56, 58, 220, 222, 225–226

Effective Schools, 3, 6, 8, 16, 50, 87, 100, 146, 148, 198, 219, 225, 228, 229, 230, 233, 242

elementary school, 103, 175, 195–196–207, 230–231

empowerment, 9, 11, 18–19, 30, 32–33, 35, 41, 44–58, 69, 71–72, 77, 82–93, 97, 107–109, 137–139, 170–177, 181–182, 185, 201–202, 207–208, 221, 223, 225–226, 228, 232–233, 237–244, 247–249
equipment and materials/supplies, 10, 14, 17, 32, 83, 85, 89, 98, 104, 134, 144, 159, 178, 193, 222, 240
expenditures, 15, 67, 106, 108, 115, 203, 227
external and internal variables, 30, 38–39, 41, 129
extracurricular activities, 101, 144, 190, 193, 211, 213

F

federal government, 62, 75, 96, 98, 109, 116–117, 129, 135, 153, 190, 219, 227, 230–233, 242
finance, 7, 13, 28, 38, 52, 108, 112, 125, 127, 133, 198, 209, 240
food service, 107, 115, 134, 159, 175
fringe benefits, 63
funds, 4, 14, 16–17, 19, 65, 70, 101, 104, 192–193, 203, 206–207, 230

G

goals, 16–17, 34–35, 41, 46, 49, 52, 56, 86, 91, 93, 97–98, 100, 126, 153, 156, 160, 166, 176, 187, 189, 196, 205, 222, 231–232, 239
governance, 5, 9, 12, 17–18, 44, 49, 51, 53, 55, 66, 74, 77–78, 82–83, 88–89, 93, 96, 103, 111, 133–134, 137–139, 143, 159, 165, 170, 172–177, 190, 212, 223–225, 227, 240–241, 245, 247, 249–250
grade level, 118, 06, 180
grants, 4, 12, 13, 14, 16, 18, 104, 227, 230–231
Great Britain, 104–105, 112, 233, 239, 242
group decision making, 35, 246
group dynamics, 13, 81, 83, 213, 216, 241
group process, 18, 55, 83, 93, 126, 181–182, 197, 207, 239
guidance, 115, 159, 198, 209–210, 240

H

handicapped pupils, 127
high school, 88, 90, 102, 195–206, 221, 230–231
hiring, 15, 18–19, 49, 57, 89, 96, 101, 106, 108–109, 111, 115, 134, 155, 199, 201–202
human relations skills, 180, 182, 241, 245
human resources, 125

I

instruction, 3–4, 7–8, 12, 15, 18, 45–46, 48–51, 54, 57, 84, 86, 89–90, 92–93, 105–107, 109–112, 115, 125–126, 131, 133–134, 137, 143–144, 147–148, 152, 158–159, 167, 171–172, 187–188, 196, 199, 203, 207–208, 211, 213, 224–225, 228–229, 240, 243–244
instructional leader, 6, 18, 49, 84, 86, 88, 143, 152, 191, 242, 248
instructional leadership, 13, 50, 58, 90, 92, 135, 137, 148, 228
instructional materials, 15, 154, 192, 210
instructional time, 213

J

job enrichment, 125

K

Kentucky, 108, 118, 138, 143–158, 161, 186, 190–194, 214–217, 241
Kentucky Education Reform Act, 120, 143–145, 157, 161, 190–194, 196, 198, 203, 207–209, 214–217, 216, 240, 242

L

law and legality, 38, 89, 101–103, 108, 110, 112, 127, 142, 152–156, 161, 214, 216, 222, 240
lead teachers, 13, 16, 54, 56, 222
legislation, 14, 28, 75–76, 112, 115, 138, 145, 147, 157, 214–217, 219, 231, 241–242
legislatures, 6, 76, 103, 142–143, 158
loose coupling, 4, 7–8, 45, 133

M

Macro Level Planning, 36
maintenance and operations, 10, 15, 98, 104, 107, 115, 127, 133, 159, 175, 193, 240
mandates, 28, 62, 71, 76, 96, 117–118, 120, 142, 143, 145, 157, 185, 187, 190, 216–217, 229, 232, 241–242, 246
master contract, 69, 72–73, 76–78, 100–101, 118, 238
media, 33, 126, 146, 152, 167, 191
Mega Level Planning, 36
mentor, 13, 49, 51, 54, 56, 88, 89
Micro Level Planning, 36
mission, 26–27, 34, 38–39, 40–41, 86, 89, 93, 98, 146, 148, 153, 156, 166, 170, 176, 196, 229, 243
multicultural, 4, 28, 126

N

National Association of Elementary School Principals, 7, 9, 57, 221
National Association of Secondary School Principals, 7, 9, 56–58, 83–84, 111, 127, 138, 180, 221, 228
National Clearinghouse on School-Based Management, 16
National Commission on Excellence in Education, 220
National Education Association, 16, 56, 58, 62, 74, 77, 99
National Governors' Association, 57–58, 220, 221, 222, 225, 229, 231
National School Boards Association, 29
needs, 16, 34–35, 38, 40, 65, 70, 102, 106, 110, 128, 168
needs assessment, 100, 126, 144, 165–167, 181, 192, 241

O

open systems, 132
organizational development, 4–5, 92, 116, 126, 226, 228, 248
organizational dynamics, 19, 237, 248
ownership, 5, 8, 26, 33–34, 84, 88–89, 93, 110, 146, 178, 212, 221, 225

P

parent teacher organizations, 164, 173, 174, 191
parents, 4, 7, 12–16, 18, 30–33, 38, 45–46, 51, 54, 56–57, 61, 71, 72, 77, 81, 83, 88–89, 91, 102–104, 107, 110, 121, 128, 129, 130, 133, 135, 142, 143, 144, 148–149, 151, 153, 177, 185, 188, 191, 193, 194, 196, 197, 199, 201, 202, 203–204, 206–208, 211–212, 220, 225–226, 228, 230, 232–233, 241–243, 245, 248
participatory management, 126
partnerships, 172, 178, 241
peer coaching, 49, 51, 56, 61, 73, 78, 109, 239
personnel, 10, 14, 16, 47, 76, 82, 98, 101, 102, 104, 106, 107, 108, 109, 115, 127, 133–134, 167, 181, 182, 201, 202, 207, 212, 222, 232, 240, 248
personnel decisions, 144, 155, 192, 237
personnel resources, 246, 249
personnel selection, 11, 47, 112, 204, 213, 239
pilot programs, 12, 15, 19, 96, 101, 107, 169
planning cluster, 36, 40, 42
planning period, 51
policy, 8–13, 15, 38, 44, 47–48, 50, 56, 65, 73, 75, 77–78, 88–89, 98, 100–102, 105, 107, 111, 115, 117, 130–131, 134, 136, 142, 144–146, 150, 153, 155–157, 159–161, 166–167, 179, 185, 188, 191–194, 196–200, 203, 205, 207–208, 211–216, 221–222, 232, 240–241, 243, 247
power, 10, 50–51, 53, 82, 84, 86, 89, 92, 97, 101, 103, 106, 111, 130, 138–139, 158, 161, 177, 180, 189, 233, 238–239
preferred future, 38–39
preparation and retraining programs, 91, 93, 136–137, 246, 249
preschool children, 29
principal, 3, 6–8, 10–11, 14–15, 17–19, 45, 47, 49–55, 57–58, 72, 75–78, 81–93, 96–97, 99, 102–103, 105–107, 109–111, 116, 121, 126, 131, 133–135, 142–144, 146, 149–152, 155, 158, 160, 171, 173–177, 179, 181, 185, 187–189, 191–194, 196–197, 199, 201–202, 206–208, 210–211, 213, 222, 224–225, 228–229, 232, 237, 239, 242–245, 247–249
private sector, 4, 103, 137, 225–226, 233

process skills, 85
professional association, 62, 149–150
professional growth and development, 13, 17, 50, 52, 54, 61, 98, 143, 145, 160, 228, 239
professional preparation, 181, 246
professionalization, 233, 238, 242
public relations, 19, 69, 125–126, 237, 246, 249
purchasing, 14, 96, 105, 108

Q

Quality Circles, 17, 64, 238
Quality of Work Life, 61, 63–64, 68, 70–72, 75, 78, 238

R

reform, 4, 8, 10, 14, 45, 48–49, 51, 56–57, 74, 77, 85–86, 96–97, 103, 111, 185–187, 190, 217, 219–235, 237, 241–243, 247–248
regulations, 97–100, 107, 109, 221–222, 226, 231–233, 237, 241, 247
resources, 11, 14, 50, 53–55, 58, 81, 84, 92, 97–98, 103, 105–106, 111–112, 127, 130, 148, 154, 158–159, 161, 181–182, 203, 214, 216, 229, 238, 240–241, 245, 249
role, 6, 18–19, 27, 41, 45, 49–50, 52, 54, 61, 77, 81–84, 86, 88–89, 92–93, 97–98, 111, 116, 131, 133–134, 136, 138–139, 142, 160–161, 215, 221, 225, 239, 245, 248–249

S

S.W.O.T. (Strengths, Weaknesses, Opportunities, and Threats), 172–173
salaries, 13, 16, 63, 69, 106, 108, 220
schedules, 32, 82, 89, 144, 192, 199, 211, 213
school based budgeting, 9, 15, 46, 106, 108–109, 130
school business manager, 107, 115, 134
school calendar, 96, 144, 192
school choice, 28, 225, 227, 232–233, 242
school improvement, 3, 7–8, 11, 13, 15, 18, 50, 64, 74, 85–86, 97–99, 102, 126, 138, 144, 147–148, 170, 181, 193, 198, 207, 212, 214, 216, 219–220, 225–226, 228–233, 241–242, 244–245, 248
scoping, 36, 41
Spain, 105, 112, 239
special education, 29, 110, 115, 157, 190, 211
staff development, 8, 12, 16–17, 47–49, 56, 65–66, 73–74, 87, 89, 98–99, 101–102, 111, 126–127, 131, 148, 159, 181, 219, 228, 240
staffing, 12, 17, 46, 83, 86, 101, 103, 109, 126, 131, 133, 159–160, 187, 189, 227, 229, 240
stakeholders, 12–13, 16, 18, 30, 32–33, 53–54, 88, 92, 106, 128, 130, 131, 166, 170–176, 178, 180, 185, 226, 233, 244, 245–247, 249–250
state department of education, 8, 12, 14, 16–17, 54, 107, 109, 117, 144–145, 154, 156, 185–217, 224, 241, 245
state legislatures, 4, 28, 101, 118, 245
statutes, 11, 100, 110, 217, 241
strategic and operational planning, 11, 13, 16, 18–19, 35–40, 54, 68, 74, 93, 99, 128, 181, 193, 237–239, 241, 245, 247, 249
students, 6–7, 12, 18, 26, 30, 33, 38, 45–49, 52–53, 70, 83, 87–88, 92, 97–98, 105–106, 110–111, 120, 128–130, 144, 146, 151, 153, 156–157, 166–167, 171–172, 175–176, 178, 190, 193, 195, 210–212, 215, 220, 225–226, 228–230, 244, 247–248, 250
superintendents, 6, 13–14, 17, 61–63, 65–67, 72, 75, 78, 98–100, 102–103, 107, 115–139, 142, 144, 149–150, 152–156, 158, 166–167, 171, 173, 175, 179, 188–189, 192, 194, 196, 200, 210, 222, 240, 245–246
supervision, 47, 49, 56, 75–76, 88, 90, 92, 102, 109–110, 115, 126, 128, 133–134, 144, 160, 193
symbolic leadership, 116, 129–130, 138, 245
systemic change, 96, 103, 226–227, 233, 242–243, 247, 249–250

T

task force, 48, 89, 107, 219, 221, 242
taxes, 28, 63, 164, 167–168
taxpayers, 69–70, 72

teacher aides, 204
teachers, 7–8, 11–17, 19, 28, 32, 44–58, 96–99, 102, 105, 107–110, 116, 121, 126, 130, 133–134, 142–144, 148–152, 155, 160, 172, 178–180, 185, 187–188, 190–191, 193–195, 197, 199–200, 202–204, 207–208, 210–212, 219–230, 232–233, 237–240, 242–251
teams, 5, 35, 38, 44, 48, 72–73, 83, 89–91, 93, 99, 108, 139, 168, 201, 205, 207, 224–225, 229, 240, 247, 249–250
Texas, 186–190, 214–217, 241
Texas Education Agency, 215
Texas House Bill 2885, 187, 189
Texas Senate Bills 1, 351, 187–189
textbook selection, 18, 32, 52, 62, 101, 106, 109, 190
Theories X, Y, and Z, 125
time to meet, 13, 19, 52, 54–55, 58, 86, 130, 136, 182, 192, 204, 207, 212–214, 216, 222, 227
training, 14, 16, 18–19, 25, 34–35, 58, 72–74, 89, 99, 102, 107–108, 110, 136–137, 139, 156, 159, 178–182, 189, 196–198, 201, 203–205, 207, 212–214, 216, 223, 237–238, 240–241, 244–247, 249–250
transfers and dismissals, 108, 144, 155, 192, 201
transformational leadership, 86
transportation services, 107–108, 115, 134, 159, 240
trends, 27, 29–30, 39, 41, 44, 56, 58, 129, 237–238, 248
trust, 31, 51, 70–71, 77, 87, 132–133, 178, 206, 223, 238

U

unions, 3, 13, 17, 28, 44, 48, 55, 99, 100–103, 116, 118, 121, 132, 142, 160, 172, 175, 215, 226, 238, 242
university, 14, 51, 136–137, 246

V

vision, 13–14, 16, 27, 31, 34–36, 38–41, 61–78, 87–89, 93, 97, 99–100, 128, 137, 146–149, 170, 176, 185, 226, 232, 244–245, 249

W

waivers, 11, 13, 15–17, 19, 96, 98, 100, 107, 111, 145, 156, 160, 185, 187, 189–190, 193, 237, 239, 246, 249
win/win collective negotiations, 61, 68–70, 78, 238